LITURGICAL MUSIC AS RITUAL SYMBOL

Liturgia condenda 9

Liturgia condenda is published by the Liturgical Institute in Tilburg (NL). The series plans to publish innovative research into the science of liturgy and serves as a forum which will bring together publications produced by researchers of various nationalities. The motto *liturgia condenda* expresses the conviction that research into the various aspects of liturgy can make a critico-normative contribution to the deepening and the renewal of liturgical practice.

Liturgisch Instituut
P.O. Box 9130
5000 HC Tilburg
The Netherlands

LITURGICAL MUSIC AS RITUAL SYMBOL

A Case Study of Jacques Berthier's Taizé Music

Judith Marie Kubicki

PEETERS

D. 1999/0602/30
ISBN 90-429-0740-1

To my Parents
who first nurtured in me a love of music
and taught me how to pray

CONTENTS

List of Illustrations XI
Acknowledgments XIII

Introduction 1

CHAPTER ONE: CONCILIAR AND POST-CONCILIAR STATEMENTS ON LITURGICAL MUSIC: ANOTHER LOOK AT THE QUESTIONS

Introduction 5

Interpreting Conciliar Texts 6

Official Documents on Liturgical Music 10

A Comparative Analysis of Common Themes 30

Restating the Questions 37

CHAPTER TWO: MUSICOLOGICAL ANALYSIS OF JACQUES BERTHIER'S MUSIC FOR TAIZÉ

Introduction 41

An Analysis of Structural Tropes 54

An Examination of Textual Inclusions 76

Summary of Analysis 91

CHAPTER THREE: PHILOSOPHIES AND THEOLOGIES OF SYMBOL: TAIZÉ MUSIC AS RITUAL SYMBOL

Introduction 93

The Nature of Symbol 96

Music as Symbol. 106

The Nature of Song as Musical Symbol. 113

Music as Ritual Symbol 119

Taizé Music as Ritual Symbol 125

CHAPTER FOUR: THE SYMBOLIC ROLE OF TAIZÉ MUSIC WITHIN
THE TAIZÉ PILGRIMAGE PROCESS

Introduction. 129

Pilgrimage as Liminal Experience. 131

The Taizé Pilgrimage Process 134

Taizé Music's Role as Ritual Symbol 139

CHAPTER FIVE: INTERPRETING TAIZÉ PRAYER IN LIGHT OF
J.L. AUSTIN'S PERFORMATIVE LANGUAGE THEORY

Introduction. 147

J.L. Austin's Performative Language Theory. 149

Implications for Liturgical Music 155

CHAPTER SIX: TAIZÉ MUSIC AS A MEDIATION OF ECCLESIAL
MEANING

Recapitulation. 169

Liturgy as *Theologia Prima* 170

Liturgy as *Theologia Ecclesia* 172

Taizé Music: Ritual Symbol Mediating Ecclesial Meaning . . . 177

Contemporary Theologies of Church 181

Taizé's Ritualization of Its Ecclesiology 186

Singing the Taizé Chants in Other Local Communities. 188

Conclusion: Toward a Critical Theory of Music as Ritual Symbol 190

BIBLIOGRAPHY 195

LIST OF ILLUSTRATIONS

FIGURE	CHAPTER TWO	PAGE
1. "Jubilate Deo" by Praetorius		47
2. Refrain of "Veni Sancte Spiritus"		57
3. Verse of "Veni Sancte Spiritus"		57
4. "Jesus, Remember Me"		57-58
5. "Crucem Tuam"		58
6. "Ubi Caritas"		59
7. Recitative verse of "Ubi Caritas"		59
8. Verse of "Ubi Caritas" for schola or cantor		60
9. Refrain of "Adoramus Te"		61
10. Verse of "Adoramus Te"		61
11. Response with 2 verses of "Veni Creator Spiritus"		62
12. "Kyrie 1"		63
13. "Alleluia 3"		64
14. "Alleluia 4"		65
15. "Jubilate, Servite"		66-67
16. Principal canon of "Prepare the Way of the Lord"		67
17. Secondary canon of "Prepare the Way of the Lord"		68
18. Principal canon of "Gloria III"		68
19. Secondary canon of "Gloria III"		68-69
20. Unison ostinato of "Veni Sancte Spiritus"		72
21. "Veni Sancte Spiritus" for women's voices		72

22. "Veni Sancte Spiritus" for men's voices 73

23. "Veni Sancte Spiritus" for mixed voices 73

24. French verse of "Veni Sancte Spiritus" 73

25. Oboe solo for "Veni Sancte Spiritus" 74

26. Refrain of "Bénissez/Chwała". 82

27. French verses 1 and 2 of "Bénissez". 83

28. Polish verses 1 and 2 of "Chwała" 84

29. "Jésus le Christ". 87

30. Refrain of "Te rogamus" 88

31. "Te rogamos". 89

32. "Chuyo, chuyo turo chusoso". 89

33. "Gospodi A" (Slovak) 90

34. "Gospodi A" (Polish) 90

CHAPTER FIVE

1. "Wait for the Lord" 161-162

2. Flute solo for "Wait for the Lord" 163

3. "Adoramus Te Christe" 165-166

ACKNOWLEDGMENTS

It is with profound joy that I acknowledge the many people without whom this study would not have been successfully completed. I am especially grateful to my religious community, the Felician Sisters, my family, especially my parents, the community of Christ the King Seminary, and all of my friends for their support and encouragement throughout the course of my doctoral studies.

I am likewise grateful to Dr. Mary Collins, OSB for challenging and inspiring my thinking, my research and my writing, to Dr. Stephen Happel, for first introducing me to the study of hermeneutics and the theology of symbol, and to Dr. Theodore Marier, for his assistance as musician and manuscript reader.

Several other people have provided support and assistance in sundry ways. I am indebted to all, but especially to Dr. Daniel Grigassy, OFM, Rev. Christopher Merry, Rev. Virgil Funk, Joseph Gelineau, SJ, Genevieve Noufflard, Germaine Berthier, the community of Taizé, especially Brother John Castaldi, Brother Dirk, and Sr. Nuria Sabé Griful, Ernestine Otis, Helen McConnell, Sr. Mary Jolene Jasinski, CSSF, Kwang-Hsiung Cheng, Dr. Chun-zen Huang, Sean Murphy, Mary Jac Reed, Betsy Pohlhaus, Deanna Light, Dr. Bernard Olszewski, OFM, Conv., the CUA Department of Religion and Religious Education and the School of Religious Studies, the staff of Mullen Library, the American Society for Aesthetics, the Church Musicians Guild of Buffalo, *Universa Laus,* and Willem Marie Speelman, for his assistance in getting this manuscript published.

You have all been a blessing! For this I give thanks!

INTRODUCTION

The relationship of music to worship, specifically Roman Catholic liturgy, has been the subject of serious reflection and study since the early days of the Church. In this century, efforts of the Liturgical Movement which preceded the Second Vatican Council bore fruit in *Sacrosanctum Concilium* (1963),[1] a document which devotes an entire chapter to sacred music. Article 112 of that document describes music as integral to liturgy. It cites as the foundation for this teaching Pius X's motu proprio *Tra le sollecitudini* (1903), which speaks of the ministerial role of music. Subsequent church documents have restated this teaching, among them the Roman instruction *Musicam Sacram* (1967) and two statements of the U.S. National Conference of Catholic Bishops, *Music in Catholic Worship* (1972) and *Liturgical Music Today* (1982). The later documents have provided elaborations on how music's integral role in liturgical rites can be understood as ministerial.

In an effort to interpret and implement these church statements on the role of liturgical music, composers and music ministers have studied these documents in the light of their experience. Their wrestling with the issues has contributed to the ongoing development of an understanding of music's role in the liturgy as both integral and ministerial.

In order to arrive at a new synthesis of an understanding of liturgical music's role as both integral and ministerial, this paper will explore the nature of music as ritual symbol. To accomplish this task this study has chosen a corpus of music whose success as ritual music renders it a suitable subject for exploring the nature of ritual music as symbol. By looking at the characteristics of this specific case, we will study data which will allow us to draw conclusions about ritual music in general. The specific case is the corpus of music Jacques Berthier (1923-1994), the Parisian composer and organist, composed for use in the ecumenical monastic community and pilgrimage site at Taizé in France. It is designed to involve pilgrims from every continent, speaking many different languages,

---

[1] *Sacrosanctum Concilium* is the Latin title of the document whose English title is *The Constitution on the Sacred Liturgy*. Both titles will be used in this study to refer to the 1963 document. Hereafter SC.

in the production of the daily liturgical prayer at the great Church of Reconciliation. In the past twenty years the music has been set to nearly twenty languages.

Two criteria have determined the music chosen for analysis in this study. Firstly, this case study will examine only that music composed by Berthier specifically for use by the brothers of Taizé with large groups of pilgrims.[2] Jacques Berthier composed numerous other works over a lifetime of musical activity, including some early works for use only by the Taizé community. Those compositions are not the subject of this study. Secondly, this study will examine only that music sung at Taizé which was composed by Berthier. Other composers, most notably Joseph Gelineau, have also composed music at the request of the brothers. Those compositions are likewise not the subject of this case study. Naturally, it is hoped that the conclusions regarding Berthier's music for Taizé will be generally applied to other instances of liturgical music. Nevertheless, for purposes of analysis, the case study will limit itself to that corpus of music which Jacques Berthier composed for Taizé.

Documents since the Second Vatican Council, as well as the various commentaries and responses to them, repeat, with theme and variation, two key points which have served as guiding principles in determining the interpretive strategies of this paper. The first is the notion that the liturgy is comprised of a dynamic complexus of symbols which are not objects, but actions that disclose relationships.[3] The second is the primacy, reiterated time and again in *Sacrosanctum Concilium* and thereafter in numerous other documents, of the active participation of the faithful in the liturgy.

Pertinent theories and theologies of symbol which specifically address the dynamics of ritual, and particularly worship, will be used to intepret how singing the Taizé chants can be understood to be symbolic activity. Louis-Marie Chauvet's theology of symbol, Polanyi's theory of symbol,

---

[2] Although Berthier's music was composed for use at the daily liturgies at Taizé, the practice of praying in a style modeled on the Taizé liturgies has been adapted by a variety of local Christian communities. For example, Sr. Suzanne Toolan, RSM, has been instrumental in promoting "Taizé Prayer around the Cross" among Catholic communities in California, The Catholic University of America has sponsored a similar service, and the Episcopal Washington National Cathedral in Washington, D.C. holds Taizé evening prayer on Sundays twice a month.

[3] Nathan MITCHELL, "Symbols Are Actions, Not Objects," *Living Worship* 13 (February 1977), 2.

and Jean-Jacques Nattiez's application of Jan Molino's tri-partite theory of musical semiotics will provide the basis for developing an understanding of symbol as a mediation of meaning between human subjects. The study of symbol will be followed by an examination of Victor Turner's ritual theory. Because of his understanding of ritual as symbolic process and his study of pilgrimages as an example of liminality, Turner's work will be used to interpret Taizé music's role in the ritual process. Lastly, because the proper object for the study of music as symbol is the action of music-making, J. L. Austin's performative language theory will be used to interpret the power of music-making as *the doing of something* rather than simply *the saying of something*.

The data from these analyses will be used to address two key questions: 1) how the act of music-making is intended to work as ritual symbol through its interplay with text and assembly in the production of the ritual event; and 2) what ecclesial meanings might be mediated in the intended ritual process. The conclusions will be used to move toward a critical theory of music as ritual symbol in order to come to a fuller understanding of music as ministerial and integral to the liturgy.

Throughout this study the terms "ritual," "worship," and "liturgy" will be used frequently and sometimes interchangeably. Of the three terms, ritual is understood to be the most general of the terms, including in its meaning not only worship and liturgy, but also a wide range of human activity not strictly understood as religious in nature. In this paper, the term "ritual" will be understood to mean "a social symbolic process which has the potential for communicating, creating, criticizing, and even transforming meaning."[4] By extension, then, "religious" ritual, will be understood to communicate, create, criticize, and even transform "religious" meaning. Moreover, the term religious ritual can be applied to any symbolic process which communicates religious meaning without necessarily involving a direct relationship with a deity.

The term "worship" can be equated, not only with the formal services or rites of a particular religion, but also with a way of life. "Worship" both expresses and mediates the divine-human relationship. Indeed, the very fact that worship is possible implies both human subjects who

---

[4] Margaret Mary KELLEHER, "Ritual," in *The New Dictionary of Theology*, ed. Joseph A. KOMONCHAK, Mary COLLINS, and Dermot A. LANE (Collegeville: The Liturgical Press, 1991), 906.

desire a relationship with God and a God who fulfills that desire."[5] This focus on worship's role as mediator of the divine-human relationship make the term more specific than ritual and also more suitable to the concerns of this project.

Liturgy, as it is used in this paper, is understood to be "the formal public worship of Christian assemblies. It is the form of ecclesial ritual action in which Christians gather to remember, express, and reappropriate their identity as co-worshippers with Christ."[6] The term "liturgy," therefore, is even more particular than worship because of its specifically Christian, communal, and public aspects. Furthermore, the combination term "liturgical worship" is often used to describe a form of ecclesial action which emphasizes the assembly's role as subject because of its union with Christ, the ultimate subject.[7]

Finally, identifying liturgical worship as a ritual action highlights the fact that it is a symbolic process since in liturgy worship is symbolically expressed or mediated.[8] Since the Roman Catholic tradition uses the term "liturgy" to designate the official public worship of the church, the focus of this paper is ultimately on the functioning of music within Roman Catholic worship.

---

[5] Margaret Mary KELLEHER, "Worship," in *The New Dictionary of Theology*, ed. Joseph A. KOMONCHAK, Mary COLLINS, and Dermot A. LANE (Collegeville: The Liturgical Press, 1991), 1105.

[6] KELLEHER, "Worship," 1105.

[7] KELLEHER, "Worship," 1105.

[8] KELLEHER, "Worship," 1106.

CHAPTER ONE

CONCILIAR AND POST-CONCILIAR STATEMENTS ON LITURGICAL MUSIC: ANOTHER LOOK AT THE QUESTIONS

INTRODUCTION

This study intends to develop a critical theory of music as ritual symbol in order to explain why music is integral to the liturgy. To achieve this purpose, I have selected Jacques Berthier's music for Taizé as a case study in order to determine how music contributes to the liturgical mediation of meaning.

The concerns of this study have a long history. Most recently, conversations on the relationship of music to the liturgy have been most profoundly influenced by the decrees of the Second Vatican Council (1962-1965). In renewing emphasis on the role of the assembly, reintroducing the vernacular, making a recommitment to ecumenical concerns, and broadening options for incorporating musical styles and instruments in the liturgy, this Council influenced theory and practice well beyond the confines of Roman Catholic worship. It was shortly after the conclusion of Vatican II that Jacques Berthier composed the corpus of music which was to become known as music for Taizé.[1] As a Roman Catholic church musician, Berthier's daily work was directly affected by the reforms of the Council.[2] Likewise, as a friend and collaborator of Joseph Gelineau, SJ (b.1920), Berthier's interpretation and implementation of the Council's liturgical reforms were influenced by those of this renowned international composer and liturgist. Further, as

---

[1] Jacques BERTHIER began working on the songs used with the pilgrims in the great Church of Reconciliation in 1974. He continued his work for Taizé until shortly before his death in 1994.

[2] See Jacques BERTHIER, "*Jacques Berthier: Un serviteur de la musique liturgique,*" interview by Pierre FAURE and Didier RIMAUD, *Célébrer* no. 236 (Janvier 1994): 14. In this interview, Berthier spoke of his willingness to compose music for the assembly and in the vernacular after the changes brought about by Vatican II. He explained that he had accepted the decision of Rome with hope: "J'ai accepté les décisions de Rome avec espoir."

a composer of music for Taizé, Berthier crafted his music for an ecumenical community of brothers who had adopted as their own, the Council's value of active participation in the liturgy.[3]

Therefore, as a first step toward developing a critical theory of music as ritual symbol, this chapter will examine the Second Vatican Council's interpretation of the nature of the relationship of music to the liturgy and its implications for musical practice. These pastoral concerns were addressed in *Sacrosanctum Concilium,* promulgated on Dec. 4, 1963. While this constitution offers many directives on the promotion and reform of the liturgy, for many concerned with the liturgy and its music, *SC* raised more questions than it answered. In fact, like other documents promulgated by the Second Vatican Council, the text of "Chapter Six: Sacred Music" invites a variety of interpretations. This was evident in the polarization which quickly developed after the Council between those who interpreted the document as a call for new approaches and those who interpreted it as a reaffirmation of traditional musical practices.

INTERPRETING CONCILIAR TEXTS

In his efforts to develop a hermeneutic for interpreting the conciliar texts of Vatican II, Hermann J. Pottmeyer points out that the method the Council used to link two concerns was essentially one of juxtaposition. He explains that "alongside a doctrine or thesis couched in preconciliar language is set a doctrine or thesis that formulates some complementary aspect."[4] While a widespread view has been to interpret this method as compromise in the pejorative sense, Pottmeyer believes that such an

---

[3] See John HEIJKE, *An Ecumenical Light on the Renewal of Religious Community Life: Taizé,* Duquesne Studies: Theological Series, no. 7 (Pittsburgh: Duquesne University Press, 1967), 38. Pope John XXIII had personally invited the Community of Taizé to send two of its members to the Council as observers. Throughout the Council, a fraternity of brothers, consisting of the Prior, his fellow-observer and three or four other brothers lived in Rome and exercised a "ministry of welcome and presence." Often, they shared meals with the various participants in the Council, including bishops, observers, theologians, and lay auditors.

[4] Hermann J. POTTMEYER, "A New Phase in the Reception of Vatican II," in *The Reception of Vatican II,* ed. Giuseppe ALBERIGO, Jean-Pierre JOSSUA, and Joseph A. KOMONCHAK, trans. Matthew J. O'CONNELL (Washington, D.C.: The Catholic University of America Press, 1987), 37.

interpretation is too superficial. Rather, he sees the method of juxtaposition itself as an example of progress, since, in complementing the older thesis, it relativizes it as one-sided and provides bearings for further development.[5]

For example, article 112 of *SC* states that the Church "approves of all forms of true art which have the requisite qualities, and admits them into divine worship."[6] On the other hand, article 114 states that "the treasury of sacred music is to be preserved and cultivated with great care." Since the promulgation of *SC*, musicians and liturgists have continued to wrestle with the possibilities of employing the so-called "treasury of sacred music,"[7] adapting old forms where feasible, and introducing new styles of music whose forms are congenial with the requirements of the liturgy.

Three decades after the Council, those involved with developing the theory and practice of liturgical music are still working to create a synthesis. Such efforts are, as church historians[8] point out, part of the very process of receiving and implementing conciliar pronouncements. In fact, examining the process whereby the decisions of Vatican II continue

---

[5] POTTMEYER, "A New Phase," 38.

[6] Sacrosanctum Oecumenicum Concilium Vaticanum, "Constitutione de sacra liturgia," in *Constitutiones, Decreta, Declarationes,* 3-70 (typis Polyglottis Vaticanis, 1966), 112. In this study the English translation is quoted from Austin FLANNERY, gen. ed., "The Constitution on the Sacred Liturgy," in *Vatican Council II: The Conciliar and Post Conciliar Documents,* 1-37, revised edition (Grand Rapids, Michigan: William B. Eerdmans Publishing Company, 1984), 112. Quotes from all church documents and documents of professional and scholarly organizations are identified by article number rather than page number.

[7] Rembert Weakland, Archbishop of Milwaukee and professional musician, has summed up his judgment of the situation in this way: "The first is that *there is no music of a liturgical golden age to which we can turn, because the treasures we have are the product of ages that do not represent an ideal of theological thinking in relationship to liturgy.* The second is *that the Romantic period made a false aesthetic judgment about the music of the past, a judgment that has found its way into official documents.*" See Rembert WEAKLAND, *Themes of Renewal* (Beltsville, Maryland: The Pastoral Press, 1995), 97.

[8] See Yves CONGAR, "Reception as an Ecclesial Reality," trans. John GRIFFITHS, in *Election and Consensus in the Church,* ed. Giuseppe ALBERIGO and Anton WEILER, 43-68, Concilium: Religion in the Seventies, no. 77 (New York: Herder and Herder, 1972); Giuseppe ALBERIGO, "The Christian Situation after Vatican II," in *The Reception of Vatican II,* ed. Giuseppe ALBERIGO, Jean-Pierre JOSSUA, and Joseph KOMONCHAK, 1-24, trans. Matthew J. O'CONNELL (Washington, D.C.: The Catholic University of America Press, 1987); and Hermann J. POTTMEYER, "A New Phase in the Reception of Vatican II, in *The Reception of Vatican II,* 27 43.

to be received and implemented is itself part of the very process of that reception. For as Giusseppe Alberigo has pointed out,

> These postconciliar stages which the Church has had to endure, and which have been so fruitful, represent a privileged phase in the life of the Church. Their function has been to authenticate the harmony between conciliar decisions and ecclesial consciousness by setting in motion latent forces and sleeping energies present in the people of God and bringing into play a dynamic rarely found in political societies.[9]

In Alberigo's assessment, the Church's postconciliar struggles to interpret and implement conciliar decisions are an important and necessary part of the conciliar process since they can enable the Church, as an ecclesial community, to harmonize theory and practice.

Yves Congar makes another important point regarding the complexity of the process. In his assessment, the reception of Vatican II, like every other reception, involves more than obedience. It also includes a degree of consent, and often of judgment which brings into play the ecclesial community's own original resources.[10]

As Pottmeyer understands it, reception requires an interpretive process which involves two steps. The first involves the interpretation of the documents of Vatican II which are found in post-conciliar legislation such as papal encyclicals and addresses, curial decisions and declarations, episcopal synods, and pastoral letters. This interpretation of legislation can be supplemented by the interpretation of new liturgical texts and forms introduced as a result of the Council. The second step involves the interpretation of theological writings, religious literature and the actual practice and implementation of local churches.[11]

If an essential element of reception is the interpretation of conciliar texts, it is clear that the reception of Vatican II is still in process. That synthesis of understandings so necessary "to authenticate the harmony between conciliar decisions and ecclesial consciousness"[12] is a goal yet to be realized. This is true for both doctrinal and pastoral concerns.

In Pottmeyer's judgment, Vatican II was probably not capable of going beyond juxtaposition to a new synthesis. That aspect of the task

---

[9] ALBERIGO, "The Christian Situation," 6.
[10] CONGAR, "Reception," 45.
[11] POTTMEYER, "A New Phase," 29.
[12] See quote, n. 9.

of reception, both official and unofficial, is reserved to the post-conciliar ecclesial community. Such a synthesis calls for an active engagement
in the interpretation of the texts.[13] Furthermore, Pottmeyer challenges
the post-conciliar Church to engage in a hermeneutical process which
takes seriously *both* juxtaposed theses and attempts to reconcile them in
a synthesis that will allow further advances.[14]

Chapter one of this study seeks to move forward the post-conciliar
effort to synthesize the legacy of the Second Vatican Council's thinking
on the relationship of music and liturgy. To do so it will begin with an
examination of the principles and directives regarding the role of music
in the liturgy as they have been articulated in *Sacrosanctum Concilium*.
By way of background, Pius X's 1903 motu proprio, *Tra le sollecitudini*
will be examined because several of its principles are explicitly reaf-
firmed in the Vatican II document.

To review the process of reception of *SC* on the regional and/or
national levels throughout the universal church is a task beyond the
scope of this study. Therefore, this study will limit itself to a consideration of the reception of Vatican II's thinking on music and liturgy to
that of the National Conference of Catholic Bishops[15] of the United
States. The two key documents published by the NCCB that will be
considered in this study are *Music in Catholic Worship* (1972) and *Liturgical Music Today* (1982).

Since the process of reception also involves an interpretation of unofficial documents,[16] our study will include an analysis of the corporate
statements of professional or scholarly groups or organizations involved
in worship and/or worship music whose work keeps them in dialogue
with the reforms of the Second Vatican Council. These will include one
international and two American documents. The international document is *De la musique dans les liturgies chrétiennes* (1980), published by
Universa Laus.[17] The documents published in the United States are *The
Milwaukee Symposia for Church Composers: A Ten-Year Report* (1992)
and *The Snowbird Statement on Catholic Liturgical Music* (1995).

Although the focus in this study is on the reception of *Sacrosanctum
Concilium* in the Church in the United States, I have made the decision

---

[13] POTTMEYER, "A New Phase," 38.
[14] POTTMEYER, "A New Phase," 39.
[15] Hereafter NCCB.
[16] See ch.1, n. 11 above.
[17] Hereafter *UL*.

to include the *UL document* in my analysis for three reasons. Firstly, this document addresses the issues regarding music and liturgy that are the focus of this study. Secondly, conversations between members of this organization, which for the most part is presently constituted of members from Western European countries, and U.S. musicians and liturgists, have already influenced U.S. efforts to deal with questions regarding music and liturgy.[18] Thirdly, because of the strong cultural and historical ties between the United States and the Western European churches, an exchange of ideas regarding these issues has already proved to be mutually beneficial.[19]

The study of the documents will be presented in three parts. The first section will identify key elements in seven documents which address the relationship of music to the liturgy. The next section will identify three ideas which appear as common themes in all the documents and offer a comparative analysis of the manner in which each document treats these key notions. The final section will offer some preliminary observations regarding the tradition within which the questions emerged, the shifts in emphasis which have occurred, and an alternate way of formulating the questions so that a new synthesis might be achieved.

OFFICIAL DOCUMENTS ON LITURGICAL MUSIC

This section will examine official documents on liturgical music in order to discover whether they make any connection between music's ministerial function and the fact that music can be said to be integral to the liturgy. The first part will consider official church statements, both conciliar and post-conciliar, and the second part, statements of professional and scholarly organizations.

---

[18] A great deal of exchange of ideas has already occurred between the European group, *Universa Laus* and the American organization, the National Association of Pastoral Musicians (NPM), largely through the efforts of Virgil Funk, president of NPM.

[19] Joseph Gelineau, SJ, an influential member of *Universa Laus* since its very beginning in 1966 and friend and collaborator of Jacques Berthier, has also been an important conversation partner with NPM, as lecturer at its conventions and contributor to its journal, *Pastoral Music*. In addition, Joseph Gelineau has been a persistent presence to developments in liturgical music on both sides of the Atlantic through his published music, books, and articles.

Official Church Statements: Vatican II

Sacrosanctum Concilium, the Constitution on the Sacred Liturgy promulgated by the Second Vatican Council, devotes an entire chapter to sacred music.[20] It is specifically article 112 of that sixth chapter, however, that offers a key to the council fathers' understanding of the purpose and nature of sacred music as it pertains to its role in the liturgy.

The opening sentence of article 112 states that traditionally music has been esteemed by the universal Church as a treasure greater than that of any other art. This statement is significant for two reasons. In the first place, it implies that the nature of music sets it apart from the other arts, and secondly, it acknowledges that music's unique nature makes it eminently suitable for worship.

One way in which music differs from the other arts is in its relationship to the artist. For while the visual arts such as sculpture, painting, and architecture produce a permanent object which can be appreciated apart from the artist, music-making, while not requiring the presence of the original composer, nevertheless depends on the personal activity of a music-maker.

Some may argue that recent technological advances in sound reproduction through electronic means eliminate the requirement of the personal presence of the music-maker. However, *Liturgical Music Today*, a 1983 statement of the NCCB, has clarified limitations on the use of recorded music in the liturgy.[21] The value invoked in this case is explained in the context of describing music as a sign:

> "The liturgy is a complexus of signs[22] expressed by living human beings. Music, being preeminent among those signs, ought to be "live" (*LTM* 60).

[20] The English translations of *Sacrosanctum Concilium* and of documents promulgated earlier in the twentieth century beginning with *Tra le sollecitudini* use the term "sacred music" to describe the music used in Roman Catholic liturgy. Documents written after the Second Vatican Council, in addition to using that term, also use the terms "liturgical music", "ritual music", and "sung prayer" to refer to the same music. Further on this paper will trace how the use of different terminology reflects different understandings of the role of music in the liturgy and its relationship to the ritual, the text, and the assembly.

[21] Bishops' Committee on the Liturgy, *Liturgical Music Today* (Washington, D.C.: USCC Publications Office, 1982), 60-62. Hereafter *LTM*.

[22] Like *Music in Catholic Worship*, for which *Liturgical Music Today* serves as a kind of appendix, the words "sign" and "symbol" are used interchangeably to describe the same reality. Cf. articles four, five, seven, eight, nine, and twenty-three of *MCW* where sign and symbol are used without differentiation.

Two ideas that will be pivotal to this paper's development of a theology of symbol in chapter three are being juxtaposed in this statement. The first is the fact that music, like the liturgy itself is a sign or symbol. The second is the fact that liturgical symbols require human presence for their expression.

Because of the values and guidelines articulated in *LTM* regarding the arts and the liturgy,[23] the assumption of this study is that live music-making is the norm for Roman Catholic liturgy. Furthermore, the very nature of music which requires a personal presence and engagement in the act of music-making, uniquely enables it to promote the active participation of the assembly, one of the Council's primary goals in *SC*.[24]

The second paragraph of article 112 of *SC* cites[25] Pius X's motu proprio[26] *Tra le sollecitudini (1903)*,[27] as the foundation for its understanding of the ministerial function exercised by music.[28] A comparison between

---

[23] Cf. Bishops' Committee on the Liturgy, *Environment and Art in Catholic Worship* (Washington, D.C.: USCC Publications Office, 1978). This document upholds similar values to those expressed in *LTM*. Article sixty-seven offers the following criteria regarding any object used in liturgy: "None should be made in such a way that it is far removed from the print of the human hand and human craft." This principle can be applied, *mutatis mutandis* to music since the document also states that the criteria it presents for quality apply to "any art form that might be employed in the liturgical environment or action," that is, "music, architecture, sculpture, painting, pottery making, furniture making, as well as to dance, mime or drama" (*EACW* 20).

[24] Cf. *SC* 11, 14, 113, and 114.

[25] By mentioning the pontiff's name in this context, the council fathers implicitly confirm his work. See Ernest Moneta CAGLIO, "Chapter Six: Sacred Music," in *The Commentary on the Constitution and on the Instruction on the Sacred Liturgy*, ed. Annibale BUGNINI and Charles BRAGA, trans. Vincent P. MALLON (New York: Benzinger Brothers, 1965), 244.

[26] A motu proprio is a papal document written on the pope's own initiative. The full title is *apostolic letter motu proprio*. Such documents are of a serious and legislative nature and addressed to the universal Church. See R. Kevin SEASOLTZ, *New Liturgy, New Laws* (Collegeville: The Liturgical Press, 1980), 174.

[27] PIUS X, *"Tra le sollecitudini,"* in *Acta Sanctae Sedis* 36 (1904): 329-339. In this study the English translation quoted is from R. Kevin SEASOLTZ, *The New Liturgy: A Documentation, 1903-1965*, (New York: Herder and Herder, 1966), 3-10. Hereafter *TLS*.

[28] See Yves CONGAR, "Reception," 53. Congar points out that in ancient times a council would begin with a reading of the decrees of previous councils. While such a practice was intended as a new stage in the process of transmission, it was also an act of reception. Such a citing is also another example of the method of juxtaposition whereby a preconciliar statement is set alongside a new insight.

article one of the motu proprio and article 112 of the constitution reveals how influential the former was in shaping the latter. *TLS* states:

> Sacred music, as an *integral part of the solemn liturgy*, participates in its general object, which is *the glory of God and the sanctification and edification of the faithful* (emphasis added) (*TLS* 1).

SC states:

> The musical tradition of the universal Church ... as a combination of sacred music and words ... forms a necessary or *integral part of the solemn liturgy* ... Accordingly, the sacred Council [acknowledges] the purpose of *sacred music*, which is *the glory of God and the sanctification of the faithful* ... (emphasis added) (*SC* 112).

The two-fold common goal of the liturgy and sacred music expressed in *TLS* is echoed in *SC* in the very same language. That is, both documents employ the term "sacred music," describe it as "integral" to the liturgy, and attribute to it the purpose of giving "glory to God" and promoting the "sanctification of the faithful."

In the same article, *TLS* goes on to list additional effects or purposes of sacred music when it states:

> It [sacred music] tends to increase the decorum and the splendor of the ecclesiastical ceremonies, and since its principal office is to clothe with befitting melody the liturgical text proposed for the understanding of the faithful its proper end is to add greater efficacy to the text, in order that by means of it the faithful may be the more easily moved to devotion and better disposed to receive the fruits of grace associated with the celebration of the most holy mysteries (*TLS* 1).

This section describes music as ancillary both to the rite and to the liturgical texts. This is expressed when the text credits music with increasing the decorum and splendor of the ceremonies. It is further evident when music's proper purpose is identified as "clothing" the texts so as to promote devotion.

Sacrosanctum Concilium's reiteration of Pius X's document is expressed in this way:

> ...sacred music ... making prayer more pleasing, promoting unity of minds, or conferring greater solemnity upon the rites ... admits [music] ... into divine worship (*SC* 112).

This section echoes *TLS's* notion that music's purpose is at the service of the rite. The description of music's role in regard to liturgical texts had come earlier in the article when it stated that music "as a combination of sacred music and words" is an "integral part of the solemn liturgy" (*SC 112*).

The influence of *TLS* on the formulation of *SC* is clearly evident. There are, however, some points on which *SC* begins to move beyond the articulations of *TLS*. One such point is the understanding of what qualifies music as "sacred."

In article two of *TLS*, Pius X had defined sacred music as that which possesses the qualities proper to the liturgy, that is, sanctity and goodness of form. Neither term is defined nor explained, except for the fact that the document holds up Gregorian chant and classic polyphony, especially of the Roman school, as models of music possessing these qualities.[29] The second paragraph of article two of *TLS* provides further clues to what "sanctity and goodness" of form refer when it states:

> It [music] must be holy, and must accordingly, exclude all profanity not only in itself, but in the manner in which it is presented to those who execute it.

The term "profanity" is not defined, nor are examples of profane music offered. Helmut Hucke, however, believes that Pius X uses the term "profane" to refer to a specific style of musical performance. In comparing the usage of this term at the Council of Trent and taking into account the historical context of *TLS*, Hucke's judgment is that, "without a doubt, for Pius it referred to the practice of bringing into the church the questionable 'virtuosity' of Italian opera at that time."[30]

On the other hand, even though *SC* employs the same terminology as *TLS* in requiring that sacred music be "holy", there is a subtle shift of focus when *SC* says:

> Therefore sacred music is to be considered the more holy, the more closely connected it is with the liturgical action, whether making prayer more pleasing, promoting unity of minds, or conferring greater solemnity upon the sacred rites (*SC* 112).

[29] *TLS*, 3-4.
[30] Helmut HUCKE, "The Concept of Church Music in History," trans. Gordon E. TRUITT, in *Aide-Mémoire UL: Excerpts from the UL Bulletin 1979-1983* (Washington, D.C.: Universa Laus and the National Association of Pastoral Musicians, 1996), 6.

Where *TLS* had defined sacred music as that music which is holy because it excludes all profanity, *SC* now explains that sacred music is holy the more closely it is connected with the liturgical action. By giving several examples of how music might be so connected, *SC* returns to the notion that music is at the service of the rite.

Despite these subtle shifts, there are still significant areas of agreement between *TLS* and *SC*. In the first place, both documents identify the purpose of sacred music in the liturgy to be the same as the purpose of the liturgy itself. That is, the goal of sacred music, like the liturgy, is the glory of God and the sanctification of the faithful. Secondly, both documents identify music's role as ministerial. That is, music's value in the liturgy is located in its ability to enhance the ecclesiastical ceremonies, to highlight the liturgical text, and to inspire the faithful.

Further on in *TLS*, Pius X reiterates the ministerial function of music in the liturgy when he states that "it must be considered to be a very grave abuse when the liturgy in ecclesiastical functions is made to appear secondary to and in a manner at the service of the music, for the music is merely a part of the liturgy and its humble handmaid" (*TLS 23*).

In the light of the excesses of the historical period which inspired this remark,[31] the pontiff's caution that the liturgy not become a mere backdrop for musical performance is understandable. Nevertheless, his rhetoric of subordination seems inconsistent with the lofty role he assigns it in article one. There he describes it as "an integral part of the solemn liturgy," a role by which it "participates in its general object, which is the glory of God and the sanctification and edification of the faithful." While *The Constitution on the Sacred Liturgy* acknowledges the influence of Pius X on its understanding of the subordination of music to the liturgy, it prefers the phrase "ministerial function" to describe "sacred music in the service of the Lord."

---

[31] See Gustav FELLERER, *The History of Catholic Church Music*, trans. Francis A. BRUNNER (Baltimore: Helicon Press, 1961), 134. In this book, Fellerer identifies the historical period beginning with the Baroque era as that time when music's relationship with the liturgy could be described as "music at worship." By using the preposition "at" Fellerer highlights the facts that beginning in the 16th century and continuing into the 17th and 18th centuries, the idea of church music as integral to the liturgy was lost. The liturgical action was no longer the focal point.

Even with the shift from "humble handmaid" to "ministerial function," there appears to be some ambiguity regarding the actual role of music in the liturgy. Pottmeyer's hermeneutic of juxtaposition would suggest that here is an area which challenges our postconciliar period to work toward a new synthesis.

The documents do make a connection between music's ministerial function and the fact that it can be said to be integral to the liturgy. That is, they suggest that music's role as integral is determined by its relationship to the ritual, the text, and the assembly. The documents appear to be saying that it is this relationship which in some way renders music "sacred." In this way, music which is at the service of the ritual, the text, and the assembly, can in some way be called "sacred" and thereby capable of sharing in the twofold goal of the liturgy: the glory of God and the sanctification of the faithful.

However, neither *Tra le sollecitudini* nor *Sacrosanctum Concilium* explain how music fulfills such a lofty role. We look next to postconciliar statements to see whether there are any further developments in understanding music as ministerial and integral to the liturgy.

Official Church Statements: Post-conciliar

Musicam sacram (1967), an instruction[32] on music in the liturgy by the Sacred Congregation for Rites,[33] was published to clarify and amplify *Sacrosanctum Concilium* (1963). Article five develops the principles set out in article 112 of *SC:*

> A liturgical service takes on a nobler aspect when the rites are celebrated with singing, the ministers of each rank take their parts in them, and the congregation actively participates. This form of celebration gives a more graceful expression to prayer and brings out more distinctly the hierarchic character of the liturgy and the specific make-up of the community. It

---

[32] See R. Kevin SEASOLTZ *New Liturgy, New Laws* (Collegeville: The Liturgical Press, 1980), 175. Seasoltz defines an instruction in this way: "An *instruction* is a doctrinal explanation or a set of directives, recommendations, or admonitions issued by the Roman curia. It usually elaborates on prescriptions so that they may be more effectively implemented. Strictly speaking, an instruction does not have the force of universal law or definition."

[33] The Sacred Congregation of Rites was an office of the Roman Curia established by Pope Sixtus V in 1588 to protect the legitimate rites of the Church. This congregation was replaced by Pope Paul VI in 1969 by the Congregation for Divine Worship.

achieves a closer union of hearts through the union of voices. It raises the mind more readily to heavenly realities through the splendor of the rites.[34]

This explanation focuses specifically on singing rather than on the broader category of liturgical music which would include instrumental music. It highlights the ministerial role of singing in regard to the rites and to the community assembled with only indirect references to the texts.

The first paragraph of article five of *MS* closes with the following significant remark:

> It [singing] makes the whole celebration a more striking symbol of the celebration to come in the heavenly Jerusalem.

This is the first instance in the documents thus far reviewed in this study where an explicit mention of the notion of symbol has been connected in any way with the role of music in the liturgy. The sentence says that singing makes the liturgy "a more striking symbol." This English translation[35] makes explicit reference to the symbolic function of music in connection with the description of music's eschatological character. Earlier, the article also expresses an implicit understanding of music's symbolic role in its description of music's ability to bring out the specific makeup of the community and to promote unity among its members.[36] These statements, then, articulate an inchoate understanding of music as symbol in the liturgy.

But aside from this new insight regarding symbol, *Musicam Sacram (1967)* reflects many of the same assumptions first expressed in *Tra le*

---

[34] Sacred Congregation of Rites, "*Musicam Sacram,*" in *Acta Apostolicae Sedis* 60 (1967): 5. In this study the English translation is taken from *Documents on the Liturgy 1963-1979: Conciliar, Papal, and Curial Texts* (Collegeville: The Liturgical Press, 1982). Hereafter *MS* and *DOL*.

[35] The original Latin for the final sentence of paragraph one of article five reads: "*Per hanc enim formam oratio [cum in cantu] suavius exprimitur, mysterium sacrae Liturgiae eiusque indoles hierarchica et communitatis propria apertius manifestantur, unitas cordium per vocis unitatem profundius attingitur, mentes per rerum sacrarum splendorem ad superna facilius extolluntur, et universa celebratio illam clarius praefigurat, quae in sancta civitate Ierusalem peragitur.* Cf. *Acta Apostolicae Sedis* 60 (1967): 301. The Latin *praefigurat* has been translated as *making a symbol* in the *DOL* translation. Cf. Robert F. HAYBURN, *Papal Legislation on Sacred Music: 95 A.D. to 1977* (Collegeville: The Liturgical Press, 1979), 547. This translation of article five reads: "through this form [singing] ... the whole celebration more clearly *prefigures* that heavenly liturgy ...

[36] See above.

sollecitudini. For example, its understanding of "sacred" music as that which is "composed for the celebration of divine worship and possesses integrity of form" (*MS* 4) echoes the motu proprio. On the other hand, *Musicam sacram* reaffirms Vatican II's judgment that the repertoire of music that fulfills these criteria includes, not only Gregorian chant and classic polyphony, but also "modern" polyphony, "sacred music for organ and for other permitted instruments, and the sacred, i.e., liturgical or religious, music of the people" (*MS* 4).

Shortly after the publication of the instruction *Musicam Sacram,* the Bishops' Committee on the Liturgy of the NCCB issued its own statements on the role of music in the liturgy. Two key documents will be considered in this section. The first, *Music in Catholic Worship (1972),* is the foundational document.[37] The second, *Liturgical Music Today (1982),* serves as an appendix to the first.

Using the statements of the previous documents as its starting point, *Music in Catholic Worship* advances an understanding of music's role in worship by juxtaposing the notion of music as integral, symbolic and ministerial. It begins by bringing together the notions of music as integral and symbolic:

> Among the many signs and symbols used by the church to celebrate its faith, music is of preeminent importance. As sacred song united to words it forms a necessary or integral part of the solemn liturgy.[38]

This quote makes two assertions about music. The first is that it is a *sign* or *symbol*[39] of preeminent importance by which the church expresses it faith. The second is that it is *integral* to worship when it is united to the words of the liturgy. This is an important distinction. Being of preeminent importance is not the same as being integral. The integral role is specifically assigned to music's link with the words of the liturgy.

The article goes on to say:

---

[37] The Bishops' Committee on the Liturgy had actually published an earlier document entitled *The Place of Music in Eucharistic Celebrations (1967).* However, this document was soon superseded by *Music in Catholic Worship (1972),* as the authoritative and foundational statement regarding music in worship in the United States.

[38] Bishops' Committee on the Liturgy, *Music in Catholic Worship* (Washington, D.C.: USCC Publications Office, 1982), 23. Hereafter *MCW.*

[39] This is one of those instances previously noted above where *MCW* appears to make no distinction in its usage of the terms "sign" and "symbol."

> Yet the function of music is ministerial; it must serve and never dominate. Music should assist the assembled believers to express and share the gift of faith that is within them and to nourish and strengthen their interior commitment of faith. It should heighten the texts so that they speak more fully and more effectively ... It imparts a sense of unity to the congregation and sets the appropriate tone for a particular celebration (*MCW* 23).

This section of the article introduces the notion of music's ministerial role and describes it in terms of music's relationship to the rite, the assembly and the texts. Note that this formulation follows the earlier statement, cited above, that music is a sign and symbol and that it is integral to the liturgy. By juxtaposing these ideas, article twenty-three makes a clear connection between music as integral and music as ministerial.

It is in the subsequent article, however, that an explanation is offered regarding how music may function as symbol, that is, as an embodiment of meaning:

> In addition to expressing texts, music can also unveil a dimension of meaning and feeling, a communication of ideas and intuitions which words alone cannot yield. This dimension is integral to the human personality and to growth in faith. It cannot be ignored if the signs of worship are to speak to the whole person (*MCW* 24).

This article suggests that the power of music to communicate meaning may extend beyond that of the power of language. So even though this point follows the statement that music is integral to the liturgy insofar as it is connected to the liturgical texts, yet there is an acknowledgement of an additional dimension to music, one which is tied to both our human and our spiritual life.

Thus *Music in Catholic Worship* is the first document to describe music as one of the many "signs or symbols" used by the church in liturgical celebrations. Exactly how music functions as sign or symbol in expressing faith, heightening texts, imparting a sense of unity or expressing meaning and feeling is not explained. Nevertheless, the importance of what music accomplishes in the liturgy is clearly asserted.

Ten years after publishing *Music in Catholic Worship*, the Bishops' Committee on the Liturgy issued *Liturgical Music Today (1982)*, an anniversary supplement to the original statement. This document makes two subtle shifts regarding the articulation of music's role in the liturgy. The first shift has to do with the notion of music as integral. Instead of saying that music is integral to the liturgy, *LMT* describes the Church's liturgy as "inherently musical" (*LMT* 5). Further on, the document describes various parts of the liturgy as "sung prayer" (*LMT* 5, 7). In discussing particular ritual moments which call for sung prayer, *LMT* explains that certain acclamations "demand song, since they are by nature musical forms" (*LMT* 8).

The second shift has to do with the notion of music as ministerial. Articles nine and ten differentiate two ritual functions of song. The first instance is when "song is meant to accompany ritual actions. In such cases the song is not independent but serves, rather, to support the prayer of the assembly ... The music enriches the moments [sic] and keeps it from becoming burdensome" (*LMT* 9). In the second instance, "the sung prayer itself is a constituent element of the rite. While it is being prayed, no other ritual action is being performed" (*LMT 10*).

Nevertheless, even in describing music as a minister of the rite, *LMT* reiterates the fact that music is integral when it concludes by saying that "[I]n each of these cases the music does not serve as a mere accompaniment, but as the integral mode by which the mystery is proclaimed and presented" (*LMT* 10).

Despite the fact that *LMT* acknowledges a close identification between music and the liturgy, certain reservations are expressed. For example, the document cautions that "the musical form employed must match its liturgical function" (*LMT* 11), and that it is necessary to guard "against the imposition of private meanings on public rites" (*LMT* 12). These cautions indicate a concern that the music chosen serve the ritual.

While the 1982 *Liturgical Music Today* develops several of the principles set out in the 1972 *Music in Catholic Worship*, the terms "sign" and "symbol" are conspicuously absent. Such phrases as "inherently musical" and "sung prayers," as well as such descriptions of acclamations as "by nature musical forms" begin to blur the lines of distinction between the music and the texts, the ritual, and the assembly. The result is a new articulation of music as integral to worship based on an understanding of music and liturgy as coterminus: making music – at least under those conditions when that action serves the liturgy's texts, assembly, and ritual – is understood to be a mode of doing liturgy.

Documents of Professional and Scholarly Organizations

The documents discussed in the previous section are the key statements officially promulgated by the Church that have guided both the composition of music and the practice of music-making in the Roman Catholic liturgy in the United States in the late twentieth century. Organizations of professional musicians and liturgical scholars have referred to them in their efforts to respond to the reforms of the Second Vatican Council in their own particular areas of expertise. Several of these groups have published their own documents based on their experience and their interpretation of the official church documents.

This section will focus on three documents published by professional groups. The representative documents have been chosen for the following reasons: 1) The documents address the key issues of concern in this paper, that is, the notions of music as symbolic, ministerial, and integral to the liturgy; 2) The members of the group have been active in the practice and research of music and/or liturgy; 3) The insights articulated in the documents promise to be helpful in moving toward a synthesis of the principles set forth in *Sacrosanctum Concilium*.

The first organization to be considered is *Universa Laus*, an international group founded for the study of singing and instrumental music in the liturgy in 1966. While its membership is international and interdenominational, its western European and Roman Catholic components are the strongest. Several members of *UL* had already been working together for many years before the groups' founding. Some had been doing so as private individuals, while others collaborated through affiliation with the groups publishing such journals as *Musik und Altar* in Germany or *Eglise qui chante,* in France.[40] When it became clear that liturgy would be a first priority at the Second Vatican Council, these same liturgists and musicologists devoted their efforts to supporting the work of those whose task it was to present texts and schemas to the council fathers.[41]

---

[40] *Eglise qui chante* is a publication of the Association Saint-Ambroise which was founded for the promotion of the singing of the people in 1957 by David Julien, René Reboud, Lucien Deiss, and Joseph Gelineau.

[41] Universa Laus, *Musique et liturgie* (Paris: Les Editions du Cerf, 1988). Translation in Claude DUCHESNEAU and Michel VEUTHEY, eds., *Music and Liturgy: The Universa Laus Document and Commentary*, trans. Paul INWOOD (Washington, D.C.: The Pastoral Press, 1992), 1, 11. Hereafter *Music and Liturgy.* The French title, *Musique et liturgie,* is

After researching and reflecting on the "ritual function" of liturgical chants in the years immediately following Vatican II, the group decided, a quarter of a century later, that it was time to issue a joint statement which could serve as a point of reference and attempt to define a number of useful concepts.[42] The result was the document *De la musique dans les liturgies chrétiennes* (1980).[43] It is comprised of two sections: 1) "Points of Reference," an "organically arranged" presentation in ten chapters; and 2) "Beliefs Held in Common," consisting of forty-five aphorisms restating the points of reference in a more incisive form.[44] While the document is the result of the corporate thinking of *UL*, the version that was finally approved by the group was the draft submitted by Joseph Gelineau.[45]

The *UL* document discusses music in three ways: as symbolic practice, as ritual practice, and as ministerial. Each of these understandings will be considered in turn.

Several articles of the document refer to the symbolic nature of music. Concerning singing in Christian assemblies, the document states:

> The liturgy, namely the communal action of a people who gather together in the name of Jesus to celebrate the mysteries of their faith, is made up of a number of symbolic practices: rites and sacraments. Music has a special place among such practices.[46]

---

the title of the publication which includes both document and commentary. The English publication is called *Music and Liturgy*. The title of the actual document found in *Musique et liturgie* is "De la Musique dans les Liturgies Chrétiennes." The English title of the document is "Music in Christian Celebration."

[42] *Music and Liturgy*, 2-3.

[43] *Universa Laus*, "De la musique dans les liturgies chrétiennes," in *Musique et liturgie* (Paris: Les Editions du Cerf, 1988). In this study, the English translation is taken from Claude DUCHESNEAU and Michel VEUTHEY, eds., "Music in Christian Celebration," in *Music and Liturgy: The Universa Laus Document and Commentary*, trans. Paul INWOOD (Washington, D.C.: The Pastoral Press, 1992). Hereafter *MCC*. The document is divided into two parts, "Points" and "Beliefs." However, since the section entitled "Beliefs" is simply a concise restatement of the principles developed at greater length in "Points," only the part entitled "Points" will be analyzed here. See *Music and Liturgy*, 3.

[44] *Music and Liturgy*, 3.

[45] *Music and Liturgy*, 5.

[46] *MCC*, 1.1.

In its very first article, the *UL* document identifies music as a symbolic practice which holds a special place in the liturgy. This assertion becomes foundational for developing the argument for music's role in the liturgy.

In the section discussing Christian ritual music in various cultures, *UL* explains that "liturgical celebration is a symbolic whole; and all its elements, musical or not, are interdependent" (*MCC*, 2.8). Likewise, when referring to the notion that ritual music is for everyone, the document points out that "the music performed in an assembly is offered to the assembly[47] as a symbolic sign of what the assembly is celebrating" (*MCC*, 4.1). Even when referring to the ritual functions of music, the document expresses the idea in terms of "symbolizing festivity" (*MCC*, 7.1).

When considering music-making as ritual practice, *MCC* acknowledges that music takes on a variety of different roles:

> Liturgical celebration calls for a wide variety of vocal acts and verbo-musical genres because different functions of language are brought into play ... Each of these types of language corresponds to a different relation between text and music (*MCC*, 5.3).

This statement takes into account the fact that music relates in a variety of ways to liturgical texts just as the texts themselves embody a variety of responses to the requirements of ritual.

The next article acknowledges that music also relates in a variety of ways to the ritual itself:

> In certain cases, a musical act may constitute a rite in itself: e.g., the ringing of bells or music for meditation. In other cases it may be integral to a rite: e.g., a procession or an action without singing (*MCC*, 6.4).

In other words, music-making is capable of relating to ritual in several ways.[48] Different musical forms correspond to different ritual forms so that appropriate choices may enhance the ritual moment (*MCC*, 7.3).

---

[47] In this document, the phrase "offered to the assembly" describes both the instance when the assembly is called upon to sing and to listen. This meaning becomes evident in the commentary: "Music becomes a rite ... accomplished in the very bosom of the assembly, for the assembly and, often, by the assembly. But such a role has its demands. It presupposes ... that the music offered to the faithful is suited to their abilities, when they are to sing, and to their perceptive faculties, when they are to listen." See *Music and Liturgy*, 60.

[48] This article regarding music's role in ritual echoes articles nine through eleven in *Liturgical Music Today*. See above.

Even though *MCC* has adopted the term "ritual music," the document does not understand this role in narrow, functional terms. Rather, *MCC* relates music's ritual functions to its ministerial and symbolic function. This is evident in the section entitled "Ritual Functions," where the document equates music's effectiveness in serving the text and the ritual action, and by extension, the assembly, with its success as ritual music. In addition, this section returns to the notion of music as symbol and adds further development to principles which had been introduced earlier:

> However, the role of music in the liturgy extends well beyond what one can see of how well it works. Like every symbolic sign, music "refers" to something beyond itself. It opens the door to the indefinable realm of meanings and reactions. Taken in terms of faith, music for the believer becomes the *sacramentum* and the *mysterion* of the realities being celebrated (*MCC*, 7.4).

The very first statement of this document had identified liturgy as an action composed of symbolic practices.[49] Therefore, when the document states that music serves the ritual, that is, the liturgy, it is saying that music serves a complexus of liturgical symbols. It might be more accurate to say that music serves the purpose that all symbols serve. That purpose is to point to something beyond itself.[50] In the context of the liturgy, music, in interacting with other liturgical symbols, points beyond itself to the mystery of faith being celebrated.

In neither of the two sections of the *Universa Laus* document is the meaning of symbolic practices, symbolic sign or symbolizing defined. However, both the French and the English translation include a commentary of the document which does pursue the meaning of these notions and how they pertain to music in the liturgy.[51] In addition, a glossary, compiled by a group of collaborators from French-speaking countries, offers somewhat lengthy explanations of what the document means by "symbol" and "symbolic practices."

---

[49] *MCC*, 1.1.

[50] See Paul TILLICH, *Dynamics of Faith* (New York: Harper and Row, Publishers, 1957), 41-42. This ability of symbol to point to something outside itself is sometimes referred to as the *indexical* property of sign or symbol. See Jean-Jacques NATTIEZ, "Reflections," 124, for a discussion of Nattiez's interpretation of Jean Molino's description of music as icon, index, and symbol.

[51] The Commentary to this document was written by Michel VEUTHEY who has served as General Secretary of *UL* since its inception.

For its explanation of "symbol," the glossary refers back to the origin of the word in the Greek verb *sumbalein* which means "to gather together" and to the ancient practice of fitting together two broken pieces in order to identify parties in an alliance.[52] Applying this ancient understanding to an understanding of symbol in ritual, the glossary explains that the "whole of symbol … is a material element (flag, light, music …) which allows us to be 'gathered together' into a reality which is far from us because it is abstract or immaterial, or invisible.[53]

In explaining its use of the term "symbolic practices," the glossary points out that liturgical action as symbolic practice "means that no liturgical action closes the celebrating assembly in on itself but, on the contrary, opens the assembly to the mystery of the active presence of the Lord and to communion with the Lord and with the entire body of Christian brothers and sisters spread throughout the world."[54]

Thus the commentary and the glossary which supplement *Music in Christian Celebration* support and expand the kernel statements of the *UL* document itself. Two key ideas which it shares with earlier documents and for which it offers further development are the notion of Christian worship music as liturgical and symbolic.

Some sixteen years after *Universa Laus* formally constituted itself, a group of American church music composers and liturgists came together in 1982 to study and dialogue on the question of the role of music in the liturgy. In 1992, after ten years of such dialogue, the group drew up a report on their efforts in a document entitled *The Milwaukee Symposia for Church Composers: A Ten-Year Report.* The foreword describes the document as "a report on ten years of observation, study, reflection and dialogue concerning the nature and quality of liturgical music in the United States, especially within the Roman Catholic Tradition."[55] As such, the report offers a further opportunity to examine current thinking among composers and liturgists regarding the nature of liturgical music.

Like the members of *UL,* the Milwaukee participants adopt the term "ritual music," or more specifically, "Christian ritual music" to describe

---

[52] *Music and Liturgy,* 167.

[53] *Music and Liturgy,* 167.

[54] *Music and Liturgy,* 168.

[55] *The Milwaukee Symposia for Church Composers: A Ten-Year Report* (Washington, D.C.: The Pastoral Press and Chicago: Liturgy Training Publications, 1992), foreword. Hereafter *The Milwaukee Symposia*

music's inseparability from the ritual of which it is the part. Article six of the preamble states: "Our document continues this emphasis on music's function in ritual by adopting the more accurate term 'Christian ritual music.' This term underscores the interconnection between music and the other elements of the rite: distinguishable facts of a single event."[56]

The document begins by setting out certain foundational principles. Among these is the fact that Christian liturgy is a symbolic event.[57] In the next section, the document returns to this notion of symbol as something dynamic rather that static when it points out that, "although symbols employ the created world, they are themselves actions."[58]

Music, then, is part of the symbolic language of worship. Its sacramental power is rooted in its nature as a sound phenomenon.[59] Article thirteen offers concrete examples of how music as sound symbolizes God's self-revelation:

> Sound's temporality, for example, symbolizes a God active in creation and history; its seemingly insubstantial nature symbolizes a God who is both present and hidden; its dynamism symbolizes a God who calls us into dialogue; its ability to unify symbolizes our union with God and others; its evocation of personal presence symbolizes a God whom we perceive as personal.[60]

The article builds its argument for the symbolic nature of music on various aspects of its nature as a sound phenomenon. Its correlation of the various qualities of sound with qualities of God known through God's self-revelation reflects Edward Foley's research in sound theology.[61]

The Milwaukee composers, like the framers of the *Universa Laus* document, link a discussion of music's role as minister to the text and rite with music's role as symbol.[62] For when article fifteen speaks about music's power to "open up new meaning in sung texts as well as the

---

[56] *The Milwaukee Symposia*, 6.
[57] *The Milwaukee Symposia*, 9.
[58] *The Milwaukee Symposia*, 12.
[59] *The Milwaukee Symposia*, 13.
[60] *The Milwaukee Symposia*, 13.
[61] See Edward FOLEY, "Toward a Sound Theology," *Studia Liturgica* 23 (1993): 121- 139. This essay develops Foley's sound theology in greater detail. How music can be said to operate as symbol will be discussed in chapter three of this study.
[62] See n. 49 in this study and *MCC: Points* 7.4.

liturgical unit that is the setting for such texts,"[63] it is not simply citing examples of music's ministerial function. It is implicitly referring to music's symbolic power.

Furthermore, in a way similar to the *Universa Laus* document, the Milwaukee report refers to Christian ritual music as a "sacramental event" when it explains:

> Texts, musical forms, styles of musical leadership, and even the technology employed in our ritual music making express and shape our faith. They are, therefore, foundational elements in the church's first theology, the liturgy.[64]

In other words, just as the liturgy has been traditionally referred to as the church's *theologia prima* or first theology,[65] so too, can the individual elements of the liturgy, including the musical elements, be recognized for their role in expressing and shaping our faith.

The afterword sums up this theological focus in these words:

> Divine grace, the power of Word and spirit, is mediated in and through concrete cultural means especially music by which a community praises and enacts the mystery of God's self-giving. The sacramentality of music is known in and through the art of the assembly.[66]

Several key points are contained in this summation. The first is that our experience of God is mediated through culture. Music as a product of culture is therefore judged to be capable of mediating a community's prayer. The second is that the assembly is the location for this mediation. As the principle music-makers of the liturgy, the assembly's experience of music's power is known first of all in their own bodies. The third is that this mediation can occur through music in a way that can be described as sacramental. Here the term "sacramental" is understood in its broader application: that which serves as a vehicle for God's self-revelation.

Thus, the Milwaukee composers have contributed to an interpretation of Vatican II's understanding of the relationship of music to worship by

---

[63] *The Milwaukee Symposia*, 15.

[64] *The Milwaukee Symposia*, 17.

[65] This notion of the liturgy as the *theologia prima* will be developed further in chapter six of this study.

[66] *The Milwaukee Symposia*, afterword.

focusing on music's role as servant of the ritual and mediator of the revelation of God based on its nature as a sound phenomenon. In doing so,
they have begun to explore the symbolic nature and sacramentality of
liturgical music in its relation to the assembly.

Finally, the third statement by a professional group to be considered
in this study is *The Snowbird Statement on Catholic Liturgical Music*.
This document is the most recent contribution to date to efforts to har-
monize further the principles set forth in *Sacrosanctum Concilium* and
subsequent documents with the experience of musicians in the field.
The statement results from a series of consultations and discussions
among Catholic liturgists and musicians in the English-speaking world.
Musicians from the United States, Canada, the United Kingdom and
Ireland met under the auspices of the Madeleine Institute in Salt Lake
City at Snowbird, Utah in 1992. A second meeting took place in Salt
Lake City, Utah in 1993. Subsequently, the group released a corporate
statement entitled "The Snowbird Statement on Catholic Liturgical
Music," on November 1, 1995.[67]

This document is a further example of the process of reception that
has been such a part of the life of the Church after Vatican II. The statement crafted by the group reflects their roles as musicians serving large
churches or cathedrals and scholars involved in academic work.

The focus of the document is on beauty and excellence in liturgical
music. Article three states: "We believe that beauty is essential in the
liturgical life and mission of the church. Beauty is an effective – even
sacramental – sign of God's presence and action in the world."[68] The
signers of the document are concerned that "styles of worship and liturgical art are promoted which lack aesthetic beauty."[69] As a result, they
hope, through the Snowbird Statement, "to affirm standards of excellence in the composition and performance of all musical forms in the
church's liturgy ..."[70]

Throughout the document, the authors of the statement dialogue
with several of the writings that have preceded their own. One example
is their acknowledgment of the importance of the concept of ritual

---

[67] "The Snowbird Statement on Catholic Liturgical Music," *Pastoral Music* 20
(February-March, 1996): 13. Hereafter *Snowbird*.

[68] *Snowbird*, 3.

[69] *Snowbird*, 3.

[70] *Snowbird*, 4.

music, yet their criticism of its failure to address artistic and aesthetic concerns. In fact, Snowbird identifies the current understanding of ritual music as the source of several problems with church music when it points out:

> Unfortunately, much ritual music in the Catholic church today is hampered by an excessive academicism and an artless rationality ... We call for further development in the concept and practice of ritual music so as to avoid utilitarian functionalism and to advance a liturgical music practice that is beautiful and artistically well-formed.[71]

This article criticizes a functional approach to music practice which promotes styles of worship and music which lack aesthetic beauty. Furthermore, it locates the source of this approach in the concept of ritual music. What is absent from the Snowbird statement's treatment of ritual music is a consideration of the symbolic nature of music.[72]

A second area where the Snowbird Statement dialogues with earlier statements is article six where the authors note the inadequate development of criteria for the musical judgment, a concept which was first introduced in *Music in Catholic Worship* (1972).[73] *Snowbird* takes exception to *MCW's* statement that comparison is valid only within a particular style.[74] Rather, *Snowbird* insists that all music is not of the same quality and that musical judgments can be based on objective criteria.[75]

This document, then, focuses on the issues of beauty and aesthetics and the development of objective standards for musical judgments as the key to promoting excellence in liturgical music. It does not directly address the question of how or why music is integral to worship. Rather, it affirms that beauty is essential in the liturgical life and mission of the church. Music, the document asserts, contributes to that life and mission

---

[71] *Snowbird*, 6.

[72] Both *Music in Christian Celebration* and *The Milwaukee Symposia* included a discussion of music as symbol in the context of their discussion of ritual music.

[73] Articles twenty-six through twenty-nine of *MCW* discuss the importance of the musical judgment as part of the threefold judgment which must be made in choosing music for worship. The other two judgments are the liturgical and the pastoral.

[74] *Snowbird*, 6. *Music in Catholic Worship* states in article 28: "We do a disservice to musical values, however, when we confuse the judgment of music with the judgment of musical style. Style and value are two distinctive judgments ... We must judge value within each style."

[75] *Snowbird*, 6.

only when it is beautiful, since, as the document asserts, "even a liturgy which serves the truth of faith and the justice of the Gospel is insufficient when the beauty of God's self-revelation is inadequately expressed and celebrated."[76]

A COMPARATIVE ANALYSIS OF COMMON THEMES

Since the promulgation of *Sacrosanctum Concilium* in 1963, ecclesial communities have been engaged in the process of interpreting and implementing its principles and guidelines regarding the practice of liturgical music. This ongoing reception is part of an effort to arrive at a synthesis of the principles put forth in *SC*, principles which often are juxtaposed in pairs which couple traditional articulations with new insights. The foregoing survey has surfaced a number of common themes that run through the documents and that develop and change with each repetition. These common themes include the notions of music as integral, music as ministerial, and music as symbolic. This section will compare and contrast the treatment and interpretation of each of these notions in the documents surveyed.

Music as Integral

Before comparing the writings surveyed to discover both the continuities and discontinuities of the various articulations, it is helpful to examine the meaning of the terms "integral" and "integrity." Webster defines the adjective "integral" as whole; entire; lacking nothing; complete as an entity; making part of a whole, or necessary to make a whole.[77] The noun "integrity," is defined as the quality or state of being complete; wholeness; entireness; unbroken state; the entire, unimpaired state or quality of anything; perfect condition; soundness.[78]

Although the definitions of both *integral* and *integrity* include the notion of wholeness, there is a difference in its application. On one hand, the adjective *integral* characterizes that which participates in making a whole by being a part of it. On the other hand, the noun *integrity*

---

[76] *Snowbird*, 3.
[77] *Webster's New Universal Unabridged Dictionary*, 2d ed., s.v. "integral."
[78] *Webster's New Universal Unabridged Dictionary*, 2d ed., s.v. "integrity."

describes a quality which belongs to something in itself, that is, a state of perfection or soundness. In this sense, then, to say that music is *integral* to worship is to say two things: 1) that music is a part that contributes to the whole, and 2) that music's contribution to making up that whole is irreplaceable, that is, it cannot be accomplished by another ritual element. To speak about music which possesses *integrity*, is to speak of music which possesses a state of perfection or soundness, presumably as music, but particularly as worship music when used in the present context.

The documents state that music is integral to worship in a variety of different ways. *Sacrosanctum Concilium*, *Tra le sollecitudini*, and *Music in Catholic Worship* explicitly state that music is integral to worship. *Musicam sacram*, even though it is an instruction on *Sacrosanctum Concilium*, does not do so. Instead, the instruction seems to be more concerned, not with the integration of music into the liturgy, but the identification of music as "sacred" because it possesses "integrity of form." Referring back to the two definitions, we see that *SC*, *TLS*, and *MCW* all focus on music as contributing to the whole – worship – and in relationship to the other parts of worship. *MS*, on the other hand, focuses on the wholeness or perfection of the music as a requirement for its insertion into worship.

A further development in understanding music's relationship to worship is evident in *Liturgical Music Today* which moves from speaking of music as "the integral mode by which the mystery is proclaimed and presented"[79] to speaking of liturgy as "inherently musical" and of worship as "sung prayer."[80] These phrases create a sense of identification between music and liturgy so that they can be grasped as a unified whole. Again, a definition of terms will clarify the difference.

Webster defines "inherent" as existing in someone or something as a natural and inseparable quality, characteristic or right; innate, basic; inborn.[81] Using the term *integral* to describe music's relationship to worship says that music contributes to the whole. Using the term *inherent* to describe worship as inherently musical, says that worship is naturally musical. Such usage places the focus on the nature of worship or ritual as musical rather than on the nature of music as a contributing aspect.

---

[79] *LMT,* 10.
[80] *LMT*, 5.
[81] *Webster's New Universal Unabridged Dictionary*, 2d ed., s.v. "inherent."

The corporate statements of professional and scholarly organizations also deal with the question of music's relationship to worship. However, like *LMT,* some have moved from describing music as "integral to worship" to speaking of ritual music. Both the *Universa Laus* document and *The Milwaukee Symposia* adopt the term "ritual music" or "Christian ritual music" to underscore the interconnection between music and the rite. In article thirteen, *The Milwaukee Symposia* describes music as "part" of the symbolic language of worship. At first glance this usage appears to be weaker than "integral." However, in this statement the document is linking music to the system of symbols that is integral to worship. *The Milwaukee Symposia,* then, is reiterating the earlier understanding of *Sacrosanctum Concilium, Tra le sollecitudini,* and *Music in Catholic Worship* which focuses on music's contribution to the whole. *The Milwaukee Symposia's* unique contribution is its linking this contribution to the fact that music is part of the symbol system of worship.[82] Thus, music, as one of those symbols, is integral to the liturgy.

Finally, *Snowbird* implicitly affirms that music is integral to worship by stating that beauty is essential to worship. By doing so, this statement qualifies the music which is integral to worship. In *Snowbird's* judgment, only music which measures up to an objective standard[83] of beauty and excellence is integral to worship. Thus *Snowbird's* concern for beauty and excellence focuses on the *integrity* of the music itself. In this way it is harkening back to *Musicam Sacram* when that instruction expressed concern for "sacred music" which possesses "integrity" of form.

It is clear that although all of these documents appear to be employing the same or similar terminology, there are important nuances to be taken into account. In one case, the focus is on music as contributing to the whole, that is, to the ritual. In a second case, the focus is on the wholeness or perfection of the music. In a third case, the focus is on ritual or worship as naturally musical.

Music as Ministerial

The notion of music as ministerial has also undergone change and development in its usage in the documents written in this century.

[82] The manner in which the documents refer to music as symbol will be discussed more fully later in this chapter.

[83] The document does not identify what the objective standards are or how they can be arrived at.

Whereas the 1903 document uses the term "handmaid," the 1963 document chooses instead the word "ministerial." Dictionary definitions shed only limited light on efforts to discover the distinction between these two terms. According to Webster, both "handmaid" and "minister" or "ministerial" refer to a person in a subordinated role who renders service.[84] Examining the meaning of "ministerial" in an ecclesial context, however, better highlights the significance of the shift.

The adjective "ministerial" comes from the noun "ministry" which has its roots in the Greek word for serving and attending upon someone. In translation, the Latin *ministerium* can easily become an office, even a servile one. In Latin Christianity it was, in fact, replaced by *officium*.[85] In common English usage, the word often refers to significant public service, as, for example, such designations as prime minister or ministry of foreign affairs.

In religious usage, until Vatican II "ministry" was often considered primarily a Protestant term. In contemporary Roman Catholic discourse, however, the word is used to described a new situation in the church. This new situation involves the expansion of ministry and a new theology of ministry. Today ministry is viewed as neither a rare vocation nor a privileged office, but a reality rooted in baptism. Its context is grace. This usage signals a return to the New Testament understanding of *diakonia* where service or ministry is grounded in the community for the sake of the building up of the Kingdom of God.[86]

The shift from "handmaid" to "ministerial," then, can be characterized as a shift from the notion of subservient service to that of mutual service. This shift, subtle though it may at first appear, is significant because it alludes to the nobler office of the sacred ministers. Using it to describe the nature of music is evidence of the discussions carried on by theologians for years prior to the council regarding the nature of music and its role in the liturgy. Such a term does not carry with it the connotation of music merely as an instrument of the liturgy, but as something vital and intrinsic.[87]

---

[84] *Webster's New Universal Unabridged Dictionary*, 2d ed., s.v. "handmaid" and "minister."

[85] Thomas F. O'MEARA, "Ministry," in *The New Dictionary of Theology*, ed. Joseph A. KOMONCHAK, Mary COLLINS, and Dermot A. LANE (Collegeville: The Liturgical Press, 1991), 657.

[86] O'MEARA, "Ministry," 657-661.

[87] CAGLIO, "Chapter VI," 244

Under the heading of "General Principles," Pius X's motu proprio describes the offices of music: to clothe with befitting melody the liturgical text, to add greater efficacy to the text and thereby move the faithful to devotion. These could be described as ministerial functions, but neither the term "handmaid" nor "ministerial" appears in this section. Interestingly enough, the term "humble handmaid" only appears near the end of the motu proprio and in regard to the length of the liturgical chants. Once again, abuses which have at times occurred in musical practice have resulted in certain cautions regarding music's role.

It is *Sacrosanctum Concilium* that first refers to music's role as "ministerial." Four years later, *Musicam Sacram* refers to the problems which have arisen regarding music's ministerial function, but does not attempt to define the meaning of the term. *Music in Catholic Worship*, on the other hand, like *Tra le Sollecitudini*, includes several examples of instances when music functions ministerially in order to clarify its use of the term.[88]

Liturgical Music Today does not use the word "ministerial" or "handmaid." However, using the term "ritual music," is another way of saying that music serves the ritual. Calling the music of the liturgy ritual music is therefore another way of identifying its ministerial function. On the other hand, in referring to the liturgy as "inherently musical," this document begins a shift from thinking of music as "ritual music" to identifying liturgy as "musical." Such terminology opens up the possibility of considering music, not as an extrinsic element that may be added to ritual performance, but as a quality which belongs intrinsically to the liturgy by its very nature.

The *Universa Laus* document, *Music in Christian Celebration*, begins in its very first article to list the principle ministerial functions of music without actually using the term. It employs the term "ritual music" to describe the relationship between liturgy and music but

---

[88] Cf. *TLS* 1 and *MCW* 23 cited above. See also Lucien DEISS, *Spirit and Song of the New Liturgy*, revised edition (Cincinnati: World Library Publications, Inc., 1976), 1-46. Deiss devotes the entire first chapter to a consideration of the ministerial function of liturgical song. An important point he makes is that the ministerial function must first of all be defined in relation to the liturgy itself and in reference to the assembly: the people of God celebrating Jesus Christ. See also Lucien DEISS, *Visions of Liturgy and Music for a New Century*, trans. Jane M.-A. BURTON (Collegeville: The Liturgical Press, 1996), 3-23.

quickly explains that "the liturgical celebration is a symbolic whole" and that "all its elements, musical or not, are interdependent."[89] Like *Liturgical Music Today*, then, this document juxtaposes a notion of music as ministerial with a notion of music as part of a larger interdependent whole. In the judgment of *UL,* while the service which music renders may take on various forms, its ultimate purpose is to mediate the encounter of "the assembly of believers with the God of Jesus Christ" (*MCC,* 7.5).

The *Milwaukee Symposia* explains that its choice of the term "Christian ritual music" was a deliberate effort to underscore the interconnection between music and the other elements of the rite. While it details several ways in which the "power" of music serves the ritual, it does not speak of music in terms of a "ministerial function."

Snowbird acknowledges that the development of the concept of ritual music has clarified how intimately music is tied to ritual forms. However, the authors of this document argue that much ritual music, hampered by an excessive academicism and an artless rationality, has resulted in a utilitarian functionalism that has at least indirectly contributed to the decline of musical excellence. In their judgment, this has happened because those who have attended to the theory and practice of ritual music, have inadequately attended to the beautiful and the artistic.[90] *Snowbird* does not argue for the ministerial function of music. Its concern is to uphold standards of musical excellence because beauty is revelatory.[91]

On this point, then, it appears that the documents and statements have come full circle. At the beginning of this century, Pius X reacts against the abuses which at times turned the liturgy into a backdrop for musical display. At the end of the century, *Snowbird* rues the loss of musical excellence because of an insistence on music's ritual function. Somewhere in between, however, is a growing understanding of the interdependent relationship between music and the various elements of ritual celebration and of the notion of the musical nature of ritual itself. This understanding is particularly evident in *Liturgical Music Today* and the *Universa Laus* Document.

---

[89] *MCC: Points,* 2.8.
[90] *Snowbird,* 5.
[91] *Snowbird,* 3.

Music as Symbolic

References to music as a symbolic element in ritual are neither plentiful nor obvious in the documents under scrutiny here. Neither Pius X's motu proprio, nor Vatican II's constitution make specific reference to the symbolic nature of music. Rather, the focus is on those qualities deemed necessary for music's participation in the liturgy. Pius X identified the following characteristics as necessary for sacred music: sanctity, goodness of form, and universality. *Sacrosanctum Concilium* reiterated the need for sanctity or holiness and true art or goodness of form, but dropped the requirement of universality. Still none of these characteristics describe music's symbolic nature.

While *Musicam Sacram* does not directly refer to music as a symbol, it is the first document where the word symbol[92] is used to describe worship when singing is an active component. Later in this study, we will show how several of the instruction's descriptions of the effects of singing on liturgical celebrations can be interpreted as describing the symbolic nature of music.

It is *Music in Catholic Worship* which presents the first clear expression of the symbolic nature of music. Significantly, this articulation is juxtaposed with the statements which identify music as both integral to worship and ministerial.[93]

As an addenda to *MCW, Liturgical Music Today* does not concern itself with theoretical issues or definitions. Rather, its purpose was to clarify issues previously raised and to address questions related to the sacramental rites and the Liturgy of the Hours. The notion of music as symbol is not directly addressed in this document. However, the development of the notion of ritual music, sung prayer, and of liturgy as inherently musical prepares the way for such a consideration in the later documents.

From the very first sentence of its manifesto-like document, *Universa Laus* clearly identifies both the liturgy as a whole and the music related to it as symbolic. In five different places in the section, "Points of Reference," the symbolic nature of music and the liturgy are mentioned. In

---

[92] See "*Musicam Sacram,*" in *DOL,* 1294; Robert F. HAYBURN, *Papal Legislation on Sacred Music: 95 A.D. to 1977 A.D.* (Collegeville: The Liturgical Press, 1979), 547. *DOL* translates "praefigurat" as "makes [making] a symbol;" the English translation in Hayburn's book translates "praefigurat" as "prefigure." See n. 36 above.

[93] See *MCW,* 23, cited in n. 38 above.

addition, "Beliefs Held in Common" mentions singing and music as a symbolic sign and makes reference to the signifying power of rites enriched by music.[94] Both the commentary and the glossary further elaborate on what the document means by symbol.

The report issued by the *Milwaukee Symposia* likewise makes several references to symbol. In the first place, it identifies the fact that Christian worship celebrates the paschal mystery by means of symbols which both express and shape Christian faith.[95] Secondly, it identifies the liturgy as symbolic and music as part of the symbolic language of worship. Thirdly, it makes the point that symbols are actions. At the conclusion of the document, the afterword moves from a description of the symbolic effects of music to a reference to the sacramentality of music.

Finally, *Snowbird* makes only one reference to symbol when it identifies modern theories of symbol and art as a resource for "a more intensive exploration of the choir's role in worship."[96] It does, however, refer to beauty as a sacramental sign of God's presence.[97]

RESTATING THE QUESTIONS

The foregoing analysis of documents of the Church and of related professional or scholarly groups reveals several important points. In the first place, the Church, specifically in this century but also throughout its history, has taken the role of music in the liturgy very seriously.[98] Implicit in all this is the acknowledgment of the power of music, for good or for ill, to significantly affect the celebration of the Church's rites and sacraments. Indeed, the Church has consistently identified the goals of the liturgy and of the music of the liturgy to be the same – the glory of God and the sanctification and edification of the faithful. The loftiness of these goals reaffirms the need to take seriously the ministry of music in worship. Furthermore, the Church has moved from a position of giving certain styles of music and certain

---

[94] *MCC: Beliefs,* 26, 33, 42.
[95] *Milwaukee Symposia,* 11, 38.
[96] *Snowbird,* 20.
[97] *Snowbird,* 3.
[98] Johannes QUASTEN, provides a scholarly treatment of this topic in his book *Music and Worship in Pagan and Christian Antiquity,* NPM Studies in Church Music and Liturgy, trans. Boniface RAMSEY (Washington, D.C.: The Pastoral Press, 1983).

instruments pride of place to a position of esteeming the musical traditions of all cultures and times.

Secondly, abandoning the position that certain styles of music or instruments possess an innate quality that somehow makes them "sacred" and "universal" opens up the possibility of exploring other characteristics which enable music to exercise its "ministerial function." One such characteristic is the notion of music as ritual symbol. This understanding has been part of the larger development of speaking of the liturgy as a complex of interactive symbols.

Thirdly, the fact that musicians and scholars have invested large amounts of time and energy into dialoguing with these Church documents and implementing them in their local practice is also significant. It witnesses both to the credibility of the Church in addressing issues involving music and to the commitment of musicians to the liturgy.

Despite these positive accomplishments, however, there are several areas which require additional effort in order to incorporate new insights into a more satisfactory synthesis. These include efforts at reconciling the notion of ritual music with the requirements of musical excellence and exploring the nature of the liturgy as inherently musical. But even before these issues can be addressed, it is necessary to work toward a new synthesis of the three prominent notions offered in the documents: music as integral, music as ministerial, and music as symbolic.

After the basic principles were set out by *Sacrosanctum Concilium* and made more concrete by specific guidelines in *Musicam Sacram*, it was *Music in Catholic Worship* which first juxtaposed the three ideas in article twenty-three. The statement bears repeating here:

> Among the many signs and symbols used by the Church to celebrate its faith, music is of preeminent importance. As sacred song united to words it forms a necessary or integral part of the solemn liturgy. Yet the function of music is ministerial; it must serve and never dominate.

In this short statement, music is described as symbolic, integral, and ministerial. Yet *MCW* does not offer a critical theory of how these three descriptions of music can be integrated into a fuller understanding of the role of music in the liturgy. Furthermore, while *Liturgical Music Today* does pursue the notion of ritual music as a way of dealing with these three characteristics of music, it is not until *Universa Laus* publishes *Music in Christian Celebration* that any further work is done on exploring these notions in greater depth.

The Milwaukee Symposia explores how music as sound symbolizes God's self-revelation. However, in its attempt to demonstrate how the various qualities of sound symbolize the various qualities of God, its explanation can be perceived as a kind of mathematical equation which undermines the very notion of symbol as polyvalent.[99] Even so, the focus of the report of *The Milwaukee Symposia* is less on music as symbolic and more on the notion of "ritual music" as a way of articulating music's role in liturgy.

It is the group of professional musicians who wrote *The Snowbird Statement* who call attention to the deficiency of viewing music simply in functional terms. But while they champion beauty and excellence, they do not offer any of the objective criteria which they insist are necessary to promote their aesthetic goals.

For the most part, it is inaccurate to say that any of the documents treat music in simply functional terms. This becomes increasingly the case with each new articulation of the role of liturgical music. Certainly by the time *Universa Laus* publishes its statement, a more and more complex picture of liturgical music begins to emerge.

Speaking of music as "ritual" music can take into account an understanding of music as both integral and ministerial. But in both instances, what is being defined is music's relationship to the whole, that is, to the liturgy. This in itself is an important consideration. However, in order to avoid the pitfall of thinking in purely functional terms, it is necessary to ask the following question: What is it in the nature of music that enables it to relate to the various elements of the liturgy – the assembly, the text, and the ritual action – so that it contributes to the wholeness or perfection of the rite?

The hypothesis of this study is that the nature of music as ritual symbol enables music to be both ministerial and integral to the liturgy. In order to arrive at a clearer understanding of the role music actually plays in liturgy, this study will now present a case study of Berthier's music for Taizé. The evident success of the Taizé songs in enabling the participation of thousands of pilgrims in Taizé worship and their widespread adoption in local communities throughout the world suggests that the music itself and the dynamic of music-making

---

[99] See *The Milwaukee Symposia*, 13.

are both ministerial and integral to liturgical prayer. The following chapter will engage in a hermeneutical analysis of Berthier's music in order to discover how this music, as it is sung by the brothers and pilgrims of Taizé, is both ministerial and integral to their liturgical prayer.

CHAPTER TWO

MUSICOLOGICAL ANALYSIS OF JACQUES BERTHIER'S MUSIC FOR TAIZÉ

INTRODUCTION

There are several reasons why Jacques Berthier's music for Taizé serves our investigation of music as ritual symbol. In the first place, Berthier's music was created in response to the pastoral experience of a particular worshiping community. The intention was to serve the assembly that gathered at Taizé for prayer by providing them with chants which would enable the active participation of all. Secondly, the music was created with the ritual prayer of Taizé in mind. That is, the chants were composed to be sung as ritual music. Thirdly, Taizé music was created with the text in mind. That is, as Berthier himself described his method of composition, the text was always the source of inspiration for the music.[1] In other words, Berthier's music for Taizé serves well as a case study for this paper because both Berthier and the Taizé community approached his music from the same perspective as that articulated by the documents reviewed in the previous chapter. That is, they viewed the music for Taizé as integral to their prayer and ministerial in relation to the assembly, the ritual, and the texts.

This chapter will begin the process of interpreting Jacques Berthier's music for Taizé by practicing a musical hermeneutic, that is, a musical interpretation, proposed by Lawrence Kramer. According to Kramer, in order to interpret music, we need to open a musical work's available hermeneutic windows and treat it as a field of humanly significant action.[2] His hermeneutic is based on the conviction that although music does not make propositions, it does have referential power. In order to discover the possible meanings to which a particular piece of music may be referring, we need to approach it with the assumption that it resists fully disclosing itself. While the music does not give itself immediately

---

[1] BERTHIER, *Un serviteur,* 15.
[2] Lawrence KRAMER, *Music as Cultural Practice, 1800-1900* (Berkeley: University of California Press, 1990), 6.

to understanding, it can be made to yield to understanding if we are able to open hermeneutic windows through which our understanding can pass.[3]

Kramer identifies three types of hermeneutic windows available for interpreting music. They include textual inclusions, citational inclusions, and structural tropes.[4] Textual inclusions refer to texts set to music, titles, epigrams, program notes, and sometimes expression markings.[5] Under citational inclusions Kramer lists various literary, visual, musical, and historical allusions.[6] By *structural trope* Kramer means "a structural procedure, capable of various practical realizations, that also functions as a typical expressive act within a certain cultural/historical framework."[7] According to Kramer, structural tropes are the most powerful type of hermeneutic window. He understands them as units of *doing* rather than of *saying* [emphasis added] that can evolve from any aspect of communicative exchange: style, rhetoric, representations, etc.[8]

Kramer develops his notion of structural tropes from Pierre Bourdieu's notion of the *habitus.* For Bourdieu *habitus* means "systems of durable, transposable *dispositions,* structured structures predisposed to act as structuring structures, that is, as principles of the generation and structuring of [cultural] practices and representations ..."[9]

Adapting Kramer's method to the task at hand, this chapter will analyze the music of Taizé by attempting to open several hermeneutic windows. In the first place, a musicological analysis will be conducted in order to discover structural tropes. This will involve an analysis of the four genres of Taizé music and an analysis of the aleatory nature of the music. Secondly, the texts of the Taizé chants will be examined in order to discover their sources, the languages employed, and the relationship of the texts to the music. Lastly, the performance notes

---

[3] KRAMER, *Music as Cultural Practice,* 6.

[4] KRAMER, *Music as Cultural Practice,* 9-10.

[5] KRAMER, *Music as Cultural Practice,* 9.

[6] KRAMER, *Music as Cultural Practice,* 10.

[7] KRAMER, *Music as Cultural Practice,* 10.

[8] KRAMER, *Music as Cultural Practice,* 10. This notion of *doing* rather than *saying* will be explored in greater depth in chapter five's discussion of J.L. Austin's performative language theory.

[9] Pierre BOURDIEU, *Outline of a Theory of Practice,* trans. Richard NICE (Cambridge: Cambridge University Press, 1977), 72.

supplied by Brother Robert Giscard[10] in the G.I.A. editions will be examined as a further source of textual inclusions.

While clear citational inclusions are not apparent in the music of Taizé, the biography of Berthier, the history of Taizé, the way of life of the brothers, their liturgical prayer, and their ministry to the pilgrims who come to pray with them are all reflected in the composition and use of the chants. Therefore, this information will also be examined as a type of hermeneutical window for interpreting the chants and identifying those characteristics which have enabled this music to be both ministerial and integral to the prayer life of the Taizé community.

The Beginnings of Taizé

Brother Roger Louis Schutz-Marsauche was born in Provence, fifteen miles from Neuchâtel, Switzerland in 1915. In 1940, during the Second World War, Roger first came to Taizé, a small village in the Burgundian Hills of eastern France.

Roger Schutz had been looking for a place where he could buy a house in order to live the Gospel with others. The desire to embrace such a lifestyle grew out of the work he was doing for a dissertation on early Christian monasticism at the University of Lausanne.[11] He was drawn to France because he saw it as a land of wartime suffering that nevertheless possessed an inner freedom. Its defeat by the Germans awakened in him a powerful sympathy and desire to discover a way to assist those most discouraged and ravaged by the war.[12]

These impulses led Roger to the ruins of the ancient monastery of Cluny where centuries before men had consecrated their lives to Christ. It was Roger's conviction that some form of traditional monastic life should be restored in Protestantism which eventually led him to

---

[10] None of the published editions include performance notes written by Jacques Berthier himself. However, because of the collaboration between Robert Giscard, the Taizé brother who was responsible for the community's music ministry, and Berthier, it is reasonable to assume that Robert's notes reflect an understanding of the music that was shared by the two men. More information on these collaborators will be provided later in this chapter.

[11] Raphael BROWN, "Taizé Community," in *The New Catholic Encyclopedia*, vol. 13 (Washington, D.C.: The Catholic University of America Press, 1967), 917.

[12] J.L. Gonzalez BALADO, *The Story of Taizé*, third revised edition (Collegeville, Minnesota: The Liturgical Press, 1988), 18.

purchase a house in nearby Taizé in 1940. From 1940-1942 he used the building to shelter Jews and war refugees.[13]

Soon other men interested in leading a life of prayer joined Roger and in 1949 seven of them bound themselves to live a community life. At first the brothers came from various Protestant denominations. By 1996 the community numbered close to one hundred Protestants, Catholics, Anglican, Lutheran and Reformed brothers from twenty-five different countries on four different continents.[14]

Brother Roger's aim was to create a monastic community at Taizé that would be, as he describes it, "a parable of community"[15] among divided Christians. Indeed, one of the dominant features of the spirituality of the Taizé brothers is their zeal for reconciliation among Christians. This is evident, not only in the makeup of their own community, but also in their active engagement in ecumenical efforts both at Taizé and in cooperation with the leaders of Christian Churches throughout the world. For example, the brothers were guests of Pope John XXIII at the Second Vatican Council and have also participated in several assemblies of the World Council of Churches.[16] In addition, Brothers Roger Schutz and Max Thurian have gone to Constantinople several times for discussions with Athenagoras, Patriarch of the Orthodox Church.[17]

However, the ecumenical efforts of Taizé are not solely dedicated to the reunification of ecclesial institutions. They are also directed toward the reconciliation of all who are separated and alienated. The brothers of Taizé view their vocation as a call to be witnesses, in a torn and

[13] BROWN, "Taizé Community," 917.

[14] This information is published in a single sheet brochure entitled "The Taizé Community," and was available at Taizé, in the spring of 1996.

[15] BALADO, The Story of Taizé, 28. In the ritual during which a brother of Taizé makes his life commitment, the following text is read: "The Lord Christ, in his compassion and his love for you, has chosen you to be in the Church a sign of brotherly love. It is his will that with your brothers you live the parable of community." The placement of this phrase at this ritual moment highlights its centrality to the vocation of a brother of Taizé. Brother Roger frequently uses this phrase in his writings and in his addresses.

[16] Brother ÉMILE, "Taizé Community," in Dictionary of the Ecumenical Movement, ed. Nicholas LOSSKY et al. (Grand Rapids, Michigan, William B. Eerdmans Publishing Company, 1991), 969.

[17] Douglas A. HICKS, "The Taizé Community: Fifty Years of Prayer and Action," Journal of Ecumenical Studies 29 (Spring 1992): 206.

individualistic world, to a mutual Christian and human unity which overcomes all barriers.[18]

By 1960 the brothers began to attract young people between the ages of 18 and 30 in increasing numbers. From the very beginning the brothers welcomed these pilgrims and shared their life of prayer with them. Eventually the little village church where they met to pray could no longer contain all the visitors. A German organization called *Sühnezeichen* (signs of reconciliation) offered a solution. This group consisted of German Christians whose purpose was to construct signs of healing in regions which had been terrorized during the war.[19] Between 1960 and 1962 this German Reconciliation Movement set up international teams of young volunteers who built the great Church of Reconciliation at Taizé.[20]

One of the primary goals of the Taizé community has been to enable young people and all of their guests to find a door open to prayer so that they can discover the prayer that is within them. To this purpose, simple songs, a few words, and the silence are used. However, the brothers do not wish to create the mistaken impression that prayer is a spectator sport. Rather, they seek to ensure that the youth can be actively engaged in the prayer.[21]

Any attempt to describe the prayer of Taizé must begin with an acknowledgment of the fact that it is a form of common prayer which has evolved over the years and remains provisional.[22] As the introduction to the English translation of their daily prayer explains, what has been constant is the community's intention to "celebrate a form of common prayer which would be at the same time firmly rooted in the great tradition of the Church's worship, but so adapted to our present-day mentalities that it would truly nourish and stimulate a daily commitment of love and service in the world today."[23] To that end, and in

---

[18] Edward DAVIS, "The Ecumenical Ecclesiology of Max Thurian, Brother of the Community of Taizé: A Catholic Appraisal" (Ph.D. diss., The Catholic University of America, 1970), 247.

[19] BALADO, *The Story of Taizé*, 43.

[20] Raphael BROWN, "Taizé Community," 917.

[21] Brother DIRK, interview by author, 22 May 1996, Taizé, France.

[22] *Praise God: Common Prayer at Taizé*, trans. Emily CHISHOLM (New York: Oxford University Press, 1977), 7. Published in French as *La Louange des Jours* (Taizé: Les Presses de Taizé, 1971).

[23] *Praise God*, 8.

keeping with their ecumenical spirit, the brothers have made a deliberate attempt to draw on many difference sources for their common
prayer.[24]

The Taizé liturgy, then, is not the official liturgy of a particular Christian church. Instead, it attempts to incorporate the strengths of the various Christian traditions: the emphasis on the Word in the Protestant
tradition, the emphasis on the Eucharist in the Roman Catholic, and
the emphasis on the presence of God and reverence for icons in the
Orthodox.[25]

The schedule of prayer includes gathering daily for morning prayer,
midday prayer, and night prayer. On weekdays, morning prayer may
include a communion service. Eucharist is celebrated once a week on
Sunday. Night prayer on Friday is "Prayer around the Cross".

The structure of the daily prayer includes the singing of the Taizé
chants at various points in the service, psalmody, the proclamation of
Scripture, responses, prayers, and intercessions. The structure of the
eucharist parallels the outline of the Roman Rite. It is divided into two
parts: the liturgy of the Word and the liturgy of the Eucharist. The
liturgy of the Word includes a gathering song, penitential rite, the Gloria, the proclamation of Scripture, responses, acclamations, the profes-
sion of faith and intercessory prayers. The liturgy of the Eucharist
includes the Eucharistic prayer with acclamations, the Lord's prayer,
communion, and closing.

Over the years, the schedule of prayer and its structure have continued to evolve. Nevertheless, the outline given above presents a general
picture of the ritual prayer to which so many pilgrims have been drawn
and for which Jacques Berthier composed his music.

The active participation of all their guests has been a priority for the
brothers whenever and wherever they have gathered for prayer. In the
early days of the community, achieving this goal was relatively easy since
the number of brothers and the number of guests who joined them were
relatively small. Eventually, however, this situation changed.

Addressing the needs of the pilgrims at prayer reached a turning point
at Easter time in 1974. This was the date of the first "Council of
Youth," a gathering of some 40,000 youth of numerous languages. The

---

[24] *Praise God*, 8.
[25] Brother ROGER, "An Interview with Brother Roger of Taizé," interview by Patrick
SAMWAY, *America* 148 (Jan. 22, 1983): 48-49.

idea for this event had been germinating for some time as a way to respond to the international interest of youth in joining together for prayer and for a sharing of their life and concerns.

Brother Robert Giscard, who was responsible for leading the group in song, realized that neither the alternative of singing in French nor of choosing the best known hymns from each language-group adequately promoted the active participation of all.[26] At first the brothers attempted to deal with the situation by working on several translations, but they soon realized the shortcomings of such an approach. Shortly after that first "Council of Youth," Brother Robert discovered that using a seventeenth century canon by Michael Praetorius, with another large multi-lingual group of youth was very successful.[27] The piece, "Jubilate Deo," is printed in Fig. 1.

Ju - bi - la - te De - o,   Ju - bi - la - te   De - o,   A - le - lu - ia.

Musique: Jacques Berthier – © Ateliers et Presses de Taizé, 71250 Taizé-Communauté, France

Fig. 1. "Jubilate Deo" by Praetorius[28]

In this instance, the text chosen was in Latin. At the time, this language was judged preferable to that of any nationality represented at the meeting since the text was so brief and it put no one group at an advantage.

That same day that Brother Robert experienced the success of the Praetorius canon, he telephoned the composer, Jacques Berthier, who had worked for the brothers of Taizé some years earlier. Robert asked Berthier to compose several new canons on such Latin texts as "Christus Vincit," "Magnificat," and others.[29] Berthier immediately went to work

---

[26] BERTHIER, *Un serviteur,* 9.

[27] Brother ROBERT, "Taizé Music ... A History," *Pastoral Music* (February-March 1987): 21.

[28] Jacques BERTHIER, *Music from Taizé,* vol. 1, vocal edition, ed. Brother Robert (Chicago: G.I.A. Publications, Inc., 1981), 100. The two English volumes of Berthier's music published in the United States by G.I.A. include both a vocal edition for the assembly, cantors, and choir, and an instrumental edition for solo instrumental parts. This will be designated by "vocal" or "instrumental" after the volume number.

[29] The texts chosen have been texts frequently used in Christian worship. The English translation of the text of "Christus Vincit" is as follows: "Christ conquers, Christ reigns, Christ rules." The "Magnificat" is so named for the first Latin word of the text

on the task. He even dictated some of the canons over the phone. Brother Robert used the canons immediately and, like the Praetorius canon, they proved very successful. This incident proved to be the beginning of many years of collaboration between Jacques Berthier and Brother Robert Giscard, a collaboration which eventually resulted in the corpus of music identified today as Taizé music.[30]

But how was it that these two men, one a brother of Taizé and the other a married Catholic layman, came together to collaborate in the genesis of the Taizé chants?[31] What was their background and how did they meet?

Brother Robert Giscard (1922-1993) was born in Lyon, France. Together with his brother, Alain, Robert became a member of the Taizé community in 1946. As a medical doctor, Robert's original ministry was caring for the people of the neighboring villages of Taizé. Eventually, however, he surrendered his medical practice to another physician in order to devote himself completely to his vocation as musician.[32]

Brother Robert worked directly with Jacques Berthier in creating the Taizé chants by compiling the texts and reacting to each of Berthier's compositional efforts, often guiding the composer through several revisions. In addition, Robert's tasks included working with the practical details of assisting the assembly to learn the songs and perform them at prayer. It was Robert's efforts to arrive at a form of sung prayer that would enable the participation of large groups of polyglot youth that was the catalyst to adopting the genres of music which Jacques Berthier composed for Taizé.[33]

---

of Luke 1:46-55 where Mary greets Elizabeth with the words which begin: "My being proclaims the greatness of the Lord."

[30] BERTHIER, "*Un serviteur,*" 9.

[31] Frequently in the interview of Jacques Berthier published in *Célébrer*, (see bibliography), the Taizé music is referred to as "*les chants de Taizé.*" Since the French word "*chants*" was used, rather than "*chansons,*" I have chosen to alternate the use of the word "chant" for "song" in my references to this music. Referring to Berthier's music as chants is not meant to equate his metered style with the unmetered monophonic music referred to as Gregorian chant. However, it is true that as chant was the foundation of Berthier's education in church music, it is also the inspiration for his own compositions. Nevertheless, the word "chant" as it is used to described the Taizé music may more aptly link his music to the chant-like mantras of the East because of their characteristic brevity and repetition.

[32] "*Nunc Dimittis:* Brother Robert of Taizé," *GIA Quarterly* 4 (Summer 1993): 9.

[33] "*Nunc Dimittis,*" 9.

Fr. Joseph Gelineau, Jesuit composer, liturgist, and key figure in *Universa Laus,* was instrumental in first introducing Jacques Berthier to the brothers at Taizé. In 1954, Fr. Gelineau had just published his first collection of psalm settings entitled "Twenty-Four Psalms and a Canticle." Both the antiphons[34] and the psalm settings were composed by Gelineau. He had done most of his work on this project at Taizé with the brothers. In fact, the first recording of these psalms in French was sung by the brothers in the old Romanesque church in which they daily worshiped.[35]

The following year, when he began work on the second collection, "Fifty-Three Psalms and Four Canticles," Gelineau solicited the assistance of some of his friends who were composers to write the antiphons. Berthier collaborated in the creation of Gelineau's second volume by contributing fifty-one antiphons in four-part mixed and three-part equal voices.[36] That same year, as a result of Gelineau's introduction,[37] the brothers of Taizé first invited Berthier to compose for them.[38] The project included settings of the Office for Christmas, as well as a setting of the Ordinary of the Mass, the Propers for the Sundays after Christmas, the Propers for Epiphany, and the responses for Christmas week.[39]

From the very beginning, then, it is clear that although the brothers of Taizé were interested in promoting the active participation of all participants in their prayer, they were equally interested in employing liturgical songs that consisted of both quality texts and quality music. Berthier's background as a classically trained church musician made him an eminently suitable partner in this project. A brief look at some of the highlights of his life will make this more apparent.

---

[34] Antiphon is the term used to describe the short refrains sung between verses of the psalms. The texts of these refrains are usually derived from a line of the psalm itself. The musical settings of these psalms are metered, that is organized in measures, in contrast to the verses which can be set to unmetered psalm tones. Gelineau's psalm settings consist of a unique ordering of the text according to the strong pulses of the poetic line.

[35] Brother DIRK, interview.

[36] BERTHIER, *"Un serviteur,"* 7.

[37] Joseph GELINEAU, interview by author, 28 May, 1996, Ecuelles, France.

[38] In her interview, Madame Berthier related how her husband, Jacques, asked the bishop of the Roman Catholic diocese of Auxerre whether it would be permissible for him to work for a Protestant community. The bishop encouraged him to do so, explaining that Brother Roger had spoken to Pius XII regarding the possibility of converting to Catholicism. Instead, Pius XII encouraged Brother Roger to set up an ecumenical community. Later, John XXIII did even more to support Brother Roger's efforts.

[39] BERTHIER, *"Un serviteur,"* 7.

Jacques Berthier was born in Auxerre, France in 1923. Both his parents were professional musicians. Jacques grew into his work with liturgical music by participating, like his father, at the liturgical celebrations of the cathedral as chorister, organist and choir director. His father, Paul Berthier, held the position of organist at the cathedral for more than fifty years. Both his father and his mother alternately directed the cathedral schola. Frequently before great feast days, choir rehearsals were held at the Berthier home.[40]

From an early age Jacques studied the organ and assisted as organist for liturgical services at the cathedral. He wrote his first serious composition at age 15, and a four-part motet for mixed voices at age 17. However, Berthier's experience and interest were not limited to church music. In fact, in those early years, the greater percentage of his compositions were secular works rather than sacred.[41]

Berthier became the organist of St. Ignace in Paris in 1960. Moving to Paris further spurred his increasing activity as a composer of music for the liturgy. For not only is Paris a center of French musical creativity, but it was also an important center of liturgical creativity at that time. In addition to composing for the Taizé community, Berthier wrote a variety of other liturgical compositions. These included music written in collaboration with the French Cistercian Commission, several Masses for youth groups and a Mass for the visit of Pope John Paul II at Lyon in 1986, a project in which he collaborated with Didier Rimaud.[42]

The composer of the music for Taizé, then, was a classically trained musician who increasingly devoted his life to the performance and composition of liturgical music. As a composer, Berthier was well respected by his contemporaries, many of whom had unsuccessfully attempted to compose liturgical music for congregational use. Olivier Messiaen encouraged Berthier to compose chants for the assembly, recognizing that Berthier was capable of doing so successfully. Messiaen admitted that although he had hoped to compose music for the assembly, he had not succeeded. Jean Langlais, who had also composed some works for the assembly, had not been able to continue on this path.

Throughout his musical career Berthier continued to be creative in many facets of musical activity. His greatest love, however, was Gregorian

---

[40] BERTHIER, "*Un serviteur*," 3-4.
[41] BERTHIER, "*Un serviteur*," 4.
[42] BERTHIER, "*Un serviteur*," 3.

chant. This is evident in the fact that so many of his improvisations are built on Gregorian chant melodies. Indeed, his entire conception of the Taizé melodies was inspired by his knowledge and love of chant.[43] Nevertheless, Berthier was totally committed to the ideal set forth by the Second Vatican Council of the primacy of the active participation of the assembly.[44]

The Genesis of the Taizé Chants

After the success of the Praetorius canon, this musical form was the place where Brother Robert and Jacques Berthier first began their efforts to create a music which would address the pastoral needs of Taizé. The canon appeared to provide the brevity and simplicity that Brother Robert intuitively believed would accommodate the constantly changing and renewed assemblies at Taizé and would enable them to join easily in the singing.[45]

However, after working for some time with the canonic form, Berthier realized that the continuous repetition of four harmonic chords can become boring. As an alternative, he came up with the idea of using the "ostinato" because it offered a few more musical possibilities.[46] In fact, it is the ostinato[47] which is most often associated with Taizé music.

An interesting and unique aspect of Berthier's music for Taizé is the process whereby this corpus of music was composed and became a part of the community's liturgical repertoire. Brother Robert would send Berthier a biblical or liturgical text. After working with the text and composing several possible settings, Berthier would send them to

---

[43] Germaine Berthier, widow of Jacques Berthier, interview by author, 29 May, 1996, Paris, France. In this same interview Berthier's widow also remarked how distressed her husband was when he realized that his Taizé chants were replacing his beloved Gregorian chant. For his funeral, Berthier had directed that only Gregorian chant be sung. Only one exception was made. Genevieve Noufflard, a flautist for whom Berthier had composed flute music for many years, performed an improvisation on an original theme by Berthier.

[44] BERTHIER, "*Un serviteur*," 14.

[45] Brother ROBERT, "Taizé Music," 21.

[46] BERTHIER, "*Un serviteur*," 9-10.

[47] The ostinato is a further development of the basic principle of the round or canon. It involves the continuous repetition of a musical unit accompanied by elements of variation. A fuller explanation of this form will be provided later in this chapter under a discussion of the four principal genres of music.

Brother Robert. He and the brothers would sing them over several times and respond by either letter or telephone. The pieces would be studied further by those involved in the music ministry and then sung several times at actual liturgies to determine whether they could easily be sung by the youth for whom they were being composed.[48]

Even after a chant was sung by the community and the pilgrims for some time, changes would still be made in the music if practical difficulties surfaced in trying to sing it well or if new needs emerged from a specific language group.[49] Both Berthier and the brothers were involved in a collaborative effort to create a repertoire of music which was on one hand quality music and on the other hand music accessible to large and varied assemblies.[50]

Robert held the view that the prayer of the community and its visitors, required "original compositions of solid quality that could be used by the people of God ... and in this sense be called *Popular.*"[51] Berthier, always committed to creating quality music, also held the conviction that liturgical song should "remain accessible to the sensibility and capacities of all the members of a community or of the people of God."[52] In fact, it is possible to say that there are several aspects of Berthier's music for Taizé

---

[48] BERTHIER, "*Un serviteur,*" 10.

[49] When I was at Taizé in May, 1996, I discovered that there are several pieces of music which have been published in slightly different versions. When I questioned Sr. Nuria about the discrepancies in some of the tones of the melodies or in the changes in the texts, she explained that it is a common occurrence at Taizé to make changes after certain difficulties emerge in the singing of a particular song. These changes were always done in consultation with Berthier. Now that he is deceased, no further changes are made in his music. However, the community continues to follow this process with the music of Joseph Gelineau. While I was singing in the choir at Taizé, the choir director cautioned us to be sure that we were singing from the right version of Gelineau's piece, "En tout, la paix du coeur," since several versions of it had already been printed and sung at Taizé.

[50] Nuria Sabé GRIFUL, interview by author, 24 May, 1996, Taizé, France. Sr. Nuria, from Spain, belongs to the community of the Sisters of St. Andrew. Several of these sisters are engaged in ministries to Taizé pilgrims. Sr. Nuria is one of the choir directors at Taizé. While Sr. Nuria discussed this compositional approach at length in her interview, Madame Berthier, Joseph Gelineau, Brother John and Brother Dirk also mentioned this laboratory approach to creating the Taizé music. In an interview for *Célébrer,* Jacques Berthier himself described this same process.

[51] Brother ROBERT, "Taizé Music," 19.

[52] Marie-Pierre FAURE, "Jacques Berthier, a Friend of God," *Liturgy: Cistercians of the Strict Observance* 29(1995): 85.

which qualify it to be described, not simply as *popular* music, but as genuine *folk music*. Certainly several of its characteristics correspond to those attributed to folk music by musicologists and ethnomusicologists.

Folk music can be described as that music which is "the product of a musical tradition that has evolved through the process of oral transmission."[53] Although Berthier's compositions have been written down, there is a fluidity about their final shape, or a *provisionality* – to use a word favored by the brothers – which is akin to music which exists in an oral tradition. Even after the chants have been written down, they continue to evolve and change as they are sung by the thousands of worshipers who participate in the liturgies at Taizé each year.

Furthermore, certain factors are considered essential to shaping the folk tradition. These include a "continuity that links the present with the past," "variation which springs from the creative impulse of the individual or the group," and "selection by the community which determines the form or forms in which the music survives."[54]

All of these factors can be identified in the evolution of the Taizé chants. In the first place, there is a continuity that links the various forms which any one chant may have taken in the process of arriving at its current form. The changes that are made are minor and gradual, always with a view to improving the accessibility of the original composition. In those cases where the demands of a new language made that impossible, Berthier would compose an entirely new piece instead.

Secondly, variations have sprung both from Berthier and from the group. Together, the composer, the music ministers, and the assembly have contributed to the variations and adaptations that have been made. Thirdly, it is the selection by the community, both through conscious dialogue and also through the successes and failures of singing the chants which has determined the form in which the music survives.

The term *folk music* has also been applied to music which "has originated with an individual composer and has subsequently been absorbed into the unwritten living tradition of a community."[55] Certainly the adoption of the Taizé music by local communities throughout the world, the "unauthorized" translation of the chants into numerous new languages by

[53] Klaus P. WACHSMANN, "Folk Music," in *The New Grove Dictionary of Music and Musicians*, ed. Stanley SADIE, vol. 6 (London: Macmillan Publishers Limited, 1980), 693.

[54] WACHSMANN, "Folk Music," 693.

[55] WACHSMANN, "Folk Music," 693.

local groups, and the adaptation of the songs to new worship situations is evidence that Berthier's music "has been absorbed into the unwritten living tradition" of numerous communities. Therefore, if it is "the re-fashioning and re-creation of the music by the community" that gives music its folk character, Taizé music can be said to be a type of *folk music.* Its "folk" quality reveals the degree to which Taizé music has been assimilated by those who sing it as an expression of their life and their prayer. It is a living expression since it is subject to re-fashioning and re-creation in the very act of performing it.

The judgment of this paper that the Taizé chants are folk music is significant to a consideration of music as ritual symbol. The notion of *folk* music suggests a type of music which presumes the active engagement of a group, not only in the performance, but also the creation of a particular musical expression. This is important, not only for the notion of active participation, but also for the notion of music as ritual symbol. For as we will propose in the chapter on symbol, music as symbol offers the possibility of active engagement, mutual recognition, and identity clarification – dynamics operative in the generation of *folk* music.

AN ANALYSIS OF STRUCTURAL TROPES

Structural Analysis of the Four Genres

Analyzing the structure of the four principal genres of Berthier's music is the first step of this study's method for discovering the structural tropes of the music. Such analysis will aid in discovering structural procedures in the chants which in turn can be said to structure the assembly in such a way that performing the music within the framework of the liturgical prayer at Taizé functions as an expressive act.[56] By describing the performance of the music as an expressive act, we are focusing on the performance as the *doing* of something rather than the *saying* of something. Furthermore, by applying Bourdieu's notion of *habitus* to these musical structures, we will show how the structures of the chants can be said to function as principles of the generation and structuring of certain practices and/or representations.[57]

---

[56] See nn. 2-8.
[57] See n. 9.

There are 232 works by Jacques Berthier sung at Taizé.[58] The corpus of music, both published and unpublished, which Jacques Berthier composed for Taizé falls into one of four genres, with some special cases.[59] These include ostinato responses and chorales, litanies, acclamations, and canons. Pieces from all four genres include basic harmonic support provided by keyboard and/or guitar. Some include vocal verses performed by one or more cantors. Most also include options for instrumental verses written for a variety of melodic instruments. The assembly's part functions as the foundation of the performance while the vocal and instrumental verses function as countermelodies.

While a more detailed discussion of the use of languages for the Taizé chants will be included later in this chapter, it is useful to recall some preliminary information at this point. In the early days of Taizé, before large groups of pilgrims joined the brothers, the prayer was conducted in French. In an initial attempt to respond to the international makeup of large groups of visitors, Latin was chosen as the language for the chants. Gradually, music was composed for specific living languages and some music was set to more than one language. As a result, the music of Taizé has been set to about twenty different languages. The examples referred to in this chapter represent several of those languages.

Ostinato Response and Chorales

As noted earlier in the section on the brief history of the Taizé chants, Berthier's idea to create the ostinato chant came out of his work with canons. In typical music practice, an ostinato is a musical unit sung in continuous repetition and accompanied by other musical elements that are continually changing. The most common type is the melodic

---

[58] Germaine BERTHIER, interview. Berthier's widow is the caretaker of all her husband's manuscripts of the music he wrote for Taizé. She has collected them together along with all the letters which Berthier had saved from his correspondence over the years with Brother Robert. The brothers at Taizé have not as yet organized their collection of Berthier's music in such a way that it could be systematically researched.

[59] I have verified this conclusion by examining the music used at Taizé in their daily services, studying the published collections in various languages for sale in their book store, procuring copies of unpublished settings from the brothers, examining Madame Berthier's collection, and speaking with the publisher of Taizé music in the United States, Robert Batastini of G.I.A. Publications, Inc.

ostinato in which a melodic unit recurs, usually in the same voice. Most often it appears in the lowest voice and is referred to as the "basso ostinato" or "ground ostinato."[60] The ostinato bass actually developed out of the efforts of early 17th century musicians to negotiate a reconciliation[61] of the old counterpoint technique with the new monody.[62] In the Taizé collections, the term "ostinato" describes a musical unit sung in continuous repetition by all.[63] These ostinati are variously accompanied by solo vocal and instrumental parts.

While Berthier did not create the ostinato form, his employment of it for liturgical song is unique, particularly because of the foundational role he assigns to the assembly. In the Western Church, it has become customary for the choir with the organ and possible ensemble of instruments to serve as the foundation of the musical performance. In the case of Berthier's music, the assembly, supported by the organ, is the principle music-maker while the choir, instrumentalists and soloists serve as the component of variation and embellishment.

The ostinati, by virtue of their musical form, are not specifically tied to a particular ritual moment. They can be employed in a variety of ways and at several places in liturgical prayer. The form can be used during the gathering rite, during processionals, during the concluding rites, and as a response to a reading. At Taizé, the ostinati are also often used as meditative chants which extend the prayer at the end of a liturgical service.

Berthier's ostinati fall into two categories: the short, designated as responses, and the long, designated as chorales. "Veni Sancte Spiritus," and "Jesus, Remember Me" are two examples of the ostinato response. The ostinato response, "Veni Sancte Spiritus," is only two measures long. This refrain, sung by the assembly functions as the repetitive element (See Fig. 2).

---

[60] Richard HUDSON, "Ostinato," in *The New Grove Dictionary of Music and Musicians*, ed. Stanley SADIE, vol. 14 (London: Macmillan Publishers Limited, 1980), 11.

[61] The fact that Berthier chose a musical form which developed out of efforts to reconcile old and new methods of musical composition should be noted since the very existence of the Taizé community was inspired by the desire to promote the reconciliation of all peoples, both the divided Christian communities and all who find themselves marginalized or alienated.

[62] Donald Jay GROUT, *A History of Western Music*, 3d ed. (New York: W.W. Norton and Company, 1980), 315.

[63] BERTHIER, *Music from Taizé*, vol. 1, vocal, 1.

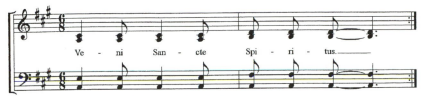

Musique: Jacques Berthier – © Ateliers et Presses de Taizé, 71250 Taizé-Communauté, France

Fig. 2. Refrain of "Veni Sancte Spiritus"[64]

Musique: Jacques Berthier – © Ateliers et Presses de Taizé, 71250 Taizé-Communauté, France

Fig. 3. Verse of "Veni Sancte Spiritus"[65]

Vocal (Fig. 3) or instrumental verses are sung or played over the assembly's ostinato (Fig. 2) with sufficient time intervals between the verses. The vocal or instrumental verses function as the variable element.

The ostinato response "Jesus, Remember Me" is eight measures long. Although there are no vocal verses, some options for instrumental verses are provided in the instrumental edition. In this ostinato, elements of repetition and variation are built into the response itself. The text is a four measure unit repeated twice for one performance of the response. The rhythmic pattern is also a four measure unit repeated the same way. However, the melody and the harmony is an eight measure unit, requiring the performance of the four measure text twice for a single completion of the response.

---

[64] BERTHIER, *Music from Taizé*, vol. 1, vocal, 36.

[65] BERTHIER, *Music from Taizé*, vol. 1, vocal, 37.

Fig. 4. "Jesus, Remember Me"[66]

"Crucem Tuam" is an example of the long ostinato referred to as a chorale or an ostinato chorale. The term "chorale" originated with the congregational hymn of the German Protestant service. Typically, the chorale possesses formal and stylistic traits appropriate to its congregational purposes: simple language, rhymed metrical verse, a strophic musical and textual form and an easily singable melody.[67]

Fig. 5. "Crucem Tuam"[68]

"Crucem Tuam" is a sixteen measure ostinato chorale. Although the text is in Latin,[69] it includes a fair amount of repetition of frequently used ecclesiastical Latin words. The ostinato is published with optional instrumental verses and accompaniments. As in the ostinato responses, the ostinato chorales are meant to be continuously repeated by the assembly while the vocal and/or instrumental verses are performed over the assembly's part.

[66] BERTHIER, *Music from Taizé*, vol. 1, vocal, 9.

[67] Robert L. MARSHALL, "Chorale," in *The New Grove Dictionary of Music and Musicians*, ed. Stanley SADIE, vol. 4 (London: Macmillan Publishers Limited, 1980), 312.

[68] BERTHIER, *Music from Taizé*, vol. 1, vocal, 6.

[69] This example is taken from the setting originally published in Latin. Subsequently, the chorale has been set in English in *Songs and Prayers from Taizé*, 1991.

Certain pieces are special cases because they do not strictly follow either of the patterns outlined above.

Musique: Jacques Berthier – © Ateliers et Presses de Taizé, 71250 Taizé-Communauté, France

Fig. 6. "Ubi Caritas"[70]

"Ubi Caritas" (see Fig. 6) is an example of such an ostinato. This chant is similar to the ostinato response in that the assembly repeats a short refrain. However, in "Ubi Caritas," the repetition may be treated in a variety of ways. The refrain may either alternate with the vocal recitative (see Fig. 7), or occur simultaneously with verses sung by a small schola (see Fig. 8).

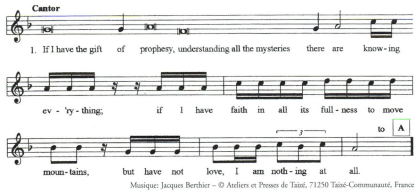

Musique: Jacques Berthier – © Ateliers et Presses de Taizé, 71250 Taizé-Communauté, France

Fig. 7. Recitative verse of "Ubi Caritas"[71]

[70] BERTHIER, Music from Taizé, vol. 1, vocal, 28.
[71] BERTHIER, Music from Taizé, vol. 1, vocal, 31-32.

When the recitative verse (see Fig. 7) is used, the refrain alternates with the verse. However, when the metered verse for cantor or schola (see Fig. 8) is used, this verse is sung simultaneously with the refrain.

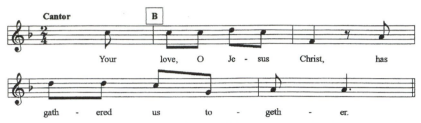

Musique: Jacques Berthier – © Ateliers et Presses de Taizé, 71250 Taizé-Communauté, France

Fig. 8. Verse of "Ubi Caritas" for schola or cantor[72]

Litanies

Berthier also composed litanies for Taizé. In these pieces, invocations are sung between very short phrases that act as refrains. The invocations are performed by cantor and the refrain by the assembly.[73]

The litany is one of the most ancient forms of liturgical prayer still used in liturgies. There is evidence of its wide use in pre-Christian religious ceremonies. The invocation-response structure of the litany lends itself to a performance practice sometimes referred to as *alternatim* or polychoral treatment. This technique allows for alternating between a unison part for soloist and a poly-voiced setting for choir.[74]

The litany form is used in the liturgy in several ritual moments. In the daily prayer of Taizé, the litany is used for intercessory prayer. In the Sunday eucharist, the litany is used for the penitential rite, the prayer of the faithful, and the fraction rite.

Two different types of litanies are included in the Taizé collection. The first type includes litanies with written out verses. "Adoramus Te, Domine" is a litany of the first type. At the conclusion of the refrain (see Fig. 9), the assembly hums on the pitch indicated at measure A. While the assembly holds the pitch, the cantor sings the verse (see Fig. 10).

[72] BERTHIER, *Music from Taizé*, vol. 1, vocal, 29.

[73] BERTHIER, *Music from Taizé*, vol. 1, vocal, 40.

[74] Michel HUGLO, Peter LE HURAY, and David NUTTER, "Litany" in *The New Grove Dictionary of Music and Musicians*, ed. Stanley SADIE, vol. 11 (London: Macmillan Publishers Limited, 1980), 75, 78.

In "Adoramus Te Domine I," the verses of the cantor, written in mixed meter, are six or seven measures long. The refrain of the assembly is three measures long. Both text and music of the assembly's refrain remain unchanged throughout the piece. Eight verses are provided for the cantor. No solo parts are provided for melodic instruments. However, several suggestions are given regarding the use of such rhythm instruments as a gong or timpani to provide an underlying pulse.

Musique: Jacques Berthier – © Ateliers et Presses de Taizé, 71250 Taizé-Communauté, France

Fig. 9. Refrain of "Adoramus Te"[75]

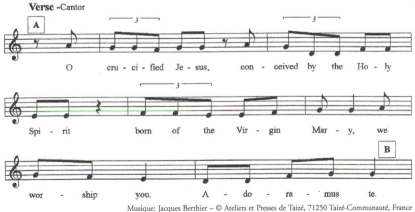

Musique: Jacques Berthier – © Ateliers et Presses de Taizé, 71250 Taizé-Communauté, France

Fig. 10. Verse of "Adoramus Te"[76]

"Veni Creator Spiritus" is another litany with a setting of verses. Like "Adoramus Te Domine I," this litany provides the assembly with a brief

---

[75] BERTHIER, *Music from Taizé*, vol. 1, vocal, 42.

[76] BERTHIER, *Music from Taizé*, vol. 1, vocal, 42.

– in this case two measure – refrain which alternates with nineteen
verses written out for the cantor.

Musique: Jacques Berthier – © Ateliers et Presses de Taizé, 71250 Taizé-Communauté, France

Fig. 11. Response with 2 verses of "Veni Creator Spiritus"[77]

Here, however, the parts of cantor and assembly are equal in length so
that a regular, rhythmic alternation, with brief overlaps, is maintained.
There is potential for a great deal of flexibility in the choice of verses by
the cantor. The performance notes for "Veni Creator Spiritus" encour-
age the adaptation of other texts, especially using other languages in
order to evoke a polylingual experience similar to that of the Pentecost
event.[78] Several solo instrumental parts are provided as well as several

---

[77] BERTHIER, *Music from Taizé*, vol. 1, vocal, 68.

[78] BERTHIER, *Music from Taizé*, vol. 1, vocal, 41. *Pentecost* is the name given to the
event which chapter two of the *Acts of the Apostles* records occurred fifty days after the
resurrection of Jesus. On that day, Jerusalem was filled with what today might be
called an international crowd of pilgrims. When the apostles began preaching, all
who listened understood what they heard in their native tongue. There are strong
parallels between the Pentecost event and the Taizé event. Both can be interpreted as
a manifestation of the work of the Holy Spirit gathering together peoples of many

instrumental accompaniments. In addition, parts for several percussion instruments are provided in order to maintain a steady pulse.

The second type of litany is designed to accommodate spontaneous verses. A simple harmonic accompaniment is written out which allows for a variety of possible texts. In this case, the final chord of the refrain is hummed by choir and assembly while the cantors proclaim the texts in free improvisation over this sound.[79]

"Kyrie Eleison I-X" is an example of the second type of litany found in *Music from Taizé*. These chants can be used during the penitential rite of the eucharist or for intercessory prayer. The series of ten "Kyrie Eleisons" allows for spontaneous or improvisatory verses. The composer provides the assembly response and the musical accompaniment for verses to be composed for specific liturgical celebrations. In other words, verses can be composed for a particular feast or season, or a particular concern of the community.

The ten Kyries vary in length from one to six measures. No melodic instrumental solos are provided since the style focuses on the vocal solo which proclaims the verses.

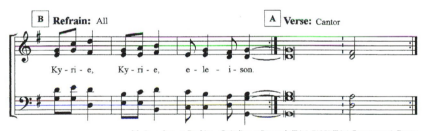

Musique: Jacques Berthier – © Ateliers et Presses de Taizé, 71250 Taizé-Communauté, France

Fig. 12. "Kyrie 1"[80]

In "Kyrie 1" the assembly sings a three measure refrain and hold the final note while the cantor improvises an invocation on the harmony at the measure marked "A." At the conclusion of the invocation the cantor moves to the harmony of the final measure, measure 5, signaling to the assembly a return to the refrain.

tongues and national origins into an experience of unity and understanding founded on faith in Jesus Christ.

[79] BERTHIER, *Music from Taizé*, vol. 1, vocal, 40.

[80] BERTHIER, *Music from Taizé*, vol. 1, vocal, 55.

Acclamations

The third genre in which Berthier composed music for Taizé is the acclamation. This musical form entails "a formula pronounced or sung corporately by a group, expressing a common sentiment, and normally referring to a specific person or object.[81] *Music in Catholic Worship* defines acclamations as "shouts of joy which arise from the whole assembly as forceful and meaningful assents to God's Word and Action."[82] Typically, they are brief, rhythmically strong, and melodically engaging. Acclamations can be sung in the eucharistic liturgy at several points. The first is the singing of the "Alleluia" before the reading of the Gospel. In addition, the assembly's parts in the eucharistic prayer – the Holy, Holy, the memorial acclamation and the great Amen – are meant to be strong acclamations of praise and assent. The two which Berthier most frequently set are the "Alleluia" and "Amen." In most cases, his settings can be used either as acclamations or as refrains with formulas for verses.

"Alleluias I-VI" may be used with or without refrains. As acclamations they can be performed as written, with the assembly following the cantor's intonation.

Musique: Jacques Berthier – © Ateliers et Presses de Taizé, 71250 Taizé-Communauté, France

Fig. 13. "Alleluia 3"[83]

In terms of liturgical usage, the Alleluias are very different from the Kyries. However, in terms of musical form, the Alleluias can also be accommodated to verses in the same way as the Kyries: the final chord is held while the cantor improvises on a chosen text.[84]

---

[81] Geoffrey CHEW, "Acclamation," in *The New Grove Dictionary of Music and Musicians*, ed. Stanley SADIE, vol. 1 (London: Macmillan Publishers Limited, 1980), 35.
[82] *Music in Catholic Worship*, 53.
[83] BERTHIER, *Music from Taizé*, vol. 1, vocal, 74.
[84] BERTHIER, *Music from Taizé*, vol. 1, vocal, 72.

Rather than simply depending on the improvisatory skills of the cantor, "Alleluia 4" actually provides two possible formulas for chanting verses over the sustained final chord of the Alleluia. The first option is written for alto or baritone and the second option is written for soprano or tenor (see Fig. 14).

Musique: Jacques Berthier – © Ateliers et Presses de Taizé, 71250 Taizé-Communauté, France

Fig. 14. "Alleluia 4"[85]

The formula tones provides melodic and harmonic shape for the cantor's improvisation. However, if necessary, the cantor can simplify the formulas by eliminating some of the passing tones.

The musical structure of the "Amens I-III" is similar to that of the Alleluias. If spontaneous verses are sung by the cantor, the assembly simply sustains the final chord as harmonic support. Otherwise, the Amens can be sung as acclamations with the assembly following the lead of the cantor. The most frequent use for the Amen is at the conclusion of the

[85] BERTHIER, Music from Taizé, vol. 1, vocal, 75.

eucharistic prayer. The acclamations do not include melodic instrumental parts since their role in the liturgy does not call for extended repetitions.

Canons

The fourth genre is the canon. As a musical term, *canon* originally referred to a formula whereby a single melody, through strict (canonic) repetition in successive voices, created a polyphonic (many voiced) musical texture.[86] The structure of the canon, sometimes also referred to as the round, employs a melodic theme based on a simple harmonic pattern. This versatile genre can be performed in a variety of ways, ranging from the simplest to the most complex. The options provide for variations in the use of voices, instruments, and dynamics. Some include both principal and secondary canons. In liturgical usage at Taizé, however, the chief role always falls to the assembly.[87]

The structure of the canon allows it to serve several moments in liturgical prayer. It can easily cover a liturgical action of an indeterminate length since it does not depend on the introduction of new verses to extend its performance. For this reason, a canon can be sung as a processional during the gathering rite or the communion rite. The canon also serves well as a response to a reading when an extended time of meditative singing is desired.

"Jubilate, Servite" is a two-voice canon for assembly. Several optional melodic instrumental parts are provided, as well as a basic keyboard accompaniment.

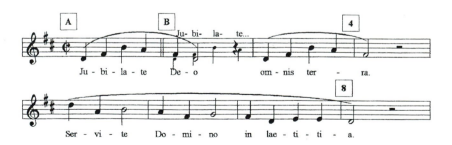

[86] Alfred MANN and J. Kenneth WILSON, "Canon," in *The New Grove Dictionary of Music and Musicians*, ed. Stanley SADIE, vol. 3 (London: Macmillan Publishers Limited, 1980), 689.

[87] BERTHIER, *Music from Taizé*, vol. 1, vocal, 82.

Al - le - lu - ia,   al - le - lu - ia,   in   lae - ti - ti - a.

in lae- ti- ti D.C.

Al - le - lu - ia,   Al - le - lu - ia,   in   lae - ti - ti - a!

Musique: Jacques Berthier – © Ateliers et Presses de Taizé, 71250 Taizé-Communauté, France

Fig. 15. "Jubilate, Servite"[88]

As is indicated in the canon in Fig. 15, a second voice enters at measure two, marked "B." In addition to this foundational canon, there are two different choir parts which may be added as embellishments. The first is a four-part humming part; the second is a two mixed voice setting.

"Prepare the Way of the Lord" is a canon which includes a principle and secondary canon, each of which can be done with up to four voices.

Principal Canon

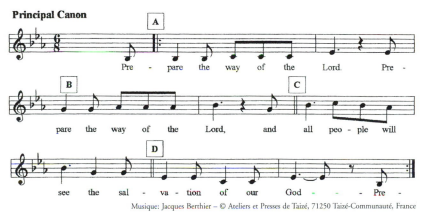

Pre - pare the way of the Lord.   Pre -

pare the way of the Lord,   and   all peo - ple will

see the sal - va - tion of our God - - - Pre -

Musique: Jacques Berthier – © Ateliers et Presses de Taizé, 71250 Taizé-Communauté, France

Fig. 16. Principal canon of "Prepare the Way of the Lord"[89]

The secondary canon may be added to the performance of the principal canon. Its inclusion provides not only an additional melody, but also a new text.

"Prepare the Way of the Lord," is a simpler canon than "Jubilate Servite," in that it does not include special choir parts. However, several instrumental parts are offered which serve as melodic instrumental solos.

---

[88] BERTHIER, *Music from Taizé*, vol. 1, vocal, 101.
[89] Jacques BERTHIER, *Music from Taizé*, vol. 2, ed. Brother ROBERT, vocal edition (Chicago: G.I.A. Publications, Inc., 1982), 50.

Secondary Canon

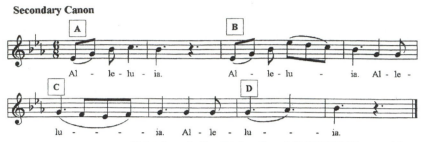

Musique: Jacques Berthier – © Ateliers et Presses de Taizé, 71250 Taizé-Communauté, France

Fig. 17. Secondary canon of "Prepare the Way of the Lord"[90]

"Gloria III" is an example of an even more complex canon. The principal canon (see Fig. 18) contains eight measures divided into four

Principal Canon

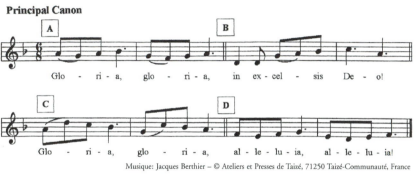

Musique: Jacques Berthier – © Ateliers et Presses de Taizé, 71250 Taizé-Communauté, France

Fig. 18. Principal canon of "Gloria III"[91]

subsections. This canon may include up to four voices, with each voice entering two measures behind the last. An optional secondary canon (see Fig. 19) can be sung in unison or in two voices.

---

[90] BERTHIER, *Music from Taizé*, vol. 2, vocal, 50.
[91] BERTHIER, *Music from Taizé*, vol. 1, vocal, 97.

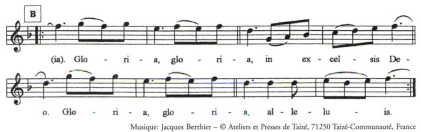

(ia). Glo - ri - a, glo - ri - a, in ex - cel - sis De -

o. Glo - ri - a, glo - ri - a, al - le - lu - ia.

Musique: Jacques Berthier – © Ateliers et Presses de Taizé, 71250 Taizé-Communauté, France

Fig. 19. Secondary canon of "Gloria III"[92]

The secondary canon is written for cantors or choir. In addition to the principle canonic melody and secondary canonic parts, a four-voiced humming part for the choir is also included. Several melodic instrumental parts are also provided.

The Four Genres as Structural Tropes

Earlier in this chapter, a structural trope was defined as a structural procedure that functions as a typical expressive act within a specific framework. Based on this definition, the four genres in which the music of Taizé has been composed can be identified as structural tropes. As such, they function as structuring structures which generate and shape particular cultural practices and representations. Our next task is to examine how each genre of Taizé music assists in structuring the assembly and the ritual.[93]

As explained above, in both the refrain and choral style ostinati, the assembly is the foundation of the musical performance. The choir, cantors, and instrumentalists support and embellish the assembly, but each of their roles is optional. The differentiation of skills is realized in the mutual convergence of all participants, but the assembly, rather than the musical specialists, exercises musical leadership.[94]

The litany form structures the assembly in a relationship of alternation with cantors or soloists. The insertion of verses in various languages provides further flexibility. Unlike the ostinato form, the litany requires the

---

[92] BERTHIER, *Music from Taizé*, vol. 1, vocal, 97.

[93] See Edward FOLEY, "Musical Forms, Referential Meaning and Belief," *Worship* 69 (July 1995), 355. Although Foley does not base his work on Kramer or Bourdieu, he offers a similar hypothesis that draws parallels between a genre of worship music and ecclesial structures. His analysis includes the example of Berthier's "Ubi Caritas."

[94] FOLEY, "Musical Forms," 330-331.

role of the cantor. As a result there is an experience both of cooperation and ministerial differentiation in doing the music.

The acclamations directly engage the assembly in the flow of the ritual. Although a cantor or other minister may exercise a leadership role in calling forth the response of the assembly, the singing of the acclamation directly engages the assembly at key moments of the rite. This is the case in the singing of the Alleluia before the Gospel or the Great Amen at the close of the Eucharistic Prayer.

As in the case of the ostinato, the assembly is the foundation for the performance of the canon. While musical specialists may embellish the assembly's principle canon with secondary canons, yet the leadership role falls to the assembly which provides both stability and variety.

Therefore, in all four of the genres of Taizé music, members of the assembly are placed in a particular relationship to one another and to the various musical and ritual specialists. In the case of the ostinato and the canon, the assembly's foundational role provides the musical leadership for the chant, a corporate leadership exercised without hierarchical differentiation. In the case of the litany, the assembly responds to the leadership of soloist in a mutually cooperative effort. In the case of the acclamations, the assembly is corporately and actively engaged in key ritual moments in a mutual relationship with other ministers.

In addition to structuring the relationships of the assembly to one another and to specific ministers, the mantra-like quality of Taizé music also structures the assembly's experience of time and space. The multiple repetitions of the chants assist in structuring the ritual and extending it in time. Furthermore, the singing of the chants structures the space within which worship takes place by creating a sonic environment[95] within which the assembly ritualizes its relationship to God and to each other.

A Study of the Aleatory Nature of the Scores

The word *aleatory* is usually associated with chance or luck. Applied to music, the term refers to a composition and/or performance that is, to a greater or lesser extent, undetermined by the composer.[96]

---

[95] See Walter ONG. *The Presence of the Word* (New Haven: Yale University Press, 1967), 163. Ong refers to this sonic environment as the phenomenon of "acoustic space," explaining that besides visual-tactile space there is also acoustic space apprehended in terms of sound and echoes. This notion will be explored further in chapters four and five.

[96] Paul GRIFFITHS, "Aleatory," in *The New Grove Dictionary of Music and Musicians*, ed. Stanley SADIE, vol. 1 (London: Macmillan Publishers Limited, 1980), 237.

Theorists have distinguished three types of aleatory technique, but it is possible that any composition may exhibit more than one of these techniques, either separately or in combination. The first technique is the use of random procedures in generating fixed compositions. This technique has been diversely exploited by John Cage. In *Music of Changes,* he tossed coins to decide pitches, durations, and other sound aspects.[97]

The second technique is the allowance of choice to the performer(s) among options stipulated by the composer. Pierre Boulez in Piano Sonata no. 3 and Karlheinz Stockhausen in *Klavierstück XI* have done this by providing performers with alternative orderings of their compositions.[98]

The third technique is employing methods of notation which reduce the composer's control over the sounds of the composition. This can be achieved by either using conventional notation in an indeterminate manner, as in Stockhausen's *Zeitmasse,* or by introducing new notations which render the sounds themselves indeterminate, as in Stockhausen's *Plus-Minus.*[99]

Jacques Berthier employed the second technique in composing his Taizé music. This technique, sometimes referred to as the *mobile form,* permits the performer(s) some flexibility in the realization of the music by providing for alternative orderings.[100] Applied to Taizé music, the term *aleatory* refers to the characteristic whereby the presentation of the score provides for both numerous choices in the combination of individual parts and also a certain element of chance in the actual performance of the music by any particular group of singers and instrumentalists. The element of chance may occur in the number of repetitions, the voice parts taken, the verses created, the time taken between the entrance of additional parts, the combination of instruments, etc.

This dimension of choice and chance comprises a defining characteristic of Taizé music. As such, it provides this study with another hermeneutical window for interpreting the structure of the music and its significance in the liturgical context.

Applied to this study, Kramer's notion of structural tropes and Bourdieu's notion of *habitus* suggests that the structure of the Taizé chants as aleatory, structures the music- makers, that is, the assembly. In this way

---

[97] GRIFFITHS, "Aleatory," 237-238.
[98] GRIFFITHS, "Aleatory," 237-238.
[99] GRIFFITHS, "Aleatory," 238-239.
[100] GRIFFITHS, "Aleatory," 238.

the aleatory performance becomes an expressive act which takes on particular meanings within the cultural/historical framework of the liturgical event. If this is so, then analyzing the aleatory structures of the Taizé
chants can provide us with a hermeneutic window for exploring the
meaning generated by this type of music. Furthermore, the music's
meaning can be understood as embodied, not only in the structures of
the music, but in the way the music organizes or structures the relationships of the music-makers to each other and to the music.

The general presentation of the Taizé chants can be described as
aleatory. In each case, several individual parts are laid out as potential
components. This includes a foundational part for the assembly, often
with options for singing in unison or in harmony. Choir parts of one to
four voices may also be added.

An analysis of the variety of options available in the vocal and instrumental score for "Veni Sancte Spiritus" will serve as an example of the
scope of possibilities available in Taizé music.

Musique: Jacques Berthier – © Ateliers et Presses de Taizé, 71250 Taizé-Communauté, France

Fig. 20. Unison ostinato of "Veni Sancte Spiritus"[101]

A unison two measure ostinato part is written for the assembly (Fig. 20).
This is supplemented by optional settings for four-part women's voices (Fig.
21), four-part men's voices (Fig.22), and four-part mixed voices (Fig. 23).

Musique: Jacques Berthier – © Ateliers et Presses de Taizé, 71250 Taizé-Communauté, France

Fig. 21. "Veni Sancte Spiritus" for women's voices[102]

The various arrangements are adaptable to the make-up of the assembly.
The setting for men's voices (Fig. 22) is similar to that of the four-part
women's setting (Fig. 21).

---

[101] BERTHIER, *Music from Taizé*, vol. 1, vocal, 36.
[102] BERTHIER, *Music from Taizé*, vol. 1, vocal, 36.

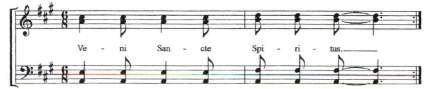

Musique: Jacques Berthier – © Ateliers et Presses de Taizé, 71250 Taizé-Communauté, France

Fig. 22. "Veni Sancte Spiritus" for men's voices[103]

Musique: Jacques Berthier – © Ateliers et Presses de Taizé, 71250 Taizé-Communauté, France

Fig. 23. "Veni Sancte Spiritus" for mixed voices[104]

In the vocal settings for the assembly and choir there are several possibilities, all dependent on the vocal resources of the group. Various combinations of the settings may be employed since none is mutually exclusive. Any or all would fit into the harmonic structure of the ostinato response.

Several vocal and instrumental verses may be added to the ostinato response. Here again, the performance notes indicate that the "vocal and instrumental verses are sung or played as desired with some space always left between the verses."[105]

Musique: Jacques Berthier – © Ateliers et Presses de Taizé, 71250 Taizé-Communauté, France

Fig. 24. French verse of "Veni Sancte Spiritus"[106]

[103] BERTHIER, *Music from Taizé*, vol. 1, vocal, 36.
[104] BERTHIER, *Music from Taizé*, vol. 1, vocal, 36.
[105] BERTHIER, *Music from Taizé*, vol. 1, vocal, 37.
[106] BERTHIER, *Music from Taizé*, vol. 1, vocal, 38.

Verse settings are provided in five languages: English, French, German, Spanish, and Italian.[107] There is a great deal of possible variety in the number of verses sung, the language of the verses, the choice of which verses are sung, the amount of time taken between verses. These possibilities are further multiplied when instrumental verses are included. In addition to the keyboard and guitar accompaniments published in the vocal edition, parts for seven solo instruments are published in the instrumental edition: flute, oboe, English horn, b-flat clarinet, b-flat trumpet, trombone and cello. Figure 25 provides eight measures of the thirty-six measures written for oboe.

Musique: Jacques Berthier – © Ateliers et Presses de Taizé, 71250 Taizé-Communauté, France

Fig. 25. Oboe solo for "Veni Sancte Spiritus"[108]

Each instrumental part stands on its own. That is, any one of the instrumental parts may be used separately, or in combination with any other. This creates a situation that is very different from an orchestral score where the instrumental parts are designed to be performed as part of a total design.

Furthermore, instrumental solos are featured in the same way as vocal solos. Solo parts can be used in various combinations in order to thicken the texture of the sound. The order and spacing of these parts is the decision of the soloists and/or music director. The scores do not indicate and the writing does not require a particular ordering of performance. These characteristics exemplify the second type of aleatory technique described earlier as the *mobile form*.

[107] In the interest of space, only one verse in French is printed here. The English edition published by G.I.A. contains some verses in French, German, Spanish, and Italian, in addition to the English verses. While the foreign languages verses are not as extensive as the English ones in the G.I.A. collection, other editions are available in several other languages which provide additional verses in their respective languages.

[108] Jacques BERTHIER, *Music for Taizé*, vol. 1, instrumental edition, ed. Brother Robert (Chicago: G.I.A. Publications, Inc., 1981), 30.

The aleatory design of "Veni Sancte Spiritus" results in a structuring of the assembly whereby a clear differentiation of roles is set up. Both vocal and instrumental parts, functioning either as accompaniment or soloist, are designed to be distinct but not separate. Parts can be moved or substituted and yet the result, each time a little different, still communicates a coherent wholeness. This is because even in the variety expressed in all the possibilities, there is an underlying harmonic and rhythmic structure to which each part adheres. Throughout, the assembly's role is foundational and consistent. It supports the variety of parts that are performed concurrently. But because of the variety of timbres and melodic lines, the soloists are not lost in the sound of the assembly.

The result of this aleatory feature is a piece of music that is strikingly versatile, dynamic, and provisional. There is no "musical work"[109] in the ordinary sense of the term. Moreover, looking at the score does not give one a definitive notion of what to expect in actual performance. The score does not define an "ideal" performance. Rather, it offers numerous possibilities. Some of these will be engaged in the making of the music in each new instance.

In the case of "Veni Sancte Spiritus," the aleatory nature of this piece constitutes it in such a way that it communicates, through its various expressive acts – that is, structural tropes – an expression and experience of what the text itself is stating. What Berthier has created is a piece of music in which a variety of different voices, both human and instrumental, invoke the Holy Spirit. The doing of the music recreates the Pentecost event.[110] Layers of sound, of different pitches and timbres, with the possibility of different texts and languages, come together to produce the harmony of the entire assembly. It is the pulse of the ostinato refrain, its persistent repetition and foundational harmonic movement, that keeps the piece together. Each singer and instrumentalist – breathing together – repeatedly invoke the Holy Spirit, the breath of God. Through their doing of this piece of music, the assembly expresses the presence of the breath of God in their midst.

---

[109] See Lydia GOEHR, *The Imaginary Museum of Musical Works: An Essay in the Philosophy of Music* (New York: Oxford University Press, 1992), for a discussion of the evolution of the concept of a musical work.

[110] See Fig. 11, p. 62.

AN EXAMINATION OF TEXTUAL INCLUSIONS

The Performance Notes

While the intention of the composer or author never limits the meaning of a piece of music or any work of art, still a look at what is behind the text, or in this case the music, is an important step in the interpretive process. In mappping out a strategy for musical interpretation, Lawrence Kramer describes textual inclusions as the most explicit hermeneutic windows.[111] In this section two types of textual inclusions will be examined: the performance notes written by Brother Robert and the texts or lyrics of the chants.

Accordingly, the remarks of Brother Robert, included in the introductory comments and performance notes in the first volume of *Music from Taizé,* vocal and instrumental editions, provide some insight into the initial design, not only of Jacques Berthier, but especially of the monks of Taizé who engaged him to compose the music. The comments and notes address several areas of concern: the music's relationship to prayer, the repetitive nature of the music, the music's relationship to the assembly, the role of the instrumental parts, the role of the music director, and the widespread use – especially in the first decade of Taizé music – of the Latin language.

Life at Taizé focuses first and foremost on prayer. Brother Robert identifies this focus when he says that the "goal towards which this music is directed is *prayer*, and most especially communal prayer, whether it be in a small group, a parish, or in a large gathering of young people, etc."[112]

It is in keeping with that focus that Brother Robert roots the repetitive nature of Berthier's chants in the mantra tradition of both the East and the West. In fact, he sees in the ostinato refrains of Taizé, echoes of the Jesus Prayer[113] among the Greek Church Fathers and the

---

[111] KRAMER, *Music as Cultural Practice,* 13.

[112] BERTHIER, *Music from Taizé,* vol. 1, vocal, x.

[113] See "Jesus Prayer, The" in *The Oxford Dictionary of the Christian Church,* 2d ed. F.L. CROSS and E.A. LIVINGSTONE, 738 (Oxford: Oxford University Press, 1974). The Jesus Prayer is a short prayer, continuously repeated in these or similar words: "Lord Jesus Christ, Son of God, have mercy upon me." Brief prayers repeated continually are referred to as mantras. The Jesus Prayer is specially recommended in Byzantine Hesychasm. Its full text is first found in a sixth or seventh century work entitled *Life of Abba Philemon.* This prayer is widely prayed in the Orthodox Church today.

rosary[114] in the Western Church.[115] Brother Robert comments on how the repetitive nature of the music touches the individual in communal prayer:

> Using few notes and words, the continuous flow of the refrain expresses something essential: it constantly penetrates further and further into the depth of a person. Early Christianity, it is true, experienced a type of prayer comprised of a few words repeated over and over again as the name of Jesus was invoked to give peace and unity to the depths of one's being. But it is *through singing* [emphasis added], for pastoral reasons, and in a manner we could not have foreseen at the beginning, that we have rediscovered a similar path. What once mediated individual prayer is now experienced as means of communion with others.[116]

Thus, the repetitive nature of the music is, in fact, at the service of ritual prayer. By fostering a unity of heart through a unity of performance, it is also clearly at the service of the assembly. Finally, by mediating this communion with God and with others, the music becomes a means whereby the brothers are able to reach out to the pilgrims who come to Taizé and provide them with a pathway for discovering their own prayer.

In explaining that the main purpose of Taizé music is to facilitate the active participation of the assembly, Brother Robert echoes all the major church documents on liturgy in the twentieth century.[117] However, Robert does not see this goal of participation as necessarily precluding *more evolved versions.*[118] By this he means that, if more elaborate musical means are available and the liturgical circumstances allow, the way is open for exploring a greater range of possibilities of alternating and combining various instruments, not for aesthetic show, but as a way of expressing spiritual animation.[119]

---

[114] The rosary is a pious devotion which consists in its entirety of fifteen decades, each of which commemorates a mystery in the life of Christ. Each decade consists of the repetition of an Our Father, ten Hail Marys, and a Trinitarian doxology. Hence, an entire rosary would consist of 150 Hail Marys. Usually only five decades of the rosary are prayed at a time.

[115] BERTHIER, *Music from Taizé*, vol. 1, vocal, x.

[116] Brother ROBERT, "Taizé Music," 21.

[117] BERTHIER, *Music from Taizé*, vol. 1, instrumental, iii.

[118] BERTHIER, *Music from Taizé*, vol. 1, instrumental, iii.

[119] BERTHIER, *Music from Taizé*, vol. 1, instrumental, iii.

The instrumental parts are conceived in two ways: some are accompaniments and others are solo parts. As accompaniments, the instrumental parts function in the standard way as harmonic support for the voices. As solos, the instrumental parts serve a more unique role. Either they can be used in conjunction with the vocal music for which they are designed or they may be arranged to form independent instrumental pieces.[120] In other words, the instrumental pieces can be treated in the same spirit, and can be performed in the same style, as their vocal counterparts.

This is an important point to keep in mind for later considerations of the relationship of music to text. Brother Robert did not consider Taizé music simply servant of the text. Rather, he sees an instrumental solo as a valid, independent option in place of a vocal solo. Furthermore, when explaining that a fuller engagement of instrumental possibilities can express a spiritual animation, he acknowledges that it can be a way of saying what words cannot say.[121]

Brother Robert's remark to the music director or conductor highlights the aleatory nature of Taizé music when, in the performance notes, he says that "the one who is in charge of the singing and its execution participates in a real way in the creation of the piece, since each one may be presented in a variety of ways. … It is up to each user of this music to find the best ways of arranging the material for his or her own circumstances and resources."[122]

Finally, comments on the rationale for the widespread use of Latin, particularly in Volume One, offer insights into the genuine effort of the Taizé community to offer hospitality to pilgrims who join them for worship. Brother Robert explains the predicament of their unique situation:

> The use of some very simple words in basic Latin to support the music and the theme of prayer was also dictated by pastoral needs. From practical experience it was the only way of solving the unavoidable problem of languages that arose at international gatherings. At first we tried to teach everybody the five or six words of a response in one of the languages represented by the participants. But very quickly it was realized that some people were being favored while others, for whom that language was 'foreign', stumbled over the pitfalls of pronunciation.[123]

---

[120] BERTHIER, *Music from Taizé*, vol. 1, instrumental, iii.
[121] BERTHIER, *Music from Taizé*, vol. 1, instrumental, iii.
[122] BERTHIER, *Music from Taizé*, vol. 1, instrumental, v.
[123] BERTHIER, *Music from Taizé*, vol. 1, vocal, vii.

In other words, since it is a dead language for everyone, Brother Robert saw the use of Latin as a way to put everyone on an equal footing. Its neutrality rather than its universality was its strong point. Variations in pronunciation due to nationality were considered inconsequential. In addition, the strong musical quality to the sound of Latin syllables was considered a further reason for choosing this language.[124]

In the notes for Volume I published by G.I.A. Publications, Inc., Brother Robert acknowledges that while this argument explains the use of Latin at Taizé, it does not address possible questions regarding its retention in the English language edition. He gives two reasons for the decision to retain the Latin responses. The first has to do with considerations for text accent and its relationship to the musical line. Concern that adaptations would weaken either element by disturbing the close link between the two had in fact prompted Jacques Berthier to compose new pieces in English rather than simply to translate the Latin. The second reason for retaining Latin has to do with the concern that the texts of the living languages would not hold up under the repetitive style of much of the Taizé music. Rather, the judgment was made that the "neutral" nature of the word or short phrases from the traditional liturgical languages such as the Greek *Kyrie,* the Aramaic *Maranatha,* or the Latin *Gloria,* would be well suited to such repetition.[125]

In fact, however, a study of later editions of various publications from Taizé indicates that, while Latin has been retained for the pieces composed in the early years of the project, increasingly, the vernacular languages of the brothers and the pilgrims who frequent Taizé have been used in the later songs.

Whether the decision to use Latin was the most appropriate, the most hospitable, or the most musical is not central to the concerns of this study. What is important is that Taizé's goal of reconciliation was furthered by their efforts to arrive at a liturgical practice whereby the language of the songs, as far as possible, included rather than excluded. The eventual combination of Latin, a dead ecclesiastical language, with the living languages of the pilgrims, can also be interpreted as an effort to reconcile the past and the present, to reconcile ecclesiastical tradition and lived experience.

---

[124] BERTHIER, *Music from Taizé,* vol. 1, vocal, vii.
[125] BERTHIER, *Music from Taizé,* vol. 1, vocal, x.

Furthermore, the provisionality of Taizé's decision to use Latin texts reflects the provisionality of the community itself. The introduction of new languages in the chants over the years, reflects both the changing makeup of the community and their outreach through international meetings and pilgrimages at Taizé. It likewise reflects the growing involvement of the pilgrims in embracing the spirit and mission of Taizé and making it their own.

The Source of Texts and the Use of Languages

Texts

The texts for Berthier's Taizé music are taken, for the most part, from two sources: Sacred Scripture and liturgical books. Some additional texts have been composed by the brothers in order to provide verses, intercessory prayers or invocations for the responses or litanies. However, even in those cases where the texts are drawn directly from Scripture, the choice and arrangement of the texts have been the work of Brother Robert or another one of the brothers.

The majority of texts are direct quotations from the Old and the New Testament, while some are paraphrases with clear scriptural references. The songs in *Music from Taizé,* Volume One, include texts from the *Book of Psalms, The Book of Daniel,* the Gospels of Matthew, Luke, and John, and *The First Letter to the Corinthians.* Several songs include phrases so brief that it is difficult to identify any one specific scriptural reference. Nevertheless, the phrases echo clear scriptural sentiments. The songs in *Music from Taizé,* Volume Two, are taken from the *Book of Psalms,* the *Book of Daniel, Isaiah, Lamentations,* the Gospels of Matthew, Luke, and John, *The Second Letter to the Corinthians,* and *Ephesians.*

There are also several settings of liturgical texts in both volumes of *Music from Taizé.* These include texts of the ordinary of the Mass such as the Gloria, Credo, Sanctus, Agnus Dei, Amen, and Alleluia, as well as excerpts from the Good Friday liturgy and the Christmas liturgy.

Languages

As mentioned earlier in this chapter, it was the problem of addressing the needs of worshipers of diverse language groups which first led Brother Robert to seek new alternatives to the French repertoire sung by the brothers and their pilgrim guests. Both the story of Taizé and the program notes indicate that concern for the accessibility of language was inspired by the immediate concern for active participation and hospitality. Ultimately, of course, all their efforts spring from Taizé's mission of reconciliation. Several solutions to the language question were attempted over the span of twenty years. A look at the latest hymnal used at Taizé indicates that none of them has been completely abandoned.[126]

For example, many of Berthier's early chants set to Latin, Greek or Aramaic texts are included in the latest edition of Taizé's hymnal. Since the texts of these pieces are very brief, almost universally familiar, and firmly rooted in the many branches of the Christian tradition, their retention not only promotes the more immediate goal of hospitality and active participation, but more importantly, promotes Taizé's mission of working toward the reconciliation of the Christian churches.

In the late seventies when the first English edition of the Taizé chants was published in the United States, despite the intention to publish new songs in English, several selections were included using the original Latin, Aramaic, or Greek texts. As explained earlier in this chapter, in the section discussing textual inclusions, this decision to retain the original Latin, Aramaic, and Greek texts was done because Latin, Aramaic, and Greek were perceived to be "neutral" languages and well-suited to repetition.[127]

Brother Robert had also attempted to deal with the variety of language groups represented at the international meetings by choosing a few classic hymns from each language. This practice is still evident in the inclusion, in the latest hymnal, of a German chorale by J.S. Bach and several pieces from the Russian Orthodox tradition.

Increasingly, however, the Taizé chants have been set to a wide variety of vernacular languages. At first this was done by retaining the Latin refrain and setting only the verses sung by the soloist in the vernacular. Jacques Berthier worked out these settings with the help of musicians who were well-acquainted with the accents of the various languages.[128] Eventually, Berthier suggested setting short ostinato

---

[126] *Chants de Taizé*, Ateliers et Presses de Taizé: Taizé, France, 1995. This latest edition of music sung at Taizé actually has a multi-lingual title. Under the words "*Chants de*," the phrase is translated into thirteen other languages.

[127] See BERTHIER, *Music from Taizé*, vol. 1, vocal, x quoted above.

[128] Sr. Nuria Sabé GRIFUL, for example, mentioned in her interview that she worked as Berthier's Spanish consultant for the song "Nada te turbe."

refrains in these vernacular languages as well. He began working on this project in 1979 with the English language. His first piece was "Jesus, Remember Me."[129]

Since then, numerous pieces have been set to a variety of languages. These include, not only such European languages as German, Italian, Polish, Slovak, and Spanish, but also Korean, Indian, and Japanese.[130] However, the process does not simply involve literal translations of a text from one language into another. Berthier never allowed translations to be simply set on the music. Rather, where necessary, he remade, or adjusted the music to the translation with the help of people from the country involved.[131]

Musique: Jacques Berthier – © Ateliers et Presses de Taizé, 71250 Taizé-Communauté, France

Fig. 26. Refrain of "Bénissez/Chwała"[132]

[129] BERTHIER, "*Un serviteur*," 10.

[130] Hymnals have been published in such vernacular languages as the English, French, German, Spanish, and Polish. These are available from the bookstore in Taizé by writing The Taizé Community, 71250 Taizé, France. Taizé's hymnal, *Chants de Taizé,* includes songs in fourteen languages. This is also available through the Taizé bookstore. G.I.A. Publications, Inc., 7404 So. Mason Avenue, Chicago, IL 60638 publishes the English settings in the USA. Geoffrey Chapman Mowbray is the publisher in England. At the time of my research, the Korean, Indian, and Japanese manuscripts were still unpublished.

[131] Germaine BERTHIER, interview.

[132] *Radość Serca: Śpiewy z Taizé,* Spiewnik (Katowice: Wydawnictwo Columb Sp zo.o, 1992), 22-23.

The following comparison of the refrain and verses of "*Bénissez le Seigneur*/Chwała Panu i cześć" (see Fig. 26) in the French and Polish settings reveals how Berthier dealt with the challenge of setting his music to different languages. The music is designed so that the cantor and assembly alternate. In other words, the rests in the refrain correspond to the solo parts in the verses and vice versa.

The music of the refrain is identical for both the French and the Polish texts. While the sense of the French is preserved in the Polish, the texts are not literal translations of each other. In English the French text is translated "Bless the Lord." The Polish text is translated "Glory to the Lord and praise."

Musique: Jacques Berthier – © Ateliers et Presses de Taizé, 71250 Taizé-Communauté, France

Fig. 27. French verses 1 and 2 of "Bénissez"[133]

[133] Jacques BERTHIER, *Bénissez le Seigneur: 27 Chants de Taizé avec versets de solistes et accompagnements,* (Taizé: Les Presses de Taizé, 1990), 6.

However, the music of the verses of the two languages is not identical as was the case with the refrains of the two languages. In this instance the music, while following the basic outline of the melodic shape in both cases includes several variations. A comparison of the settings of the French and Polish verses (see Fig. 27 and Fig. 28) reveal that the melodic lines are not identical. In order to account for the differences in the accents and the number of syllables in the two versions, a number of adjustments have been made.

Musique: Jacques Berthier – © Ateliers et Presses de Taizé, 71250 Taizé-Communauté, France

Fig. 28. Polish verses 1 and 2 of "Chwała"[134]

[134] *Śpiewy z Taizé: Głosy solowe* (Taizé: Les Presses de Taizé, 1993), 9.

The adjustments involve alterations to the melodic line. In some cases, the rhythm, and in other cases the pitches have been changed. For example, in each of the three phrases of verse one, the first syllable of the French and the Polish begin on a different beat of the measure. In verse two, the melody of the first French phrase is F-E-D. The first phrase of the Polish setting of verse two is F-A-F-E-D. The harmony and the number of measures in each case remain the same. In addition, the texts are not identical even though both are based on "The Canticle of the Three Young Men," *Daniel* 3: 51-90.

As a general rule, both Brother Robert and Jacques Berthier understood and guarded the close relationship between the text and the music in these chants. In the notes to Volume Two of *Music from Taizé*, Brother Robert explains why certain pieces composed for other languages are not included in this English edition:

> ...[M]any new pieces created at Taizé are in other languages: Spanish, French, Italian, German, etc. They have not been included in this volume, with the exception of three pieces for which adaptation into English seemed acceptable, though perhaps not perfect: "O Poverty" (originally in French), "Stay with Me" (originally in German) and "Stay with Us" (also in German). It should be repeated that in general such adaptations are formally inadvised [*sic*]. In such short pieces, the music is strongly tied to the text, its rhythmic structure and the color of the syllables. To change the text would, in most cases, mean weakening the specific message of the music. However, the composer himself may at times take up an already used musical structure and, with minor modifications, employ it for an entirely new text. This is the case with the piece, "My Soul Is at Rest," which is based on "Misericordias Domini" from the first volume. Such exceptions however do not change the general rule.[135]

These comments clearly express a keen understanding of the mutual relationship between text and music in a song. Neither the integrity of the text, nor of the music, would be sacrificed for the sake of multiplying translations. In describing his compositional technique, Berthier himself noted that for him it was always the text which inspired the music.[136] His second consideration was the general style, that is the

---

[135] BERTHIER, *Music from Taizé*, vol. 2, vocal, vi.

[136] The actual quote of this comment in French is as follows: "C'est vraiment le texte qui me fait faire la musique, toujours." Cf. BERTHIER, "*Un serviteur*," 15

genre of the piece, and the third was the people for whom the music was being composed.[137]

In the last years of Berthier's life, it appears that this practice was not strictly adhered to. Oftentimes, the music is not remade to accommodate a new language, nor are certain tunes restricted only to the original language for which they were written.

Editions of *Chants de Taizé* published in the 90's include chants which are set to several – sometimes as many as twelve – languages.[138] Although the chants in this publication are the work of Berthier and the brothers, in another sense, the development reflected in this collection is beyond the control of either the brothers or Jacques Berthier. The difficulty of monitoring the translations supports the conviction that Taizé music is a type of folk music. Simply stated, an oral tradition has developed around these Taizé chants. Different language groups who have visited Taizé or become acquainted with its music have worked out "unofficial" translations. These have been done with varying degrees of expertise. As a result, greater efforts have been made at Taizé to provide songs in the various languages in order to guarantee more careful translations.[139] The final results, however, are not literal translations and sometimes not even dynamic equivalents.[140] Rather, the same prayer sentiments are often expressed in very different ways.

The multi-language setting of "*Jésus le Christ*," is a good example of the effort to provide the same chant in several languages without attempting literal translations. In Fig. 29, the original French text is set to five additional languages.

---

[137] BERTHIER, "*Un serviteur*," 15.

[138] See no. 1, 5, and 17 in *Chants de Taizé*, 1995 for examples of this practice.

[139] John CASTALDI, interview by author, 23 May 1996, Taizé, France. Brother John is a member of the Taizé community who comes from the United States.

[140] Translating into dynamic equivalents involves attending to the idioms of the receptor language rather than the distinctive characteristics of the original language. For further discussion of this translation procedure see Lawrence BOADT, "Problems in the Translation of Scripture as Illustrated in ICEL's Project on the Liturgical Psalter," in *Shaping English Liturgy*, ed. Peter C. FINN and James M. SCHELLMAN, 405-429 (Washington, D.C.: The Pastoral Press, 1990); and Mary COLLINS, "Glorious Praise: The ICEL Liturgical Psalter," *Worship* 66 (July 1992): 290-310.

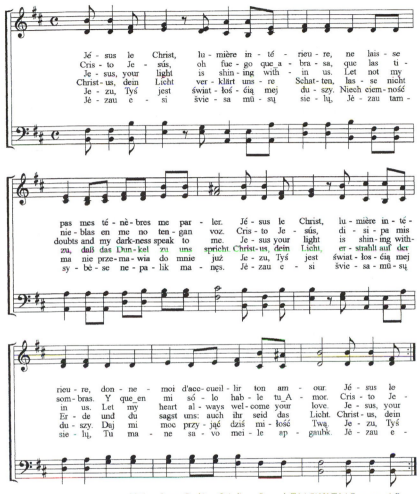

Musique: Jacques Berthier – © Ateliers et Presses de Taizé, 71250 Taizé-Communauté, France

Fig. 29. "*Jésus le Christ*"[141]

In each case, while the subject of the texts is the same, that is, Jesus as the light in the darkness, the expression of that idea is unique to each language.[142]

[141] *Chants de Taizé*, no. 9.

[142] For example, in English, the French text of verse one translates: "Jesus, the Christ, interior light, do not let my darkness speak to me. Jesus, the Christ, interior light grant that I may welcome your love." The German text of verse four translates: "Christ, your light transforms our shadows. Do not permit darkness to speak to us.

There are, on the other hand, several examples of chants which have been written specifically for a particular language. Often, they have similarities to chants set to other languages in terms of their liturgical purpose or the sentiments of the text, yet the musical setting is unique to the language for which it has been composed. The litanies are a good example of this.

In the early days of the Taizé project, Berthier wrote several litanies which could be used either in the penitential rite or for the intercessory prayers. In Volume One of *Music from Taizé*, there are a number of settings of such litanies in Greek, Latin, and English. These include the ten settings of the "Kyrie,"[143] the "O Christe audi nos,"[144] and the "Te rogamus audi nos" which is printed below.

Musique: Jacques Berthier – © Ateliers et Presses de Taizé, 71250 Taizé-Communauté, France

Fig. 30. Refrain of "Te rogamus"[145]

However, publications for specific national groups, in addition to including some of these early litanies, particularly the Kyries, also include litanies that have been written specifically for a particular language. For example, the Spanish edition of Taizé chants, *Cantos de Taizé*, includes some litanies in Spanish which are not included in other editions. "Te rogamos, óyenos" has a similar text to the Latin setting, but an entirely new melody (see Fig. 31).

Another example of a litany that Berthier composed for a specific language can be found in the unpublished collection of chants in Korean. The music of the chant printed below (see Fig. 32) is only found in the Korean setting. The English translation is "Lord, Lord, please hear us."

Christ, your light shines upon the earth, and you say to us: you also are light." The Polish text of verse five translates: "Jesus, you are the light of my soul. Let not my own darkness attract me anymore. Jesus, you are the light of my soul. Give me the strength to welcome your love today."

[143] BERTHIER, *Music from Taizé*, vol. 1, vocal, 55-59.

[144] BERTHIER, *Music from Taizé*, vol. 1, vocal, 66.

[145] BERTHIER, *Music from Taizé*, vol. 1, vocal, 66.

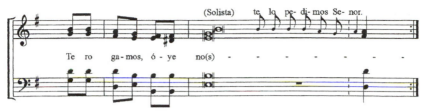

Musique: Jacques Berthier – © Ateliers et Presses de Taizé, 71250 Taizé-Communauté, France

Fig. 31. "Te rogamos"[146]

In "Chuyo, chuyo turo chusoso" the cantor's part is set to a metered melody rather than to a reciting tone. Nevertheless the melody serves simply as an outline for possible improvisations by the cantor.

Musique: Jacques Berthier – © Ateliers et Presses de Taizé, 71250 Taizé-Communauté, France

Fig. 32. "Chuyo, chuyo turo chusoso"[147]

Lastly, the 1995 edition of the Taizé hymnal includes four different settings of the "Gospodi," a litany set in Slovak and Russian which means "Lord, have mercy." These melodies are not found with texts in English, French, Spanish or German. However, the Polish edition of the Taizé chants does include three of the "Gospodi."

The first "Gospodi" (see Fig. 33) is in Slovak. The second example (see Fig. 34) is in Polish. The music is identical except for the use of bar lines.

---

[146] Jacques BERTHIER, *Cantos de Taizé*, vol. 1, edición vocal, ed. Hermano ROBERTO (Chicago: G.I.A. Publications, Inc., 1986), 72.

[147] BERTHIER, *Chants coreéns*, unpublished manuscript, The Community of Taizé, Taizé, France.

Musique: Jacques Berthier – © Ateliers et Presses de Taizé, 71250 Taizé-Communauté, France

Fig. 33. "Gospodi A" (Slovak)[148]

A comparison of the texts of Fig. 33 and Fig. 34 indicates the very close similarity between them.

Musique: Jacques Berthier – © Ateliers et Presses de Taizé, 71250 Taizé-Communauté, France

Fig. 34. "Gospodi A" (Polish)[149]

The similarities in inflection and accents among the Polish, Slovak, and Russian languages makes exchanges such as these quite natural. Furthermore, the familiarity among these language groups with the Slavic liturgical tradition enables the mutual exchange of these prayer settings to serve as a potential instrument of reconciliation among the churches.

Text and Language as Hermeneutic Windows

This analysis of the texts and language of Berthier's music highlights several important aspects of the Taizé community. In the first place, the care and effort they have taken with setting the Scripture and liturgy texts speak clearly of their respect for the Christian tradition and their commitment to the mission of promoting the reconciliation of the Christian churches and all marginalized people.

---

[148] BERTHIER, *Chants de Taizé*, no. 80.
[149] BERTHIER, *Radość Serca: Śpiewy z Taizé*," 17.

Secondly, the ongoing process of revising chants and creating new chants in new languages demonstrates, not only an awareness of the importance of the wedding of text and music in the creation of a liturgical chant, but also an acceptance of the provisionality of the community and of the music with which it worships. A willingness to take into account the oral tradition whereby the participants often unconsciously revise difficult chants or rework chants to address their own particular needs further demonstrates an awareness of and respect for the participation of the praying community not only in the ritual, but also in the creation of the music.

SUMMARY OF ANALYSIS

Following the musical hermeneutic proposed by Lawrence Kramer, this chapter has presented an analysis of Berthier's Taizé music based on the conviction that music has referential power which will disclose its meaning if we open hermeneutic windows through which our understanding can pass. In order to open these hermeneutic windows, this chapter examined the four genres of Taizé music and their aleatory nature as structural tropes or procedures capable of functioning as expressive acts within the liturgy. It has also examined the performance notes, the texts of the chants, and their various languages as textual inclusions available for interpreting the chants.

An analysis of the four genres and the aleatory nature of the chants reveals that the Taizé music situates the assembly in a foundational role which expresses both leadership and mutuality. Furthermore, the performance notes and the multi-lingual texts from Scripture and the liturgical rites situate the assembly within the Christian tradition in an expressive posture of reconciliation and mutual respect.

The results of this musical hermeneutic indicate that the music of Taizé does indeed embody meaning that in some way makes connections between the life and mission of Taizé, the purpose of the liturgy and liturgical music, and the lives of the pilgrims who come to pray. The music mediates these relationships and these understandings. The task of the next chapter is to examine both philosophical and theological theories of symbol which can assist in arriving at a critical theory of how music embodies meaning that can be applied not only to the ritual prayer at Taizé, but to all liturgical prayer.

CHAPTER THREE

PHILOSOPHIES AND THEOLOGIES OF SYMBOL: TAIZÉ MUSIC AS RITUAL SYMBOL

INTRODUCTION

If indeed music-making – and in particular, the singing of the Taizé chants – is both integral to the liturgy and ministerial, then ritual music-making provides something more than simply "a nobler aspect" to the rites or "a more graceful expression to prayer."[1] The thesis of this paper is that the symbolic nature of music and music-making provides the possibility that music is both integral to the liturgy and ministerial.

Chapter two employed a musical hermeneutics which approached the chants of Taizé as a field of humanly significant action. This hermeneutic is based on the conviction that music has referential power. It allowed us to identify textual inclusions and structural tropes which serve as hermeneutical windows for interpreting how these chants mediate meaning.

The task of this chapter is to explore several aspects of symbol theory in order to discover how music, and specifically, the music of Taizé, can be said to be symbolic. This will include an examination and application of principles of symbol theory and semiotics and also theologies of symbol which promise to assist our efforts to discover how music functions as symbol within the liturgy and how the singing of the Taizé chants can be described as symbolizing activity.

Since this paper regards music not only as symbol, but also as an art form, the ideas of various thinkers in the philosophy of art called aesthetics will be applied to the analysis of ritual music. Furthermore, because the art form being studied is performed at Taizé in Christian liturgy, various theologies of symbol will be used to address the question of music as ritual symbol. Lastly, because this paper is examining music's power to signify, that is, to mediate meaning, certain approaches in the field of semiotics will be engaged to analyze how music mediates

---

[1] *"Musicam Sacram,"* 5.

meaning, particularly in a ritual context. Since semiotics is a relatively new field of study, having developed significantly since the 1970's in both Europe and the United States, a brief introduction to semiotics and a rationale for its application to the study of liturgy will clarify its role in this study.

Charles Sanders Peirce (1839-1914) and Ferdinand de Saussure (1857-1913) are considered the two founders of contemporary semiotics, a tradition which has its roots in ancient Greece. Charles Morris, a semiotician who built on the theoretical foundations of Charles Sanders Peirce, has defined "semiosis" as the process in which something functions as a sign.[2] The related term "semiotic" was adapted by John Locke from the Greek Stoics.[3] In contemporary usage, the terms semiosis, semiotics, and semiology have all been employed to describe the signifying process and the study of the process. Charles Peirce's followers have used the term *semiotic* to describe their elaboration of his conceptual framework, while Ferdinand de Saussure's followers have used the term *semiologie* to describe their application of his conceptual framework for analyzing language to other sign phenomena.[4] In general, today semiotics is considered the discipline which concerns itself with both verbal and non-verbal signs.[5]

In his writings,[6] Peirce identifies three dimensions of approach to the analysis of signs in semiotics: the semantic, the pragmatic, and the syntactic. Wilson Coker, whose work builds on the tradition of C.S. Peirce and Charles Morris, explains these terms in this way:

---

[2] Charles MORRIS, "Foundations of the Theory of Signs," in *Foundations of the Unity of Science: Toward an International Encyclopedia of Unified Science,* ed. Otto NEURATH, Rudolf CARNAP, and Charles MORRIS, vol. 1, nos. 1-10 (Chicago: The University of Chicago Press, 1969), 81.

[3] Charles MORRIS, *Signification and Significance: A Study of the Relations of Signs and Values* (Cambridge, Massachusetts: The M.I.T. Press, 1964), 1.

[4] Jan Michael JONCAS, "Musical Semiotics and Liturgical Musicology: Theoretical Foundations and Analytic Techniques," *Ecclesia Orans* 8 (1991): 183.

[5] Gerard M. Lukken, "Semiotics and the Study of Liturgy," *Studia Liturgica* 17 (1987): 109.

[6] Peirce himself published approximately twelve thousand printed pages of his writings and lectures. In addition, the known manuscripts of unpublished materials runs to approximately eighty thousand pages. Two different editions of Peirce's writings have been consulted for this study. Because Peirce often provides several definitions for the same term, as is the case, for example, of his term *interpretant,* directly quoting a succinct definition is not possible.

The dimension of *semantics* concerns the relations of signs to their contexts and to what they signify. The kinds of signs, their ordering, and their relations to one another are the dimension of *syntactics*. And the dimension of *pragmatics* treats the relations of signs to their interpreters.[7]

Each of these dimensions looks at a different aspect of the process of signification. In engaging in semiotics, the meaning of a sign is considered in terms of its relation to all three dimensions since it is generated by their interaction.

If semiotic analysis is concerned with the analysis of signs, it follows that such analysis can be fruitful in the study of the liturgy as a complexus of symbols. The musical semiologist Gino Stefani argues for the appropriateness of applying semiotics to the analysis of the liturgy when he explains:

> The liturgy ... is to be performed following the laws of Christian worship and those that regulate the action and expression of human groups. ... [T]he liturgy is an ensemble of signs, that is to say, of actions in which the dominant value is situated in the order of signification ... That is why it is correct to consider liturgical science as a branch of semiology, the general science of signs. ... It is thus normal for semiological reflection to devolve upon the liturgy insofar as it is human communication, just as it is normal to appeal to theology to clarify the purposes and content of the liturgy insofar as it is a sacred action and to psycho-sociology to analyze the celebration insofar as it is a human action *tout court*.[8]

Stefani makes two points pertinent to the concerns of this study. The first is that liturgy is an ensemble of signs or symbols.[9] The second is that the liturgy is an action whose dominant value is situated in the order of signification. If the liturgy is an ensemble of signs or symbols, music is one of those symbols. If liturgy is an action, then music-making can be described as symbolizing activity.

---

[7] Wilson COKER, *Music and Meaning: A Theoretical Introduction to Musical Aesthetics* (New York: The Free Press, 1972), 2.

[8] The original French text is found in Gino STEFANI, "Essai sur les communications sonores dans la liturgie," *Paroisse et liturgie* 52 (1970): 99-100. This translation is by Jon Michael JONCAS and is found in his essay "Musical Semiotics and Liturgical Musicology: Theoretical Foundations and Analytic Techniques," *Ecclesia Orans* 8 (1990): 198-199.

[9] As noted above in chapter one, the terms *sign* and *symbol* are often used interchangeably to designate the same reality. Stefani's use of sign in this context appears to follow this practice.

Furthermore, the semiotic method is particularly important to the analysis of liturgical sources because it pays just as much attention to the non-verbal in these sources as it does to the verbal. Whereas it has often been the practice to analyze liturgical sources by methods adopted from literary studies, even when those sources are not literary texts, semiotics provides the conceptual apparatus for approaching the analysis of such ritual objects as actions, gestures, movements in space, the space itself, images, vestments, and music by taking into account their non-verbal aspects.[10]

The last chapter described how Berthier's music of Taizé situates the assembly in specific relationships to one another and within the Christian tradition. This ability of the Taizé chants to mediate meaning and create connections requires further philosophical and theological investigation in order to explain how the music of Taizé operates as ritual symbol. This chapter will pursue such an investigation into the nature of symbol and music's symbolic properties.

THE NATURE OF SYMBOL

Symbolic thought and symbolic behavior are among the most characteristic features of human life. Indeed, the whole progress of human culture, including the origin of language, of art, and of religion may be said to be based on these phenomena.[11] Several of the documents examined in chapter one either directly or indirectly allude to the fact that, like so many other significant human actions, doing liturgy is engaging in symbolic activity. However, in several instances[12] the terms *sign* and *symbol* appear to

[10] LUKKEN, "Semiotics," 114. Lukken is a member of a research group called "Semanet" which applies the semiotics of A.J. Greimas, of the Saussurian school, to the liturgy. While the article referred to here is specifically pointing out the relevance of Greimassian semiotics to an analysis of the liturgy, his conclusions are also applicable to the Peircean school since several of its members, including such scholars as Wilson Coker and Charles Boilès, have applied semiotics to the study of musical signification. See Gerard LUKKEN and Mark SEARLE, *Semiotics and Church Architecture: Applying the Semiotics of A.J. Greimas and the Paris School to the Analysis of Church Buildings,* Liturgia Condenda (Kampen, the Netherlands: Kok Pharos Publishing House, 1993). This work is a good example of how semiotics can provide the conceptual apparatus for analyzing non-verbal liturgical sources.

[11] Ernst CASSIRER, *An Essay on Man: An Introduction to a Philosophy of Human Culture* (New Haven: Yale University Press, 1944), 27.

[12] These examples are included in chapter one: *Music in Catholic Worship* 4, 5, 7, 8, 9, 23 and *Liturgical Music Today* 60.

be used interchangeably to describe the same reality. This study does not view the two terms as synonymous. Therefore, before discussing the nature of symbol, I will identify the primary distinctions between *sign* and *symbol* that are being assumed in using the two terms in this study.

Charles Peirce distinguishes three types of signs: *iconic, indexical* and *symbolic.* Charles Boilès, an ethnomusicologist and semiotician of the Peirceian school, offers the following definitions of the three types: A sign is *iconic* if it in some way imitates or "mimics" that which it represents. A sign is *indexical* if it points to something or indicates its existence, usually in time and space. A sign is *symbolic* if it represents something which has no direct relationship to the form or natural properties of the sign itself.[13] Furthermore, a symbol is polysemous and multivocal. That is, it presents many layers of meaning and allows for a variety of interpretations.

These brief explanations, however, do not suffice to explain the difference between *sign* and *symbol.* Since, in this study, *symbol* will be distinguished from *sign* and studied within a philosophical and theological framework, several distinctions commonly made in these disciplines will be examined.

The theologian Paul Tillich points out that there is one important characteristic which signs and symbols have in common: both point to something beyond themselves. The decisive difference between the two is that signs do not participate in the reality to which they point. Symbols do.[14]

Tillich enumerates several characteristics which distinguish symbols from signs. Symbols open up levels of reality which are otherwise closed to us. This is particularly true of the arts, for they create symbols which provide access to a dimension of reality that cannot be reached in any other way. In addition, symbols also provide access to dimensions of a person's inner life which correspond to those levels of reality. Lastly, symbols cannot be produced intentionally nor invented. Rather, they grow out of the individual or social unconscious and die when the situation changes.[15]

In his book, *Meaning,* the philosopher Michael Polanyi presents a detailed discussion of the difference between indicators – his term for

[13] Charles L. BOILÈS, "Processes of Musical Semiosis," *Yearbook for Traditional Music* 14 (1982): 34-35.

[14] TILLICH, *Dynamics of Faith*, 41-42.

[15] TILLICH, *Dynamics of Faith*, 42-43.

signs – and symbols. Polanyi's schema for explaining the different dynamics involved in signs and symbols can help to elucidate Paul Tillich's distinctions.

According to Polanyi's schema, indicators, that is signs, point in a subsidiary way to that focal integration upon which they bear. These indicators possess little interest in themselves. Rather, the interest lies in the object to which they point.

Polanyi uses the example of the name of a building and the building itself. The name of the building functions as the subsidiary (S) pointing to the building which is the true object of focal attention (F).[16] Polanyi diagrams the operation of indicators in this way:

$$-ii \qquad\qquad +ii$$
$$S \longrightarrow F\,[17]$$

The name of the building, the subsidiary, is labeled "-ii" to indicate that it lacks interest. The building itself, the focal meaning, is labelled "+ii" to indicate that it possesses interest. Polanyi notes that the integration resulting from this dynamic is self-centered because it is made *from* the self as center, including all the subsidiaries in which we dwell, *to* the object of our focal attention.[18]

On the other hand, Polanyi presents symbols as that phenomena of meaning in which subsidiary clues do not function as indicators pointing our way to something else. Rather, in the act of symbolizing it is the subsidiary clues that are of intrinsic interest to us because they enter into meanings in such a way that we are "carried away" by these meanings. Within this dynamic, our persons are involved in a way quite different from that described in the self-centered integration of indicators. In the case of symbols, our involvement is of such a nature that the relation of "bearing upon" and the location of intrinsic interest is much more complex.[19] Polanyi diagrams symbolization in this way:

$$+ii \qquad\qquad -ii$$
$$S \longrightarrow F\,[20]$$

[16] Michael POLANYI and Harry PROSCH, *Meaning* (Chicago: The University of Chicago Press, 1975), 70-71.

[17] POLANYI, *Meaning*, 70.

[18] POLANYI, *Meaning*, 71.

[19] POLANYI, *Meaning*, 71.

[20] POLANYI, *Meaning*, 72.

The position of the plus and minus signs are reversed in order to demonstrate that now the subsidiary clues are more interesting to us than the focal object. Using the American flag as an example, Polanyi explains that what gives the flag meaning is that we put our whole existence as lived in our country into it. Without that surrender of ourselves into that piece of cloth it would remain only a piece of cloth and not a flag, that is, a symbol of our country. It is our diffuse and boundless memories of our nation's existence and our life in it that give the flag meaning by becoming embodied and fused in it.[21]

A straight arrow cannot illustrate this dynamic. Therefore Polanyi devises an arrow loop in order to illustrate the way our perception of the focal object in symbolization also "carries us back toward (and so provides us with a perceptual embodiment of) those diffuse memories of our lives (i.e., of ourselves) which bore upon the focal object to begin with."[22]

Thus the symbol can be said to "carry us away," since it is in surrendering ourselves that we, as selves, are drawn into the meaning of the symbol. Polanyi illustrates this integration of our existence by redrawing the diagram in this way:

$$+ii \qquad\qquad -ii$$
$$S \longrightarrow F^{23}$$

What is significant in Polanyi's scheme is his illustration of the participation of the subject in the coming to meaning of the symbol. In surrendering ourselves, we accomplish the integration of those diffuse parts of ourselves that are related to the symbol. Thus our surrender to the symbol is at the same time our being carried away by it.[24]

Polanyi's insights highlight important distinctions between signs and symbols. On the one hand, signs function on the level of cognition, providing us with information. Symbols, on the other hand, function on the level of recognition, providing instead not information but integration, both within a subject and between subjects. Furthermore, Polanyi's scheme demonstrates how meaning comes to subjects through their past experiences and within a particular cultural and social milieu

---

[21] POLANYI, *Meaning*, 72-73.
[22] POLANYI, *Meaning*, 73.
[23] POLANYI, *Meaning*, 72.
[24] POLANYI, *Meaning*, 73.

which involves relationships with other subjects. Thus Polanyi's analysis of the apprehension of meaning provides a basis for building a theory of symbol appropriate to ritual music.

The etymology of the word symbol corroborates Polanyi's insights. The word "symbol" derives from the Greek word "symballein" which literally means "to throw together." The ancient practice of "symbolon" involved cutting an object in two. Partners in a contract would each retain one part of the symbolon, which separately possessed no value, but which when joined with the other half "symbolized" or confirmed the agreement between two partners. Thus it was the agreement between two partners which established the symbol. It functioned as an expression of a social pact based on mutual recognition in the rejoining of the two halves. In this way it was a mediator of identity.[25]

Our contemporary understanding of symbol has developed and broadened beyond this original usage. The theologian Louis-Marie Chauvet, in referring to the ancient practice of "symbolon," observes that "the semantic field of the word 'symbol' has been extended to every element (object, word, gesture, person ...) that, exchanged within a group, somewhat like a pass-word, permits the group as a whole or individuals therein to recognize one another and identify themselves."[26] A common element in the original usage of the term, as well as in Polanyi's and Chauvet's understanding of the symbolic process, is that a symbol mediates recognition within a community or social world.

In distinguishing between sign and symbol, Chauvet adopts Eugene Ortigues's distinctions.[27] In *Le discours et le symbole,* Ortigues explains that the sign refers to something of another order than itself. The symbol, on the other hand, introduces us into an order to which it itself belongs. This order is a cultural realm completely different from that of immediately experienced reality, one presupposed to be an order of meaning in its radical otherness.[28]

Louis-Marie Chauvet captures the radical nature of symbolizing to human life when he explains:

---

[25] Louis-Marie CHAUVET, *Symbol and Sacrament: A Sacramental Reinterpretation of Christian Existence*, trans. Patrick MADIGAN and Madeleine BEAUMONT (Collegeville: The Liturgical Press, 1995), 112.

[26] CHAUVET, *Symbol and Sacrament*, 112.

[27] Ortigues's distinctions are similar to those made by Tillich. Cf. p. 97.

[28] Eugene ORTIGUES, *Le discours et le symbole* (Paris: Aubier-Montaigne, 1962), 65, 210. Cited in Louis-Marie CHAUVET, 112-113.

Reality is never present to us except in a mediated way, which is to say, constructed out of the symbolic network of the culture which fashions us. This symbolic order designates the system of connections between the different elements and levels of a culture (economic, social, political, ideological – ethics, philosophy, religion . . .), a system forming a coherent whole that allows the social group and individuals to orient themselves in space, find their place in time, and in general situate themselves in the world in a significant way – in short, to find their identity in a world that makes "sense," even if, as C. Levi-Strauss says, there always remains an inexpungible residue of signifiers to which we can never give adequate meanings.[29]

In this statement, Chauvet identifies the foundational principle of his sacramental reinterpretation of Christian existence. It is the principle that all reality is mediated. His explanation includes two points which are important for examining the nature of music as symbol in liturgy. The first is that symbols mediate reality by negotiating connections. These connections, secondly, allow subjects both as members of a social group and as individuals to make sense of their world and to find their identity by discovering relationships. Symbolizing, then, is a dynamic which involves the active participation of subjects in mediating connections and in discovering their identity and place in their social world.

Michael Lawler, also working in the area of sacramental theology, has likewise underscored the importance of understanding the dynamics of symbolizing in the liturgy. Like Chauvet, Lawler highlights the importance of the action of the human subject in symbolizing when he explains:

It is the symboling activity of the human subject that makes possible symbolic transformation, that is, the transformation of a mere sensible reality into a more than merely sensible symbol embodying meaning. Such transformation depends ultimately on the human subject, not on some communion of natures between a sensible reality and a meaning which leads, by some ineluctable law, to their union as symbol and meaning. The total process of symbolization from beginning to end, from the first moment of the interpretation of the sensible reality into a symbol to the final moment of the transformation of that symbol, is controlled by the human symbolizer, and not by either the symbol or its meanings.[30]

[29] CHAUVET, *Symbol and Sacrament*, 84-85.
[30] Michael G. LAWLER, *Symbol and Sacrament: A Contemporary Sacramental Theology* (New York: Paulist Press, 1987), 11.

The distinction between signs and symbols, then, turns on whether sub-jects are taken into account.[31] The symbol clearly stands on the side of the subject who produces him/herself in producing the symbol. Fur-thermore, the effects of meaning produced by the symbol are under-stood as effects of the subject, whereby the subject recognizes him/her-self in the effects and identifies him/herself with them.[32] Both Chauvet and Lawler focus on the importance of the subject in the creation of a symbol's meaning.[33]

Thus far we can say that a symbol is a mediation of recognition which evokes participation and allows an individual or a social group to orient themselves, that is, to discover their identity and their place within their world. This is especially true of the symbols operative in rit-ual since ritual provides those most contingent and culturally deter-mined aspects which are the very epitome of mediation.[34]

Chauvet further elucidates his understanding of the nature of symbol and sacrament by highlighting the foundational nature of embodiment. According to Chauvet, the body is the primordial and arch-symbolic form of mediation and the basis for all subjective identification.[35] That is, the body is "the primordial place of every symbolic joining of the 'inside' and the 'outside.'"[36] It is the body that places human beings in the world and it is the body that is the entry place where the entire sym-bolic order takes root in us as human beings.[37]

To support his assertion, Chauvet quotes D. Dubarle, who explains that the living body is indeed, "the arch-symbol of the whole symbolic order."[38] Chauvet realizes that such a premise is important for a theology of the sacraments since the ritual symbolism which constitutes them has the body for its setting. Furthermore, such a premise is important for a theory of music as ritual symbol since music-making, more than any other artistic enterprise, involves the body in an intimate and integral

---

[31] CHAUVET, *Symbol and Sacrament*, 110.

[32] CHAUVET, *Symbol and Sacrament*, 116, 119.

[33] Other scholars, notably Susanne K. Langer and Jean-Jacques Nattiez, also situate the symbol's source of meaning in the subject. Their ideas regarding symbol will be pre-sented later in this study.

[34] CHAUVET, *Symbol and Sacrament*, 110-111.

[35] CHAUVET, *Symbol and Sacrament*, 111.

[36] CHAUVET, *Symbol and Sacrament*, 147.

[37] CHAUVET, *Symbol and Sacrament*, 147.

[38] CHAUVET, *Symbol and Sacrament*, 151.

way. Indeed, according to Church tradition, the most "spiritual" communication of God, even that of the Holy Spirit itself, takes place through a process of symbolizing which is eminently "sensory and bodily."[39]

Using his theology of symbol as a foundation, Chauvet develops a theology of sacrament by focusing on the body as arch-symbol. In this respect he is proceeding with a method similar to that of Karl Rahner who constructed his theology of sacrament on his understanding of the symbolic relationship of the body to the soul. A brief look at the development of Rahner's ideas will further elucidate those of Chauvet.

Rahner begins his enquiry into the notion of symbol by looking at the ontology of symbolic reality in general. His first axiom is that "all beings are by their nature symbolic, because they necessarily 'express' themselves in order to attain their own nature."[40] Rahner sets out "to look for the highest and most primordial manner in which one reality can represent another ..."[41] This supreme and primal representation, in which one reality renders another present, Rahner calls a symbol.[42] Further, Rahner explains that the symbol, strictly speaking, "is the self-realization of a being in another, which is constitutive of its essence."[43] For Rahner, a symbol is not primarily considered a relationship between two different beings which are given the function of indicating one another by a third. Rather, a being is symbolic in itself because the expression which it retains while constituting itself as the "other" is the way in which it communicates itself to itself.[44]

For Rahner, the paradigmatic symbol is the human subject. Following Thomistic doctrine that the soul is the substantial form of the body, Rahner explains that the soul exists insofar as it embodies itself, that is, expresses itself in the body. The body, though distinct from the soul, is not a separate part. Rather, the body is the phenomenon, that is, the mode of the soul's presence and appearance.[45] Thus the body is the

---

[39] CHAUVET, *Symbol and Sacrament,* 140.

[40] Karl RAHNER, "The Theology of Symbol," in *Theological Investigations,* vol. 4, *More Recent Writings,* trans. Kevin SMYTH (Baltimore: Helicon Press, 1966), 224.

[41] RAHNER, "The Theology of Symbol," 225.

[42] RAHNER, "The Theology of Symbol," 225.

[43] RAHNER, "The Theology of Symbol," 234.

[44] RAHNER, "The Theology of Symbol," 230.

[45] Louis ROBERTS, *The Achievement of Karl Rahner* (New York: Herder and Herder, Inc., 1967), 35.

symbol or self- realization of the soul which "renders itself present and makes its 'appearance' in the body which is distinct from it."[46] In other words, "the body is the manifestation of the soul, through which and in which the soul realizes its own essence."[47]

The body, then, is truly the symbol of the self. Since the body so completely comes from the self and expresses the self, it is indeed *the* way in which we are present to self and to others. It would be impossible to be ourselves or be present to one another without being embodied.[48]

To highlight this aspect of corporality, Chauvet explains that "the human being does not have a body, but is body."[49] This "I-body" – his designation for each person's physical body – is irreducible to any other and yet similar to every other. Furthermore, this "I-body," exists only as woven, inhabited and spoken by the triple body of culture, tradition, and nature. In other words, it is the place where the triple body – social, ancestral, and cosmic – is symbolically joined.[50]

For Louis-Marie Chauvet both the body and language are in their essence symbolic since both function, not as instrument, but as mediation. Following Rahner's line of reasoning, Chauvet concludes that, just as human subjects come to be through the mediation of their bodies, so do they come to be in language which is constitutive of all truly human experience.[51]

But exactly how does Chauvet define language? In chapter three of *Symbol and Sacrament* he states that "there is no human reality, however interior or intimate, except through the mediation of language or quasi-language[52] that gives it a body by expressing it."[53] He continues, quoting E. Ortigues, who explains that "whether the expression be verbal, facial, or gestural, it 'indicates an act of presence which acts itself out for

---

[46] RAHNER, "The Theology of Symbol," 247.

[47] Karl RAHNER, *The Church and the Sacraments,* trans. W.J. O'HARA (Herder and Herder, 1963), 37.

[48] Michael SKELLEY, *The Liturgy of the World: Karl Rahner's Theology of Worship,* forward by Rembert G. WEAKLAND (Collegeville: The Liturgical Press, 1991), 37-38.

[49] CHAUVET, *Symbol and Sacrament,* 149.

[50] CHAUVET, *Symbol and Sacrament,* 149-150.

[51] CHAUVET, *Symbol and Sacrament,* 87.

[52] CHAUVET, *Symbol and Sacrament,* 87, n. 8, Chauvet defines the term "quasi-languages" to include both "supra- language": that made up of gestures, mime, and all artistic endeavor, as well as "infra-language": that made up of the archaic impulses of the unconscious.

itself …'"[54] In other words, "every impression can take form (a human, significant form) only in the expression that accomplishes it, and every thought 'forms itself by expressing itself.'"[55]

Thus, in using the term "language," Chauvet's definition is broad enough to include a variety of forms of expression beyond strictly "words," or "morphemes."[56] Just as he had pointed out that the semantic field of the word "symbol" had been extended beyond that of the word "symbolon," so, too, does he extend the definition of "language."[57]

Similarly, Michael Polanyi talks about the need to expand the concept of a class of meanings that covers all cases of meaning distinct from the meanings of perception, skills, and such part-whole relations as we meet in nature. He suggests that the word "semantic" be used for all kinds of artificial meanings. By these he means all those contrived by human persons. Normally, the use of the term "semantics" is limited to the meanings achieved by language.[58] His suggested expansion will allow us later in this investigation to apply the term "semantic" to include meanings conveyed by music. This is important, since in order to adequately explore the nature of meaning in music, it is essential not to define meaning solely as a reflection of some linguistic meaning.[59] Therefore,

---

[53] CHAUVET, *Symbol and Sacrament*, 90.

[54] CHAUVET, *Symbol and Sacrament*, 65.

[55] CHAUVET, *Symbol and Sacrament*, 65.

[56] Webster defines a morpheme as any word or part of a word, as an affix or combining form, that conveys meaning, cannot be further divided into smaller elements conveying meaning, and usually occurs in various contexts with relatively stable meaning.

[57] Scholars in the field of musical semiotics debate the appropriateness of using linguistic models to interpret musical meaning. I have chosen to adopt the position of such semioticians as Willem Marie SPEELMAN who regard music as a discourse and therefore a type of language. On page ix of *The Generation of Meaning in Liturgical Songs: A Semiotic Analysis of Five Liturgical Songs as Syncretic Discourse,* Speelman explains that, "the word semiotics is used to indicate languages, e.g. music and literature are semiotics …"

[58] POLANYI, *Meaning*, 74. Since about 1970, a great deal of work has been done in the fields of general semiology and the semiology of music by scholars both in Europe and in the United States. Cf. Coker's definitions of Peirce's three dimensions of semiotics on p. 95. According to Coker, semantics is the study of the relations of signs to their contexts and to what they signify. In addition to Coker, Peirce's categories have been employed by Charles Boilès in several of his essays. In his comparative semiology, Jean-Jacques Nattiez was originally interested in the music-language comparison.

[59] Jean-Jacques NATTIEZ, *Music and Discourse: Toward a Semiology of Music,* trans. Carolyn ABBATE (Princeton, New Jersey: Princeton University Press, 1990), 9.

unless otherwise indicated, this study operates with these expanded definitions of "language" and "semantics" in order to allow the broadest possible interpretation and application of these notions to the functioning of music as symbol.

MUSIC AS SYMBOL

Thus far we have determined that the definition of symbol operative in this paper can be expressed in this way: a symbol is a mediation of recognition which evokes participation and allows an individual or a social group to orient themselves, that is, to discover their identity and their place within their world. If we are to be justified in calling music a "symbol," we need to demonstrate that music does indeed function in this way. In addition, we need to address the specific questions regarding the method or framework for analyzing the symbolic nature of music and music-making.

Philosophers since the time of the ancient Greeks have been struggling with the question of music and meaning. Indeed, many of our suppositions about the potential of music to embody meaning and to influence human life and behavior go back to the writings of such thinkers as Aristotle. In his *Poetics,* Aristotle includes music, along with epic poetry, tragedy, comedy and dithyrambic poetry as forms which in their general conception are modes of imitation. Aristotle explains that in instrumental music, imitation is produced by rhythm or "harmony."[60] What music imitates is action, defined by Aristotle not as physical activity, but a movement-of-the-spirit that results from a combination of thought and character. By "imitation," Aristotle means, not a superficial copying, but rather the representation of the countless forms which the life of the human spirit may take, in the medium of a particular art. In music, that medium is sound.[61]

Aristotle's *Politics* discusses the nature of music as imitation in this way:

> ...even in mere melodies there is an imitation of character, for the musical modes differ essentially from one another, and those who hear them are differently affected by each ... The same principles apply to rhythms;

---

[60] *Aristotle's Poetics,* trans. S.H. BUCHER, introduction by Francis FERGUSON (New York: Farrar, Straus and Giroux, 1961), I, 2-5.

[61] *Aristotle's Poetics,* VI, 5-6.

some have a character of rest, others of motion, and of these latter again, some have a more vulgar, others a nobler movement.[62]

In this description of music as imitation, Aristotle expresses the belief that music can influence the character or disposition of persons so that their characters or dispositions change. This is possible, Aristotle reasons, because music has character and the means to communicate this character to the listener.[63]

Although Aristotle does not speak explicitly about the nature of music as a symbolic phenomenon, many of his ideas provide the ground work for building a symbolic theory of music. His idea that music imitates a "movement of the spirit" and represents "the countless forms of the life of the human spirit" situates the locus of music in the human subject and in the potential of music to evoke recognition and thereby influence integration or the formation of character.

Since Aristotle, further questions have evolved regarding the nature of music, its ability to signify, its power to refer, and the possibility of apprehending and analyzing its meaning. Since it is beyond both the scope and the purpose of this study to present a comprehensive presentation or critique of the various theories which have been developed, only representative theories which have a direct bearing on the questions of this study will be included here.

The question of musical reference continues to perplex scholars. The typical articulation of the argument is that if music can be said to possess signification, that is, to have meaning, it must be possible to establish reference. In other words, if music has meaning, it must refer to something. Furthermore, theories of reference usually distinguish between internal and external reference.

Those theorists who emphasize music as pure form, such as Eduard Hanslick, conclude that the ideas expressed by music are first and foremost purely musical ideas.[64] In other words, music refers primarily to itself. This dynamic is often referred to as internal reference.

---

[62] ARISTOTLE, *The Politics*, ed. Stephen EVERSON (Cambridge: Cambridge University Press, 1988), 1340 a, 18-22.

[63] Göran SÖRBOM, "Aristotle on Music as Representation," *The Journal of Aesthetics and Art Criticism* 52 (Winter 1994), 41.

[64] Eduard HANSLICK, *On the Musically Beautiful: A Contribution Towards the Revision of the Aesthetics of Music*, trans. and ed. Geoffrey PAYZANT from the eighth edition (1891) of *Vom Musicalisch-Schonen: ein Betrag zur Revision der Asthetik der Tonkunst* (Indianapolis: Hacket Publishing Company, 1986), 10.

Most scholars, however, subscribe to the theory that music is capable of both internal and external reference. For example, Leonard B. Meyer believes that music is capable of expressing meaning in both ways: as a pure play of forms and as a symbolic fact with the potential to refer to something. In other words, music does have the power to refer to things outside itself, thereby evoking associations and connotations relative to the world of ideas, sentiments, and physical objects. Such designative meanings are often less precise, less conceptually clear, and less logically articulated than those arising in linguistic communication, but this does not make them less powerful or significant.[65]

In a similar way, Gordon Epperson's study of the philosophic theory of music is built on the notion that the auditory characteristics of music – what Aristotle identifies as rhythm and harmony – are its medium of communication. Epperson defines music as "a symbolic mode of human discourse, in which meanings are aurally apprehended through auditory entities."[66]

However, any approach which sets up a one-to-one correspondence between particular musical properties or structures and a specific idea or emotion, views music, not as a symbol, but as a sign. In light of the distinctions made earlier in this paper between sign and symbol, such an exercise approaches signification in music as indexical.[67] The study of the symbolic nature of music, however, requires that music be approached, not simply as a constellation of sounds with predictable referential properties, but as the activity of human subjects.

As the musical semiologist Jean-Jacques Nattiez has observed, the anthropological perspective favored by ethnomusicologists understands music not only as "a play of forms and structures, but as products functionally related to the social, and most often ritual contexts in which they appear ... "[68] Thus Nattiez does not see the two perspectives on musical reference incompatible. Rather, he points out that it is "probably right to see in music an element which is at once *endosemantic* (the structures refer to structures) and *exosemantic* (referral to the outside

---

[65] Leonard B. MEYER, *Music, the Arts, and Ideas: Patterns and Predictions in Twentieth Century Culture* (Chicago: The University of Chicago Press, 1967), 6.

[66] Gordon EPPERSON, *The Musical Symbol: A Study of the Philosophic Theory of Music* (Ames, Iowa: Iowa State University Press, 1967), 214.

[67] Cf. Peirce's distinction of three types of signs p. 97.

[68] Jean-Jacques NATTIEZ, "Reflections on the Development of Semiology in Music," trans. Katharine ELLIS, *Music Analysis* 8 (1989): 22.

world).[69] Furthermore, the relative importance which is attributed to these two dimensions, in Nattiez's judgment, "varies according to historical period, aesthetics, culture and the individual."[70]

In this respect, Nattiez echoes Jean Molino's illustration of music's multiple signifying properties:

> The sonic phenomena produced by music are indeed, at the same time, icons: they can imitate the clamors of the world and evoke them, or be simply the images of our feelings – a long tradition which cannot be so easily dismissed has considered them as such; indices: depending on the case, they may be the cause or the consequence or the simple concomitants of other phenomena which they evoke; symbols: in that they are entities defined and preserved through a social tradition and a consensus which endow them with the right to exist.[71]

Molino attributes to music the properties of all three of the dimensions of signs originally identified by Peirce. In response to Molino's description of music as, at the same time, an icon, an index, or a symbol, Nattiez concludes that if music can be all three, "it is proof that music is first and foremost a *symbolic fact*."[72]

Nattiez's musical semiotics synthesizes in a coherent theory many of the issues regarding the symbolic nature of music. A careful look at his approach will assist in synthesizing philosophical and theological notions of symbol and in elucidating music as symbolizing activity.

Two principles are foundational to Nattiez's semiology of music. The first is that the *interpretant* is the root of the symbolic operation. The second is that a symbolic form necessarily has three dimensions: the *poietic,* the *immanent* or *neutral,* and the *esthesic.*[73]

---

[69] NATTIEZ, "Reflections on the Development of Semiology in Music," 22.

[70] NATTIEZ, "Reflections on the Development of Semiology in Music," 22.

[71] Jean MOLINO, "Fait musical et sémiologie de la musique," *Musique en jeu* 17(1975): 45. Cited in Jean-Jacques NATTIEZ, "The Contribution of Musical Semiotics to the Semiotic Discussion in General," in *A Perfusion of Signs,* ed. Thomas A. SEBEOK (Bloomington: Indiana University Press, 1977), 123.

[72] NATTIEZ, "The Contribution of Musical Semiotics," 124. Also cf. BOILÈS, "Processes of Musical Semiotics," 34-35. Nattiez's own work follows Boilès's understanding of Peirce's three distinctions.

[73] NATTIEZ, "Reflections on the Development of Semiology in Music," 57. Nattiez derives his use of the term "esthesis" from a lecture of Paul VALÉRY for the Collège de France in 1945. Valéry coined the neologism for that lecture, using it instead of "aesthetic" in order to avoid possible confusions. Since the word "aesthetic" is commonly

Nattiez's understanding of the role of the interpretant in the symbolic operation is built on Charles Peirce's notion of the infinite interpretant. For Peirce, the interpretant is the habit by which a sign is interpreted.[74] Incorporating Peirce's notion of interpretant into a working definition, Nattiez describes a symbolic form as "a sign, or a collection of signs, to which an infinite complex of interpretants is linked ... "[75]

The notion of the interpretant enables Nattiez to describe the dynamic of symbolic meaning as "a proliferation of interpretants when an object of any kind is placed for the individual relative to his or her lived experience. The meaning of an object of any kind is the constellation of interpretants drawn from the lived experience of the sign's user – the "producer" or "receiver" – in a given situation."[76]

There are two significant points in Nattiez's definition. The first is that there is a proliferation or constellation of interpretants. This notion corroborates the generally accepted view that symbols are by nature multi-vocal or polysemous. The second is that the source of meaning is in the lived experience of the sign's user. The richness and variety of that lived experience thus accounts for an infinite possibility of interpretants.

Nattiez applies the Peirceian notion of the infinite and dynamic interpretant to specific examples, including music, when he says:

> ...an object, whatever (a sentence, a painting, a social conduct, a musical work...), takes on a meaning for an individual who perceives it when he relates the object to his *experience-domain,* or the set of all other objects, concepts, or data of the world which make up all or part of his experience. To be more direct: meanings are created when an object is related to a horizon or a background.[77]

Applying Nattiez's summation specifically to his example of a musical work, we can say that musical meanings are created when a piece of music is related to a horizon or background. This focus on the "experience-domain" accounts for the multiple layers of symbolic meaning. It

---

associated with a response to beauty in the arts and good taste, Nattiez chose the word "esthesic" in order to emphasize the fact that the process he is referring to is more complex. This will be explained in greater detail later in the chapter. See NATTIEZ, *Music and Discourse,* 12.

[74] BOILÈS, "Processes of Musical Semiosis," 31.
[75] NATTIEZ, *Music and Discourse,* 8.
[76] NATTIEZ, *Music and Discourse,* 10.
[77] NATTIEZ, "The Contribution of Musical Semiotics," 126.

also accounts for the inability of philosophers of music to establish strict rules of reference, despite countless attempts.

In addition to his application of the Peircean notion of the interpretant to his musical semiotics, Nattiez's incorporation and development of Jean Molino's theory of tri-partition is likewise an essential part of his musical semiotic. Nattiez explains it in this way:

> For him, [Molino] the domains that semiology studies are symbolic facts, insofar as there are no texts or musical works which are not the product of compositional strategies (the domain studied by poietics) and which do not give rise to strategies of perception (the domain covered by esthesics). Between these two there lies the study of the neutral or immanent level, i.e. the study of structures which are not prejudged *a priori* as pertaining either to poietics or to esthesics.[78]

Musical works, therefore, are symbolic facts resulting from the interaction of three dimensions: the strategy of composition Molino calls poietics, the strategy of perception he calls esthesics, and the structures of the musical work, which he calls the neutral or immanent level.

Nattiez underlines the fact that this schema does not follow the usual direct lines we understand in a simple act of communication. The classic schema for communication can be diagrammed in the following manner:

$$\text{"Producer"} \longrightarrow \text{Message} \longrightarrow \text{Receiver}^{79}$$

But semiology is not concerned with the science of communication. Instead, Nattiez substitutes the following diagram, one that only makes sense when interpreted from the perspective of the theory of the interpretant:

$$\begin{array}{ccc} \text{Poietic Process} & & \text{Esthesic Process} \\ \text{"Producer"} \longrightarrow & \text{Trace} & \longleftarrow \text{Receiver}^{80} \end{array}$$

By reversing the direction of the second arrow, Nattiez is pointing out that a symbolic form – which he calls *trace*[81] – is not simply an intermediary

---

[78] NATTIEZ, "Reflections on the Development of Semiology in Music," 35.

[79] NATTIEZ, *Music and Discourse,* 16.

[80] NATTIEZ, *Music and Discourse,* 17.

[81] *Trace* is Nattiez's term for what Molino calls the *immanent* or *neutral* level. He uses the term to refer to the material reality of the work, i.e., its live production and the score that result from the poietic process. According to Nattiez, the symbolic form is

in the process of communication. Rather, the symbolic form is the result of a complex *process* of creation, the poietic process, which involves both the form and the content. But the symbolic form is also the point of departure for a complex process of reception, the esthesic process, which *reconstructs* a "message." Using Molino's schema, Nattiez presents a theory of symbolic function which sees communication as only one of several possible results of the symbolic process.[82]

One of the significant aspects of Molino's tripartite schema is that it recognizes the importance of going beyond analysis of immanent structures. In this respect, it allows us to move beyond the limitations of a strict musical reference and still take into account the messages manifested on the level of musical syntax. However, analysis cannot be limited to the neutral or immanent level. The poietic level lurks beneath the surface of the immanent even as the immanent is the springboard for the esthesic. The interpretive task is to identify the interpretants from the point of view of each of the three dimensions and establish their relationships to each other.[83]

This does not mean that efforts to determine a correspondence between meaning and musical material as such are abandoned, but that identifying such correspondence is only one aspect of the process. There can be no stable or predictable relation between a particular music feature and a given meaning because the relation is always the result of a complex combination of variables which includes not only the immanent, but also the poietic and esthesic dimensions.[84]

Notice that this schema situates the immanent or neutral level between the poietic and esthesic in such a way that the symbolic object mediates a dynamic process of creation and a reception which actively engages the "recipient" in a reconstruction achieved against the horizon of his/her experience. This horizon corresponds to Polanyi's description of "our whole, lived existence" and our "boundless memories" which become embodied and fused in the focal object.[85] Furthermore, this

---

embodied physically in the form of a *trace* accessible to the five senses. He uses the word *trace* to indicate that the poietic process cannot immediately be read within the symbolic form since the esthesic process is heavily dependent on the lived experience of the *receiver*. See NATTIEZ, *Music and Discourse*, 12, 15.

[82] NATTIEZ, *Music and Discourse*, 17.

[83] NATTIEZ, *Music and Discourse*, 28-29.

[84] NATTIEZ, "The Contribution of Musical Semiotics," 128.

[85] POLANYI, *Meaning*, 72-73.

schema supports Chauvet's and Lawler's conviction that symbolizing activity is rooted in the activity of human subjects.[86]

The Nature of Song as Musical Symbol

Thus far we have explored various theories and theologies of symbol and semiotics of music. The next task is to consider the particular characteristics of the musical genre under study in this paper – liturgical song – in order to discover how the combination of music and text may be said to operate symbolically. Since many of the documents discussed in chapter one described music's role in relation to liturgical texts, this question is pertinent to the present study.

For the most part, the Taizé chants were composed to be performed as songs.[87] That is, each piece is a unit consisting of music and text. Several theories have attempted to describe or account for the relationship between music and text. A common position is that the purpose of the music is to communicate or supplement the meaning of the text. Several of the church documents on liturgy and music examined in chapter one subscribe to this point of view.[88] On the other hand, Friedrich Nietzsche, in discussing the poetry of the folk song, has argued that melody is primary and universal, and that the poetry of the folk song is stretched to the utmost that it might imitate music.[89] While Nietzsche's philosophy of music may not be considered a prime source of insight into liturgical music, his thesis does provide the opportunity to reexamine presuppositions regarding the relationship of music to text.

In answer to the question regarding how the Church has incorporated singing and music in its liturgy, Joseph Gelineau explains:

[86] CHAUVET, *Symbol and Sacrament*, 110 and LAWLER, *Symbol and Sacrament*, 11.

[87] BERTHIER, vol. 2, instrumental, iii. The foreword explains that while the instrumental parts were meant to be performed in conjunction with the vocal music, they may also be performed as independent instrumental pieces in the same spirit and style as their vocal counterparts. Therefore, even in those instances when a vocal piece is performed as an instrumental, that is, without the singing of the text, the conception of the piece remains vocal.

[88] Those documents which most explicitly hold this view include *TLS* 1; *SC* 112; and *MCW* 23.

[89] Friedrich NIETZSCHE, *The Birth of Tragedy*, in *Basic Writings of Nietzsche*, trans. and ed. Walter KAUFMANN (New York: The Modern Library, 1968), 53.

Today, music is a discipline with a separate existence, and singing is clearly distinguished from mere speech. These distinctions did not obtain in the cultural milieu of the early Church. Hebrew and Greek have no separate word for music. The frontier between singing and speaking was far less precise.[90]

Gelineau's comment about the lack of clear distinctions between speech and song in the early Church's experience at worship reflects a way of thinking which views speech and song as two poles on a continuum of human vocal expressiveness. The musical anthropologist John Blacking, on the other hand, views the distinctions in another way:

It is often assumed that song is an extension or embellishment of speech, which is the primary mode of communication, and that there is a continuum of increasing formalization from speech to song. But song is not inherently either a more or a less restricted code than speech: the relative dominance of song or speech, as of their affective and cognitive elements, in any genre or performance of a genre, depends not so much on some absolute attributes that speech and song might have, as on people's "intentions to mean" in different social situations, and on their motivation and the psychological assumptions that they invoke.[91]

Blacking takes the anthropological perspective that situates meaning neither in musical structures nor in text because of some innate power of either, but in the intentions of the human subjects within a specific context. If the church, in the liturgical rite as a "social situation," intends to highlight the texts, Blacking's statement suggests that the "intention to mean" is what gives the text "relative dominance."

In Peircean terms, Blacking is saying that the syntactic dimension, that is, the structures of the music and the text, are not the sole determinant of meaning. Rather, the social situation or context in which the songs are sung, that is, the semantic dimension, and the people's intention to mean, that is, the pragmatic dimension, all contribute to the overall meaning and significance of a song.

---

[90] Joseph GELINEAU, "Music and Singing in the Liturgy," in *The Study of the Liturgy,* eds. Cheslyn JONES, Geoffrey WAINWRIGHT, and Edward YARNOLD (New York: Oxford University Press, 1978), 444.

[91] John BLACKING, "The Structure of Musical Discourse: The Problem of the Song Text," *Yearbook for Traditional Music* 14 (1982): 19.

Others in the field of musical semiotics have tackled this question from another perspective. Armen T. Marsoobian, who builds her semiotic approach on Peirce's infinite interpretant, "eschews the notion that communication is primarily the transmission of some content or message between individuals or groups."[92] Refining Peirce's notion of the interpretant in order to make room for nonpropositional forms of meaning, she distinguishes between exhibitive and assertive propositions. For example, understanding the meaning of a poem, Marsoobian points out, has as much to do with the "how" of its structure as with the "what" of its reference. In other words, the relations exhibited or manifested within the poem give us its poetic meaning. In Peirceian terms, the "exhibitive" interpretant is the aesthetic meaning of the poem.[93]

Marsoobian makes the following distinction. When the process of shaping and the product as shaped is central, we produce in the exhibitive mode. When citing evidence in behalf of our product is central, we produce in the assertive mode.[94]

Marsoobian applies these principles to a semiotic analysis of opera, reading the entire operatic drama as a complex and integrated phenomenon. In doing so, she refuses to reduce the meaning of the opera to the meaning of the libretto. Rather, she explains, "the interplay between the words and the formal structures of the music (its so-called syntax) articulates the meaning of the opera. Meaning here ... is not asserted in the propositional content of the libretto but exhibited in the interplay between words and music."[95]

These insights can be particularly helpful when applied to liturgical analysis. The language of the liturgy is not propositional but confessional. Both the glory of God and the faith of the assembly are confessed and manifested or *exhibited*. Therefore, the ritual "as shaped or arrayed" is of central concern. Its meaning is not asserted, but exhibited by means of a variety of ritual symbols. Ritual song is one of those ritual symbols. From a Peirceian perspective, then, we can say that a song, as an exhibitive art form, is greater than the sum of its parts.

The musical semiotician, Willem Marie Speelman is of a similar opinion regarding the nature of song. Although the framework for his

---

[92] Armen T. MARSOOBIAN, "Saying, Singing, or Semiotics: '*Prima la Musica e poi le Parole*' Revisited." *The Journal of Aesthetics and Art Criticism* 54 (Summer 1996): 269.
[93] MARSOOBIAN, "Saying, Singing, or Semiotics," 269-271.
[94] MARSOOBIAN, "Saying, Singing, or Semiotics," 271.
[95] MARSOOBIAN, "Saying, Singing, or Semiotics," 274.

semiotic approach is explicitly Greimassian – a semiotician from the Saussurian rather than the Peirceian school – his work on liturgical songs reaches similar conclusions to those of Marsoobian.

In his analysis of liturgical songs, Speelman acknowledges that to analyze the musical and literary discourses separately is not yet to have analyzed the song, since the song is a specific function between music and text.[96] Therefore, even though he approaches music and text, and the expression and content of both, as quasi-autonomous discourses, yet he views this autonomy as relative. All four aspects are related to the song as an integrity, creating what Speelman calls a *syncretic discourse.* In other words, the musical discourse conditions the literary discourse and vice versa, and the expression and content forms of both condition one another.[97]

Furthermore, in addition to the fact that Speelman views these four aspects – the musical expression and content and the textual expression and content – as all contributing to the integrity which is the song, he also views the context as an essential element in the enunciation of the song. In the specific case of the liturgy as context he says:

> A point of departure is that the liturgy conditions the song, but that the song realizes the liturgy together with other liturgical discourses, like architecture, movements, vestments, icons, texts, etc. These heterogeneous discourses constitute liturgy in their togetherness. Liturgy in its turn conditions these discourses; it is the enunciative domain in which they are brought together.[98]

Speelman's point is that meaning is the result of a complex interplay between the great variety of symbols which constitute the liturgical action. Song is one among many liturgical discourses enunciated within the context of the liturgy.

Throughout this study, social or cultural context has been identified as an important factor in the coming-to-be of a symbol and its meaning. Polanyi alludes to this when he speaks of the subsidiaries and diffuse memories which bear upon a symbol's meaning. Similarly, Lawler points out that meaning comes to subjects within a particular social and

---

[96] Willem Marie SPEELMAN, *The Generation of Meaning in Liturgical Songs: A Semiotic Analysis of Five Liturgical Songs as Syncretic Discourse,* Liturgia condenda 4 (Kampen: Kok Pharos Publishing House, 1995), xi.

[97] SPEELMAN, *The Generation of Meaning in Liturgical Songs*, xiii, 32.

[98] SPEELMAN, *The Generation of Meaning in Liturgical Songs*, xiv.

cultural milieu. Indeed, Chauvet sees the social or cultural context as the very symbolic network through which all of reality is mediated. Symbols do not operate in isolation. Rather, they mutually condition and illuminate one another.[99] Like the "half" in the ancient practice of symbolon, a symbol retains its value only through the place it occupies within the whole or to the extent that it represents the whole. That is why every symbol of necessity must bring with itself the cultural and social context within which it operates. Ultimately, it is by this indirect reference to the "whole" that the symbol becomes an agent of recognition and identification between subjects.[100]

Although musical "purists" or "formalists" such as Eduard Hanslick, Igor Stravinsky, and Leonard Bernstein have argued that the musically significant needs to be identified first and foremost with the purely musical,[101] other theorists, particularly those influenced by post-modernist writings and the contemporary emphasis on pluralism, insist that musical meaning can only be interpreted within the institutional and societal context where the musical works are created, presented, and enjoyed.[102] Philosophers such as Lydia Goehr and Claire Detels have made explicit efforts to link our understanding of music to its social, political, and cultural contexts.[103] What they are suggesting is the use of "experience-based" categories which would study music within the contexts in which it is composed, performed, heard, taught, danced, moved, worked, or prayed.[104] These observations correspond to Nattiez's insight that individuals perceive meaning within the horizon of their "experience-domains."

Charles Boilès is particularly noted for his emphasis on the importance of attending to the cultural context in any systematic interpretation of musical symbols. He believes that the interpretation of a symbol will vary according to the context in which that symbol is used. As a

[99] Avery DULLES, *The Craft of Theology: From Symbol to System* (New York: The Crossroad Publishing Company, 1992), 19.

[100] CHAUVET, *Symbol and Sacrament,* 115.

[101] NATTIEZ, *Music and Discourse,* 112.

[102] Philip ALPERSON, "Introduction: New Directions in the Philosophy of Music," *The Journal of Aesthetics and Art Criticism* 52 (Winter 1994), 8.

[103] Lydia GOEHR, "Political Music and the Politics of Music," *The Journal of Aesthetics and Art Criticism* 52 (Winter 1994), 101.

[104] Claire, DETELS, "Autonomist/Formalist Aesthetics, Music Theory, and the Feminist Paradigm of Soft Boundaries," *The Journal of Aesthetics and Art Criticism* 52 (Winter 1994), 119-122.

result, although some symbols may appear to have the same physical properties, the contexts may indicate that they are not identical even if they appear to be so. This accounts for the situation in which a given sign object may have two or more unrelated meanings.[105]

Closely related to the issue of context is the necessity of attending to *cultural codes*. Borrowing from the semiologist Roman Jakobson, Nattiez points out that, in addition to requiring a context, a message, if it is to be operative, also requires a code which is fully, or at least partially common to the addresser and the addressee. In addition, a *contact,* that is, a physical channel and psychological connection between the two are necessary to enable them to enter and to remain in communication.[106] That is, every symbolic expression tends toward a discourse of cognition where something is said. A minimum knowledge is required if a symbol is to be able to exercise its power. In regard to music, this would include some knowledge of the cultural codes which enable the listener or performer to understand the music. Without this, music, like any other symbol about which nothing could be said, would dissolve into pure imagination. Such a situation would reduce the musical symbol to the Romantic ideology of art for art's sake. [107]

Umberto Eco has written extensively on the importance of interpreting codes within a cultural context when he pointed out that "one hypothesis of semiotics is that underpinning every process of communication there exist rules or codes, which rest upon certain cultural conventions."[108] While Eco points out that everything depends on "knowing" the codes, he nevertheless acknowledges that they may be different for producer and receiver. In other words, Eco recognizes the fundamental discrepancy between the poietic and the esthesic. Furthermore, in his conception of multiple meanings, he cites as a fundamental precept the notion of the Peirceian interpretant.[109]

---

[105] BOILÈS, "The Processes of Musical Semiosis," 32.

[106] NATTIEZ, *Music and Discourse,* 18.

[107] CHAUVET, *Symbol and Sacrament*, 128.

[108] See NATTIEZ, *Music and Discourse,* 20. A discrepancy in Nattiez's citation made it impossible to verify the source of this direct quote. A parenthetical reference cites the following: Umberto ECO, *A Theory of Semiotics,* Advances in Semiotics series, gen. ed., Thomas A. SEBEOK, (Bloomington: Indiana University Press, 1976), 13. It appears that information on pages 8 and 13 are the source for Nattiez's own formulation of Eco's ideas.

[109] NATTIEZ, *Music and Discourse,* 21.

As Chauvet points out, whether ritual elements be religious, political, mythic or poetic, they can only function symbolically insofar as they are correlative to the other elements that are constitutive of the ritual in which they are located.[110] Therefore, since understanding music's ability to symbolize in a liturgical setting – the goal of this present study – can not be achieved while isolating music or removing it from that context, the next section of this paper will examine music's symbolic role within that ritual called liturgy.

MUSIC AS RITUAL SYMBOL

Tom Driver's description of religious ritual helps to set the scene for this section of our study:

> Religion's being danced out, sung out, sat out in silence, or lined out liturgically, with ideation playing a secondary role, is not something confined to religion's early stages but is characteristic of religion as long as it is vital. This does not mean, of course, that ritual is mindless, nor anti-intellectual. It means that its form of intelligence is more similar to that of the arts than to conceptual theology, just as the intelligence of poetry is a different order from that of philosophy or literary criticism.[111]

Here Driver points out that the symbolism of the arts has always been an essential element of religious ritual. This is not a characteristic limited to the rituals of primitive religion. Furthermore, this role of the arts takes precedence over the role of the intellectual or conceptual because, by its nature, ritual is more closely akin to the arts than to propositional discourse.

In other words, the language of ritual is the language of the arts. And Driver rightly claims that artistic discourse is of a different order than philosophy, theology, or literary criticism. In Marsoobian terms, we can say that the language of ritual is *exhibitive,* and for that reason possesses a greater affinity with music than with theological discourse. In both cases, the process of shaping and the product as shaped are of primary importance.[112]

---

[110] CHAUVET, *Symbol and Sacrament*, 115.

[111] Tom F. DRIVER, *The Magic of Ritual: Our Need for Liberating Rites that Transform Our Lives and Our Communities* (San Francisco: HarperCollins Publishers, 1991), 84.

[112] Cf. Wade T. WHEELOCK, "The Problem of Ritual Language: From Information to Situation," *The Journal of the American Academy of Religion* 50 (1982): 56-58. In this

The theologian Avery Dulles argues that the deeper insights of revelatory knowledge are not imparted first of all through theology's propositional discourse. Instead, Dulles identifies the ecclesial-transformative approach to theology as one in which symbolism in worship plays a key role in apprehending revelation. This approach views symbolic communication as imbued with a depth of meaning that surpasses conceptual thinking and propositional speech.[113] In this approach,

> the primary subject matter of theology is taken to be the saving self-communication of God through the symbolic events and words of Scripture, especially in Jesus Christ as the 'mediator and fullness of all revelation.' A privileged locus for the apprehension of this subject matter is the worship of the Church, in which the biblical and traditional symbols are proclaimed and "re-presented" in ways that call for active participation (at least in mind and heart) on the part of the congregation. The interplay of symbols in community worship arouses and directs the worshipers' tacit powers of apprehension so as to instill a personal familiarity with the Christian mysteries.[114]

According to Dulles, then, theology is expressed symbolically in worship. More specifically, one of the primary purposes of that symbolic expression is the apprehension of revelation. This is achieved through the active participation of the congregation in the symbols celebrated which allows for discernment of meaning and communion with the sacred mysteries. Symbols transmit the message of faith by forming the imagination and affectivity of the worshiping community who appropriate the symbols and "dwell in" their meaning.[115]

One of the key elements of ritual is participation, understood in this context to be an engagement in participatory knowledge. The symbols interactive within ritual lure us into situating ourselves within the universe of meaning and value which it opens up to us.[116] Nathan Mitchell

---

article Wheelock argues that an essential difference between ritual utterances and ordinary language is that ritual utterances convey little or no information. In other words, they are not propositional, but exhibitive. This is true whether the text be tied to song or not. A discussion of the nature of ritual language will be more fully developed in chapter five.

[113] DULLES, *Craft of Theology*, 18.
[114] DULLES, *Craft of Theology*, 19.
[115] DULLES, *Craft of Theology*, 23.
[116] Avery DULLES, *Models of Revelation* (Garden City, New York: Doubleday and Company, Inc., 1983), 58.

points out that ritual symbols are not objects to be manipulated, but an environment to be inhabited: places to live, breathing spaces that help us discover life's possibilities.[117] Because of the power of symbols to make present the reality which they symbolize, inviting participation in themselves enables the worshipers to participate in the reality to which they point – the saving presence and action of God. Lawler describes this reality as "living into" the symbols.[118]

In a unique way, music as symbol invites the worshiper to participate in and inhabit its world. Such activities as singing, playing, listening, or moving with the rhythms of the music can mediate a participatory knowledge, a "living into" the music, that allows our bodies and our spirits to breath with its rhythms and phrases in such a way that they reveal the saving presence of God and our communion with the entire assembly. Such participation engages us on the level of subjects in an acoustic space which is fluid. For unlike visual space, acoustic space does not contain a thing but is itself a sphere delineated by activity. This acoustic activity is translated by the human imagination as evidence of the presence of life, of animation, and particularly, of human presence.[119]

Victor Zuckerkandl's investigation of the reason why people engage in song, particularly folk song, led him to a number of important insights regarding the activity of singing. In examining a variety of different activities and settings in which people sang, he concluded that the common element in all the situations is that people sing when they abandon themselves wholly to whatever they are doing. This abandonment is not for its own sake, that is, in order to forget themselves. Rather, this self-abandonment is an enlargement, an enhancement of the self which results in the breaking down of barriers: it is a transcendence of separation which is transformed into a togetherness.[120]

In this way, participation in ritual song corresponds to that dynamic described by Polanyi: by drawing us into the activity of music-making, singing carries us out of ourselves. This movement introduces us into realms of awareness not normally accessible to discursive thought. As a result, ritual song as symbol puts us in touch with the power to which

---

[117] MITCHELL, "Symbols Are Actions, Not Objects," 1-2.
[118] LAWLER, *Symbol and Sacrament*, 23, 19.
[119] Edward FOLEY, "Toward a Sound Theology" *Studia Liturgica* 23 (1993), 127.
[120] Victor ZUCKERKANDL, *Sound and Symbol*, vol. 2, trans. Willard R. TRASK (Princeton, New Jersey: Princeton University Press, 1969), 23.

it points and opens up to us levels of reality which might otherwise be closed to us.

Nattiez's application of the tri-partition schema (the poietic, immanent, and esthesic levels) to music as symbol provides another way for understanding how music draws us in. Music as ritual symbol enables participation because its infinite web of interpretants engages our imagination so that we might interpret the music's meaning from within our unique "experience-domain." This occurs when music as ritual symbol becomes the point of departure for the complex process of reception, the esthesic process, which reconstructs a meaning or message.

Religious symbols have a character that "points to the ultimate level of being, to ultimate reality, to being itself, to meaning itself.[121] In and through the music used in worship, the sacred is proclaimed, realized, and celebrated as present and active by those who are drawn into this symbol with the disposition of faith.[122] This effects a permanent solidarity between the worshipers and the sacred, thereby carrying out the process of hierophanization.[123]

In addition to inviting participation and pointing beyond itself, ritual symbols, insofar as they involve the knower as person, have the potential to mediate transformation. By shifting our center of awareness symbols can change our values.[124] According to Chauvet's theory of symbolizing, this dynamic is constantly in process as symbols continue to offer new opportunities for human subjects to make sense of their world and find their identity within it. This is especially true of aesthetic or art symbols within the liturgy since, in their innermost nature, they reveal both what we are and the various possible and actual appearances of the world within a Christian faith context. Therefore, as we are assimilated or integrated into the world of the art symbol, we open up to the possibility of intentional self-transcendence: we can become different persons if we allow ourselves to be carried away by

---

[121] Paul TILLICH, "Art and Ultimate Reality," in *Art, Creativity and the Sacred,* ed. Diane APOSTOLOS-CAPPADONA (New York: The Crossroad Publishing Company, 1984), 109-110.

[122] LAWLER, *Symbol and Sacrament,* 23-25.

[123] DULLES, *Models of Revelation,* 134. By hierophanization, Dulles means that process whereby religious meaning or the sacred mysteries unfold or are revealed to the worshiper.

[124] DULLES, *Models of Revelation,* 136.

new faith meanings and orient ourselves in new ways to our place within that faith world.[125]

Lawler calls a symbol that functions in this way within liturgy a "prophetic" symbol, and describes it as a provocation to personal action, interaction, and reaction that affects the worshiper's total being. Without this personal response, the symbol does not come fully alive for the worshiper.[126] This point highlights once again the centrality of the role of the subject in the act of symbolizing. As Chauvet explains, the effects of meaning produced by the symbol are effects of the subject, whereby the subject recognizes him/herself in the effects and identifies him/herself with them. In Polanyi's schema, the subject operates from within his/her diffuse memories of personal experiences and from within a particular social and cultural context, what Nattiez would call a horizon. Such engagement of the subject with the symbol effects a symbol's ability to mediate change or transformation.

According to Chauvet, by engaging with symbols and dwelling in the symbolic order, subjects build themselves by building their world.[127] This "building" of themselves suggests the process of change that is inherent in the process of transformation. By means of this "symbolic exchange,"[128] subjects weave or reweave alliances and recognize themselves as members of a social group in which they find their identity. It is a process which provides the possibility of becoming and living as subjects.[129]

By enacting this symbolic exchange ritually, liturgy can have a powerful influence on our commitment and behavior, if, as Polanyi suggests, the symbols mediate recognition and if we allow ourselves to be "carried away" by their meaning. Because liturgical symbols mediate relationships between subjects, the liturgy can direct our response beyond the ritual act itself to our daily living with our brothers and sisters. Working

---

[125] Robert E. INNIS, "Art, Symbol, and Consciousness: A Polanyi Gloss on Susan Langer and Nelson Goodman," *International Philosophical Quarterly* 17 (December 1977): 475-476.

[126] LAWLER, *Symbol and Sacrament*, 12, 25.

[127] CHAUVET, *Symbol and Sacrament*, 86.

[128] Chauvet uses the term "symbolic exchange" to describe the distinctive way in which subjects come to be in their relations to other subjects. This exchange or interaction occurs in the symbolic order and is characterized by a three-fold process of gift, reception of the gift, and return-gift. In Chauvet's view, this process structures every significant human relationship. See CHAUVET, *Symbol and Sacrament*, 99-109.

[129] CHAUVET, *Symbol and Sacrament*, 106-107.

on worshipers like an incantation, Dulles explains, the symbols of the liturgy can stir the imagination, release hidden energies in the soul, give strength and stability to the personality and arouse the will to consistent and committed action.[130] All of this assumes, of course, that the symbols employed can be deciphered within the cultural or social contexts in which they are enacted. If subjects lack the cultural codes necessary to understand a particular symbol or system of symbols, a mediation of recognition and integration is impeded.

As with all liturgical symbols, music has the potential to communicate to the worshiping assembly the challenge to live a fuller life with God in Christ. But how is it that the symbolizing activity of music in ritual actually operates as an influence in Christian transformation? Don Saliers asserts that ritual music has the power of transformation by forming, over time, the imagination and affectivity of the Christian assembly. It does this by "forming and expressing those emotions which constitute the very Christian life itself."[131]

Saliers builds his thesis on the premise that worship itself both forms and expresses a characteristic set of emotions and attitudes in participants. In this regard, his understanding of the role of worship corresponds to Susanne Langer's description of ritual when she says:

> Ritual "expresses feelings" in the logical rather than the physiological sense. It may have what Aristotle called "cathartic" value, but that is not its characteristic; it is primarily an *articulation* of feelings. The ultimate product of such articulation is not a simple emotion, but a complex, permanent *attitude*. This attitude, which is the worshipers' response to the insight given by the sacred symbols, is an emotional pattern, which governs all individual lives. It cannot be recognized through any clearer medium than that of formalized gesture; yet in this cryptic form it *is* recognized, and yields a strong sense of tribal or congregational unity, of rightness and security. A rite regularly performed is the constant reiteration of sentiments toward "first and last things"; it is not a free expression of emotions, but a disciplined rehearsal of "right attitudes."[132]

Saliers builds his argument on Langer's theory that ritual is an articulation of feelings and on her distinction between simple emotion and a

[130] DULLES, *Models of Revelation,* 137.

[131] Don E. SALIERS, "The Integrity of Sung Prayer," *Worship* 55 (July 1981): 293.

[132] Susanne K. LANGER, *Philosophy in a New Key: A Study in the Symbolism of Reason, Rite and Art,* 3d edition (Cambridge, Massachusetts: Harvard University Press, 1967), 153.

complex, permanent attitude or deep emotion. Taking Langer's remark that the ultimate product of ritual repeatedly performed is an emotional pattern which governs the lives of individual subjects, Saliers concludes that the music used in worship, particularly congregational song, assists, not only in articulating, but also in forming the deep emotions particular to the Christian life. Furthermore, it is in the process of repeatedly articulating these "right attitudes" that transformation can be effected. In other words, singing praise or thanksgiving, contrition or forgiveness has the ability to form the singers in those Christian attitudes. By *exhibiting* these Christian attitudes – to use Marsoobian's terminology – we participate through our music-making in the process of being shaped or formed in those very attitudes. Therefore, specific musical choices will either lead the assembly toward or away from the deep patterns of emotion which constitute the Christian life. Over time, for good or for ill, assemblies will be shaped by their musical choices. In this way, the emotional range of their worship music will either enhance or inhibit their ability to enter into those praisings, repentings, lamentings, hopings, longings, rejoicing, and thankings that are peculiar to the heart of Christian worship.[133]

Taizé Music as Ritual Symbol

The various theories and theologies of symbol which have been examined in this chapter provide us with the tools for investigating how Taizé music functions as ritual symbol. Several aspects of these theories and theologies have emerged as particularly applicable to this study.

Chauvet points out that human subjects, through their participation in symbolizing activity, are enabled to recognize their identity, negotiate connections, build their world, and engage in the process of Christian transformation. The specific symbolizing activity in question here is liturgical singing.

Singing the Berthier chants during the liturgies at Taizé involves each person, first of all, on the physical level. Making music – whether it be singing, playing an instrument, moving with the rhythms of the songs, or listening – is an activity which involves the body. This physical participation, furthermore, is an entree into a deeper participation. Polanyi

133 SALIERS, "Sung Prayer," 294-295.

explains that symbolizing activity involves the dynamic whereby a person is carried away by the meanings in the subsidiary clues. In the case of the Taizé chants, a person's diffuse and boundless memories of his or her life become embodied and fused in the singing so that abandonment or surrender to the meaning of the symbol becomes possible. In the process, a person can recognize him/herself as a person of faith, a person in relationship with God, and a person in relationship with others, both those present and those absent from the liturgy. Further, one experiences oneself in a common bond with the other singers. This type of recognition makes it possible to imagine a world where Christian faith can become unifying rather than divisive, where national and denominational barriers can be overcome. Even more so, the act of singing brings that world about, even if only while the liturgy lasts.

Singing the chants enables the music-makers to express such Christian attitudes as faith, trust, praise, love, thanksgiving, and repentance and to experience a world where divisions are overcome. Indeed, the very act of entering into the common effort of singing is a gesture of moving outside of oneself and allowing oneself to be carried away by the song of the group. Zuckerkandl describes this abandonment as an enhancement of the self which results in the breaking down of barriers.[134] The Taizé chants enable the singers to transcend the separation which is the existential reality of the pilgrims so that the "rehearsing" of Christian unity, that is, the unity experienced in the singing, might eventually be realized outside the ritual event. Such an experience can shift the participants' center of awareness and be transformative if they allow themselves to be carried away by meanings mediated through the singing.

Nattiez's explanation of the *esthesic* dimension offers yet another perspective on the dynamic of participation. According to the tripartite schema he appropriates from Molino, the esthesic process is a complex process of reception which reconstructs the "message." This requires an active involvement of both the "sender" and "receiver." In the case of the Taizé chants this means that the meaning mediated by singing the chants is part of the complex interplay between the process of creation, involving all those who participate in this process – composer, collaborators, performers – and the process of reception. The various activities of composing, singing, playing, listening, interpreting, and receiving the

---

[134] ZUCKERKANDL, *Sound and Symbol*, 23.

liturgical songs of Taizé draw each music-maker into participating in the generation of meaning.

This generation of meaning occurs within each person's particular horizon or experience-domain. In regard to the Taizé chants, one aspect of that horizon is the liturgical prayer of Taizé as it is celebrated within the Christian tradition. Another aspect is the international community of Christians participating in the prayer. Added to the ritual context and the entire Taizé pilgrimage experience is a constellation of interpretants experienced within the personal horizon of each individual engaged in the Taizé prayer. This personal horizon includes, not only an individual's experience of Taizé prayer and the Taizé pilgrimage experience, but also, as Polanyi describes them, the diffuse and boundless memories "of a person's life that become embodied and fused" in the symbolizing activity.[135]

Scholars of the Peirceian school remind us that three dimensions of signification determine symbolic meaning: the semantic, the syntactic and the pragmatic. For this reason, the relation of Taizé music to the ritual context and what it signifies, the various types of symbols in Taizé liturgical prayer and their relations to each other, and the relation of Taizé music to the music-makers all contribute to the generation of meaning.

In other words, the meaning of singing the Taizé chants can only be most fully interpreted within the larger context of the ritual activity. This requires taking into account the interplay between the singing of the songs, the proclamation of the Scriptures, the recitation of prayers, the gestures, and the keeping of the silences. In addition, the influence of other ritual elements such as the visual, tactile, and olfactory also need to be included in the interpretive process.

By insisting on the importance of studying symbol in context, the theories and theologies of symbol in this chapter have raised questions regarding the symbolic role of music in the ritual process. In order to address this question in greater depth, the next chapter will examine the ritual theory of Victor Turner. His work on symbolic process can further assist in focusing on Berthier's music as symbolizing activity within the setting of Taizé ritual prayer and within the larger setting of the Taizé experience as pilgrimage process. In addition, Turner's theoretical framework for interpreting symbols, in looking at three dimensions of significance, complements and supports Charles Peirce's approach to semiotic analysis as an analysis of the semantic, the pragmatic, and the syntactic dimensions.

---

[135] POLANYI, Meaning, 72-73.

CHAPTER FOUR

THE SYMBOLIC ROLE OF TAIZÉ MUSIC WITHIN
THE TAIZÉ PILGRIMAGE PROCESS

INTRODUCTION

The previous chapter examined theories and theologies of symbol in order to discover how music mediates meaning and how singing Berthier's Taizé music can be described as symbolic activity. The purpose of this chapter is to examine the setting for which the music was composed and for which the music continues to be used.[1] While it is true that the Berthier chants were composed for Taizé liturgies, nevertheless it is useful to examine the symbolic role of this liturgical music, not only within the context of Taizé prayer, but also within the broader setting of the entire Taizé experience.

It is difficult to describe the Taizé pilgrimage process fully. The first problem is the difficulty of compiling sufficient data to draw a complete picture of what happens at Taizé and how it is experienced by the brothers and the visitors. Such a task would require recourse to the social sciences and is beyond the scope of this study. The second problem is the "provisional" nature of the Taizé experience. In other words, even if a lengthy period of time were spent at Taizé compiling data on observable events and interviewing participants, still the provisional nature of the structure and content of the experience[2] would quickly render the data obsolete. There are, however, several elements of continuity in regard to the setting, the participants, and the activities. These will provide the basis for outlining a general description of the Taizé pilgrimage process.

---

[1] There is, of course, the possibility that Berthier's music can be and has been used for other purposes, for example, for private meditation or as background music to other activities. The focus of this study, however, is only on the use of Berthier's music at Taizé.

[2] See *Praise God: Common Prayer at Taizé*, trans. Emily CHISHOLM (New York: Oxford University Press, 1977), 7. Both chapter two and chapter six discuss the provisional aspect of Taizé in greater detail. The brothers describe both their monastic life and the form of their common prayer as provisional because they see it "in process," that is, continually developing and evolving.

Since thousands of people from four continents travel to Taizé each year, it is possible to speak of Taizé as a pilgrimage site.[3] Visitors seeking to participate in the Taizé experience travel to this isolated, rural village located in the Burgundian hills of France.[4] The center of the stable, monastic community of Taizé is the great Church of Reconciliation where all liturgical prayer takes place.[5]

Just as the great Church of Reconciliation is the center of Taizé, so, too, is the monastic community of brothers at the center of the Taizé experience.[6] The brothers pray the daily liturgies from a specially designated area in the center of the church dressed in white prayer robes. The pilgrims who gather for prayer are seated around them. In this way, the brothers provide, not only a stable and continuous presence, but also a strong symbolic witness to unity, unanimity and hospitality to pilgrims.[7]

Pilgrims participate in the Taizé experience throughout the entire year, though the numbers may vary from less than a hundred to several thousand, depending on the season and the feast. Together, the brothers and the pilgrims represent a diverse range of nationalities and races, of languages, and of Christian denominations.

The schedule of the day and the week also provides a strong element of continuity. Prayer is scheduled three times daily, at dawn, midday, and sunset. Sunday Eucharist is celebrated each week and a special "Prayer around the Cross"[8] takes place each Friday at sunset. In addition

[3] See Victor TURNER and Edith L.B. TURNER, "Pilgrimage as a Liminoid Phenomenon," in *Image and Pilgrimage in Christian Culture: Anthropological Perspectives* (New York: Columbia University Press, 1978), 6. Turner includes the occurrence of miracles as a criterion for designating a place a pilgrimage site. It is the miracle of spiritual healing and reconciliation that takes place in the context of this pilgrimage experience which draws so many to Taizé.

[4] Since 1976, the brothers of Taizé have periodically sponsored international meetings of youth in various cities throughout the world. While these events have become an important aspect of their ministry to youth, these meetings are not the subject of this study.

[5] Some description of the liturgical prayer of Taizé was provided in chapter two. Further descriptions will be included later in this chapter.

[6] At any given time, the majority of the community is in residence at Taizé. However, the community has founded houses in the poorest areas of several countries.

[7] During my visit to Taizé in May 1996 I became acquainted with the Sisters of St. Andrew, a religious community of Roman Catholic women who serve in such areas as hospitality, food services, health care, bookstore management, and music ministry. While they have become an important part of Taizé's ministry to pilgrims, their presence in the liturgies, in contrast to the brothers, is invisible.

[8] See Kathryn SPINK, *A Universal Heart: The Life and Vision of Brother Roger of Taizé* (San Francisco: Harper and Row Publishers, 1986), 136-137. The idea for the Friday

to the prayer schedule, there are daily gatherings of the pilgrims for guided reflections. Separate sessions for adults and for youth are held in the morning, followed by small group sharing on the morning's topic in the afternoon.

All meals are taken communally, at designated times and places, and in distinct groups. The brothers take their meals privately. Separate tents are provided for adults or families and for youth. In addition, pilgrims are assigned by teams to common tasks related to meals. Sleeping arrangements are also assigned and communal. Accommodations include barracks and, in the summer months, tents. A limited number of semi-private rooms are available for older adults.

Therefore, even though the Taizé experience is always intentionally a "provisional" one, there are constant features which provide continuity and enable us to speak of a Taizé pilgrimage experience. Within the structured experience there are several elements – for example, engaging in small group sharing in more than one language – which invite the pilgrims to be open to the new, the unfamiliar, and the "provisional."

Looking at Taizé as pilgrimage to a monastic center can provide one theoretical framework for interpreting the pilgrimage process and music's symbolic role within the prayer and the process. Victor W. Turner developed a theory of the pilgrimage process in connection with his study of ritual as social drama. This chapter will draw upon his ritual theory in order to interpret this event and the symbolic function of music-making, not only in the mircrocosm of the liturgies, but also in the macrocosm of the Taizé pilgrimage experience.

PILGRIMAGE AS LIMINAL EXPERIENCE

Victor Turner favored process theory for its capacity to take into account the critical importance of meaning and "symboling."[9] By focusing on interpreting the meaning of symbols, Turner was able to view ritual as both meaningful and transformative performance. He explains:

evening "Prayer around the Cross" was suggested by young people in Eastern Europe. Their intention was to hold this prayer service each Friday evening at the same time in each country. As the practice has spread, the prayer has subsequently served to unite both young and old at Taizé and in parishes throughout Europe and beyond.

  [9] Victor TURNER, "Process, System, and Symbol: A New Anthropological Synthesis," in *On the Edge of the Bush: Anthropology as Experience,* ed. Edith L.B. TURNER (Tucson: The University of Arizona Press, 1985), 152-153.

> [Ritual] is not, in essence ... a prop for social conservatism whose symbols merely condense cherished cultural values, though it may, under certain conditions, take on this role. Rather does it hold the generative source of culture and structure, particularly in its liminal stage. Hence, ritual is by definition associated with social transitions.[10]

While acknowledging that ritual may at times take on the role of preserving certain cultural values, Turner prefers to focus on ritual's creative and inventive possibilities. His association of ritual with social transitions and change reveals the influence of Arnold van Gennep[11] on his thinking.

In studying rites of passage, van Gennep discovered that "the processual form of ritual epitomized the general experience in traditional society that social life was a sequence of movements in space-time, involving a series of changes of pragmatic activity and a succession of transitions in state and status for individuals and culturally recognized groups and categories."[12] These transitions or rites of passage had three principle stages: separation, margin or limin, and reaggregation.

It was the notion of threshold or liminality, the second stage of the process, which particularly attracted Turner's consideration.[13] While van Gennep's work involved studying liminality in the rituals of pre-industrial societies, Turner extended and transformed his idea, applying it to such occasions as festivals, pilgrimages, and other kinds of public celebrations.[14]

Turner defines liminality as "an anti-structural moment of reversal which is the creative fond not only for ritual but for culture in general."[15] As such, liminality provides that "generative quality which lends motion

---

[10] TURNER, "Process, System, and Symbol,"171.

[11] See Arnold VAN GENNEP, *The Rites of Passage,* trans. Monika B. VIZEDOM and Gabrielle L. CAFFEE (Chicago: The University of Chicago Press, 1960).

[12] TURNER, "Process, System, and Symbol," 158.

[13] See Caroline Walker BYNUM, "Women's Stories, Women's Symbols: A Critique of Victor Turner's Theory of Liminality," in *Anthropology and the Study of Religion,* ed. Robert L. MOORE and Frank E. REYNOLDS (Chicago: Center for the Scientific Study of Religion, 1984). In this essay Bynum critiques Turner's analysis of liminality for not taking into consideration gender differences in dynamics involved in the three stages. Her argument is that women do not move out of liminality in the same way men do.

[14] Ronald GRIMES, *Beginnings in Ritual Studies,* revised edition, Studies in Comparative Religion, gen. ed., Frederick M. DENNY (Columbia: University of South Carolina Press, 1995), 152.

[15] GRIMES, *Beginnings in Ritual Studies,* 149.

to a society by forcing it out of a rigid structure into flowing process."[16] Liminality, then, is both generative and anti-structural in its nature.

When Turner speaks of ritual as "anti-structural," he is speaking in the social sense. Such anti-structure involves a stripping and leveling of human persons before the transcendent. In the liminal experience, relationships, values, and norms which prevail in the usual pragmatic structures of everyday life are reversed, expunged, suspended, reinterpreted, or replaced by another set of structures. In other words, what is *socially* anti-structural is often protected or enclosed by other *cultural* structures.[17] Turner identifies religious buildings, pictorial images, statuary, and sacralized features of the topography as sensorily perceptible symbol-vehicles which serve as the new structures of thought and feeling.[18]

"Communitas" is the term Turner uses to refer to ritual's prime anti-structural characteristic.[19] In one sense, this characteristic of "communitas" is the primary aspect of ritual for Turner. By "communitas" he means something more substantive than "community," a term which he associates with an area of common living such as a village, town, or neighborhood. Rather, "communitas" is "an essential and generic bond without which there could be *no* society.[20] Turner contrasts "communitas" with social structure. The former he describes as "spontaneous, immediate, [and] concrete ... as opposed to the norm-governed, institutionalized, abstract nature of social structure."[21] In providing the possibility for "communitas," the liminal stage is a moment when distinctions of wealth and class are suspended in favor of equality, poverty, and homogeneity.[22]

By contrasting social structure with "communitas," however, Turner is not saying that the experience of "communitas" is totally without

[16] GRIMES, *Beginnings in Ritual Studies,* 149.

[17] Victor TURNER, "Passages, Margins, and Poverty: Religious Symbols of Communitas," *Worship* 46 (August-September 1972): 390-391.

[18] TURNER and TURNER, "Pilgrimage as a Liminoid Phenomenon," 10.

[19] Turner acknowledges borrowing the term "communitas," but not its meaning, from Paul Goodman.

[20] Victor TURNER, *The Ritual Process: Structure and Anti-Structure* (Chicago: Aldine Publishing Company, 1969), 83.

[21] TURNER, *The Ritual Process,* 114.

[22] GRIMES, *Beginnings in Ritual Studies,* 149. While Grimes acknowledges such distinctions as wealth and class, others can be added to his list, including those of sex, race, and religion.

structure. Rather "communitas" is actually an instance of those "complex cultural structures" which replace social structures within the liminal experience.[23] In other words, "the liminal situation of communitas is invested with a structure that is *not* a social structure ... but a structure of symbols and ideas; ..."[24]

Turner's theoretical interest in processual units, social anti-structure, and the analysis of ritual symbols converge in his study of pilgrimage processes.[25] According to Turner, the pilgrimage experience involves a going forth and a retirement from the world which gives it a "rite of passage" character. In addition, the pilgrimage center itself, generally possesses a marked peripherality because of its location outside the main administrative centers of church or state. As Turner describes it, the experience of a pilgrim is one of moving from a familiar place, to a far away place, then returning to a familiar place.[26] Participation in the pilgrimage leads to a heightened awareness of belonging to a larger whole, an awareness promoted by participation in common rituals and ceremonies. The "communitas" thus generated moves toward universality and ever greater unity. For these reasons, Turner interprets pilgrimage as a form of symbolic anti-structure in both tribal and industrialized society.[27]

THE TAIZÉ PILGRIMAGE PROCESS

Turner chose the notion of social drama as a root metaphor for interpreting social process in order to focus on the reality of people interacting and the consequences of their interactions for the maintenance and meaning of a cultural system.[28] Social drama likewise offers a useful framework for interpreting the pilgrimage week and what is enacted at Taizé. Within that framework, the three stages Turner adapted from van Gennep offer further possibilities for interpreting the Taizé pilgrimage

---

[23] TURNER, "Passages, Margins, and Poverty," 391.

[24] TURNER, "Passages, Margins, and Poverty," 400.

[25] Victor TURNER, *Dramas, Fields, and Metaphors: Symbolic Action in Human Society*, Symbol, Myth and Ritual series, gen. ed., Victor TURNER (Ithaca: Cornell University Press, 1974), 166.

[26] TURNER, *Dramas, Fields, and Metaphors*, 195.

[27] TURNER, *Dramas, Fields, and Metaphors*, 177-195.

[28] Mary COLLINS, "Ritual Symbols and Ritual Process: The Work of Victor W. Turner," *Worship* 50 (July 1976), 341.

process since it involves movement from a familiar, routinized existence to a place of peripherality, followed by a return to ordinary existence. Of the three stages, it is the second stage, liminality, which can provide important insights into the dynamics of Taizé as a pilgrimage process.

A review of Turner's definition of social structure can provide a basis for understanding anti-structure as an element of the Taizé experience. Borrowing Robert Merton's terms, Turner defines social structure as "'the patterned arrangements of role-sets, status sets, and status-sequences' consciously recognized and regularly operative in a given society."[29] Several of such patterned arrangements can be identified as part of the social structure out of which the pilgrims of Taizé normally operate, including such patterns as wealth, race, nationality, sex, political position, and religious affiliation.

As an experience of liminality, the rituals of the Taizé experience provide "anti-structural moments of reversal" which have the capacity to move pilgrims "out of rigid structure into flowing process."[30] This moving out of rigid social structures occurs as pilgrims of different racial, ethnic, linguistic, economic, and denominational backgrounds share in such everyday activities as taking meals together, sleeping in barracks or other multiple occupancy housing, joining in such common tasks as serving meals and doing dishes, sharing in small group discussions which require translators, and participating in liturgies in several languages.

The result is what Turner describes as "flowing process." When barriers are suspended, strangers begin to interact freely with each other. The behavior among the pilgrims becomes characteristically "egalitarian and cooperative" and "distinctions of rank, office and status are temporarily in abeyance or regarded as irrelevant."[31]

The description of the constant elements in the Taizé process provided above precludes any notion that the pilgrimage process, even though liminal and therefore anti-structural, lacks structure. Turner himself pointed out that "process is intimately bound up with structure and that an adequate analysis of social life necessitates a rigorous consideration of the relation between them."[32]

---

[29] TURNER, "Passages, Margins, and Poverty," 397.
[30] See GRIMES, *Beginnings in Ritual Studies,* 149.
[31] See TURNER, "Passages, Margins, and Poverty," 398.
[32] TURNER, "Process, System, and Symbol," 156.

Margaret Mary Kelleher takes this caution into account. She explains that "ritual emerges gradually from within the dynamics of the social process, the interplay between two different needs, the need for structure or social order and the need to experience the more basic human bonding that is prior to any order."[33]

In the same way, the rituals of Taizé can be said to be shaped by the brothers in order to address different needs and promote specific ends of the pilgrimage process. These rituals include, not only the liturgies, but the rituals of sharing meals, gathering for reflection, and various other dimensions of life at Taizé. All of these rituals, as aspects of the social drama enacted at Taizé, have as their primary goal the reconciliation of all Christians. Both the writings of Brother Roger Schutz and Brother Max Thurian attest to the centrality of this purpose.[34] In addition, there is the broader goal of achieving reconciliation among all people who suffer any type of alienation and/or are separated by barriers of creed, race, national origin, language, or economic status.

The more immediate goal of the rituals, however, is to provide a provisional experience of reconciliation at Taizé. To achieve this goal the pilgrimage process sets in motion the dynamics of both anti-structure and generativity. The anti-structure suspends the social structures already identified above. In their place are set up new symbolic structures. These serve as alternate cultural structures which, Turner explains, protect and enclose the liminal experience and generate new structures of thought and feeling.[35]

Turner calls these cultural structures sensorily perceptible symbol-vehicles. At Taizé they include the traditional Christian symbols of Sacred Scripture, eucharist, sacred music, icons, especially the crucifix, and public witness to the values of hospitality, unity, and reconciliation. These values are incorporated into the patterns of the daily schedule, including the structure of daily prayer, meals, guided reflections, small group discussions, work tasks, free time, and rest.

---

[33] KELLEHER, "Ritual," 906.

[34] See the following: Roger SCHUTZ, *Unanimity in Pluralism,* trans. David FLOOD, Brother PASCHAL, and Brother THOMAS (Chicago: Franciscan Herald Press, 1967); SCHUTZ, *Unity: Man's Tomorrow* (New York: Herder and Herder, 1963); Max THURIAN, "L'Unité visible," *Verbum Caro* XVI (1962): 150-160; idem, *The One Bread, trans.* Theodore DuBOIS (New York: Sheed and Ward, 1969).

[35] See TURNER, "Passages, Margins, and Poverty," 390-391; TURNER and Edith L.B. TURNER, "Pilgrimage as a Liminoid Phenomenon," 10.

The ritual symbols of the Taizé liturgies, including the Berthier chants, are an integral part of that structure. In fact, the patterns of the musical genres of the Berthier chants[36] themselves serve as "structuring structures"[37] which enable the temporary suspension of social and denominational barriers and promote patterns of hospitality, unity, and reconciliation. Following Pierre Bourdieu and Lawrence Kramer's schema, we can say that if "structuring structures" are those which generate and shape practices and representations, Berthier's chants serve in this way by generating and shaping the representation and experience of "communitas" and reconciliation.

This immediate goal of experiencing provisional reconciliation at Taizé corresponds in many ways to Turner's notion of anti-structure's primary characteristic, "communitas." It is an experience of spontaneous, immediate, and concrete community at Taizé, made possible by the liminal dimension of the Taizé pilgrimage process.

For Turner, this characteristic of "communitas," of belonging to the whole, is promoted through participation in common rituals. While the various rituals of Taizé assist in promoting reconciliation and "communitas," the daily and weekly rhythm of liturgical prayer is key in several respects. In the first place, the visible presence of the brothers at the center of the liturgies serves as symbol of the communion toward which the mission of Taizé is directed. In addition, the liturgies engage the primary symbols of Taizé, enable active participation, and serve as a microcosm of the "macro" ritual known as the Taizé pilgrimage.

This conviction that the daily prayer of the community is intimately bound up with the daily life of the community is articulated in *Praise God: Common Prayer at Taizé.*[38] The introduction expresses the conviction that prayer for the Christian has a dual purpose: "to worship God and to express the fact that our communion with him is social as our humanity itself is social."[39] The history of the community, as outlined in chapter two, indicates that the prayer of the community, expressed to a great extent as sung prayer, has grown, changed and developed out of the social reality of the community and of its growing number of international members and visitors.

[36] See chapter two for a discussion of the musical genres of the Taizé chants.

[37] See chapter two for a discussion of Lawrence Kramer's musical hermeneutics which includes his notion of "structuring structures."

[38] This is the 1977 English edition of the Taizé liturgy of the hours published by the community.

[39] *Praise God,* 8.

Several aspects of that "social drama" – of brothers interacting with each other and with large numbers of pilgrims – can be identified. In the first place, the Taizé community is rooted in the Christian tradition from which the members and visitors come. That Christian tradition, in turn, is the source of the liturgical prayer of Taizé and the mission of the community. As the introduction to *The Taizé Office* explains, the community seeks to remain "in the biblical and liturgical tradition of the Church" even as it desires "a contemporary form of prayer."[40] An important aspect of the social process is negotiating the tradition by discovering and celebrating common elements among members of the various Christian denominations, whether they be brothers or pilgrims.

The three periods of prayer assist in negotiating relationships among the worshipers and between each worshiper and God. By design, the prayer periods are intended for both the brothers and the guests. Invariably, both of these groups comprise members from the various Christian denominations – Protestant, Roman Catholic, and Orthodox churches. The daily prayer of Taizé brings together separated Christians in a shared space and time, during which they pray the psalms, listen to the proclamation of Scripture, sing and speak prayers of praise, petition, and thanksgiving. The assembly thus participates in a unity enacted within the ritual setting, but not yet fully achieved.

Finally, because Taizé prayer is common prayer, it likewise mediates a relationship between a community, as a social entity, and the God whom they worship. The biblical foundations of the prayer serve as a constant reminder to the worshipers that they are members of the People of God and participants in the drama of salvation history which God is accomplishing for his people.[41] And while they profess the Christian belief that redemption has been won through Jesus Christ, yet they continue to experience its unfolding in their life together as they live in joyful hope for the coming of the Kingdom when the unity prayed for by Christ will at last be realized.

The primary symbols of Christian reconciliation are "rehearsed"[42] at the three daily liturgies in the great Church of Reconciliation. Singing

---

[40] *The Taizé Office* (London: The Faith Press Limited, 1966), 9. Originally published in French as *Office de Taizé* (Taizé: Les Presses de Taizé, 1963).

[41] See 1 Pt. 2:9-10.

[42] See LANGER, *Philosophy in a New Key,* 153. Chapter three includes a discussion of Susanne K. Langer's notion of religious ritual as a "rehearsal" of right attitudes and Don E. Saliers development of this idea for interpreting Christian worship.

the Berthier chants is an important aspect of the symbolic process because, as a symbol which structures a disparate group of individuals into an assembly which acts as one, it is able to mediate both reconciliation and "communitas."

In addition to the daily cycle of prayer, the weekly cycle is marked by the celebration of eucharist each Sunday and the "Prayer around the Cross" each Friday evening. Because these liturgies contain key symbols of Christian identity, their weekly celebration likewise serves to express and promote the ongoing mediation of Christian community among the brothers and visitors. In order to further discover Taizé music's symbolic role both in the liturgies and in the pilgrimage process, the next section will use aspects of Turner's method of processual symbolic analysis to interpret Berthier's chants.

TAIZÉ MUSIC'S ROLE AS RITUAL SYMBOL

Processual Symbolic Analysis

Victor Turner described his approach to ritual studies as processual symbolic analysis. His method involves "the interpretation of the meaning of symbols considered as dynamic systems of signifiers, signifieds, and changing modes of signification in temporal sociocultural processes."[43]

For Turner, symbols, both verbal and non-verbal, are the units or molecules of which rituals are composed. Furthermore, the great rituals of humankind convey meaning by means of multi-vocal symbols, that is symbols having many meanings or significations.[44] In order to interpret the many layers of meaning in ritual symbols, Turner identifies three major dimensions of significance: the exegetic, the operational, and the positional.[45] Each of these dimensions can assist in interpreting Taizé music as ritual symbol.

[43] TURNER, "Process, System, and Symbol," 170-171.
[44] Victor TURNER, "Symbols and Social Experience in Religious Ritual," in *Worship and Ritual: In Christianity and Other Religions,* Studia Missionalia (Rome: Gregorian University Press, 1974), 1, 7. In this section, Turner distinguishes between the terms "multivocal" and "multivalent." He explains that the first distinguishes human from animal ritualization since while "valent" includes the notion of motivation, "vocal" includes also cognitive and ideological components.
[45] TURNER, "Symbols and Social Experience," 11. While there are some differences in the organization of the categories, Turner's three dimensions of significance correspond in

The Exegetic Dimension

The exegetic dimension consists of the whole corpus of explanations of a symbol's meaning offered by indigenous informants. It may take the form of myth, piecemeal interpretations, doctrine, or dogma. In the case of myth, exegesis may be expressed through story-telling about sacred beings or the origins of all things.[46] Piecemeal interpretations may be explanations "based on appearances or normative 'common sense' cultural perceptions."[47] In the case of doctrine or dogma, it may involve more systematic explanations which supplement or replace myth. Questions regarding the exegetical dimension focus on what is said about a ritual symbol, what explanations are offered, and what names are given to a symbol.[48]

No data is available from indigenous informants regarding the meaning of Taizé or of the Berthier chants. Only official explanations, for example those published by Brother Robert in the various music editions, offer some insights into possible exegetical interpretations.[49]

The Operational Dimension

The operational dimension has to do with a symbol's use, that is, what participants of ritual do with the symbol. Regarding this dimension, it is necessary to consider, "not only the symbol itself but also the structure and composition of the group which ... handles it or performs mimetic acts with clear and direct reference to it."[50] Questions regarding the operational dimension also focus on the roles distributed within the group, the distinctions which appear within the ritual process and

---

many ways with Peirce's categories: the semantic, the syntactic and the pragmatic and Nattiez's concept of the horizon or experience-domain. In addition, Turner's understanding of the multi-vocality of symbols has some correlation with Peirce's infinite interpretant. See chapter three.

[46] TURNER, "Symbols and Social Experience," 11-12.

[47] COLLINS, "Ritual Symbols and the Ritual Process," 343.

[48] Margaret Mary KELLEHER, "Liturgical Theology: A Task and a Method,: *Worship* 62 (January 1988): 14.

[49] Several of the textual and citational inclusions analyzed in chapter two are examples of official explanations of the meaning of Taizé and Berthier's music. In addition, chapter six will look at statements in publications of Taizé regarding official explanations of its ecclesiology.

[50] TURNER, "Symbols and Social Experience," 12.

public reactions or expressions of feeling resulting from the way symbols are used.[51]

The diversity of the groups participating in Taizé liturgies has already been established. This characteristic influences the manner in which the pilgrims are able to engage in the symbolic activity of singing. It likewise determines the meaning this symbolizing activity can mediate for them. However, while there is a great deal of diversity in the make-up of the pilgrims, there is one common factor in the great majority of cases. That is the fact that the symbolizing activity of Taizé is being interpreted from at least one common experience-domain, that of Christian faith.[52]

The potential for singing the chants is provided for everyone although there is some distinction regarding parts and roles.[53] That is, while everyone is encouraged to participate, the singing does structure the group in certain ways. For example, a choir rehearsal, open to all pilgrims, is held each day so that some of the participants can sing the choir parts which supplement the assembly's. In addition, both men and women, and sometimes youth, serve as cantors. The musicians, including the music director, cantors, choir, and accompanists, fulfill their roles without distinction. That is, the cantors and choir perform their roles while seated among the assembly and instrumentalist play their instruments from unobtrusive locations.

Thus singing the songs enables the assembly to actively participate in the liturgies. Distinctions in musical roles do not set individuals apart from the assembly, but rather support and embellish the assembly's song. In addition, it makes possible the assembly's active participation in this element of the pilgrimage process. By means of this symbolic activity, social structures are suspended and new relationships are negotiated. That is, engagement in singing the Berthier chants is participation in a ritual activity which makes such distinctions as race, nationality, status, and denomination irrelevant. In addition, such engagement provides

---

[51] KELLEHER, "Liturgical Theology," 13-14.

[52] See chapter three for a discussion of Charles Peirce's notion of the infinite interpretant and Jean-Jacques Nattiez's understanding of the experience domain of the interpreter as significant factors in determining symbolic meaning.

[53] Chapter two presents a more detailed account of how Berthier's chants are designed to enable the active participation of all those present at the liturgies. Not only are the chants composed to be accessible, but music books are available to all who enter the church, even when the number of participants is in the several thousands

the assembly with a tangible experience of unity, reconciliation, and "communitas" in the very act of singing. These are part of the dynamics involved in the pilgrimage process. Singing the Taizé chants sets these dynamics in motion in a unique way.

The Positional Dimension

The third and last dimension, the positional meaning of a symbol, is derived from its relationship to other symbols. Here, "we see the meaning of a symbol as deriving from its relationship to other symbols in a special cluster or *gestalt* of symbols whose elements acquire much of their meaning from their position in its structure, from their *relationship* to other symbols. Often a symbol becomes *meaningful* only in its relationship to another symbol in terms of binary oppposition or complementariness."[54] Furthermore, the structure of the relationship between symbols may specify which meaning is situationally relevant out of the vast potential of meanings which a symbol may in fact mediate.[55]

The Taizé chants are strategically positioned in the daily liturgies in two ways. In the first place, they either accompany or constitute key elements of the liturgies. This includes gathering songs, acclamations, psalmody, responses, intercessions, processionals, and songs for reflection. Secondly, the chants give voice to the assembly and enable each worshiper to participate actively in the prayer.

The daily liturgies, in turn, are strategically positioned in the rhythm of the day and of the week. The day begins and ends with a celebration of one of the hours of prayer. Another hour marks the day's midpoint. As a result, the singing of the chants permeates the entire structure and meaning of the pilgrimage experience.[56]

The significance of the position of the chants and of the liturgies in terms of *rhythm* raises another significant aspect of the chants. That aspect is the organic and temporal rootedness of music and of ritual. Victor Turner recognized that ritual is not only a cultural, but also an

---

[54] TURNER, "Symbols and Social Experience," 12-13.

[55] TURNER, "Symbols and Social Experience," 13.

[56] During my visit to Taizé in the spring of 1996, I also witnessed the custom of using one of the Taizé chants as the prayer before meals. Two of the three daily meals followed one of the daily liturgies. In this way, the prayer which occurred in the liturgies in the great Church of Reconciliation was carried into the other rituals of the day in a tangible way through the singing of the chants.

organic phenomenon. In observing the specific connection between music and organic life, Susanne K. Langer points out that the same principle that organizes all vital activity – rhythm – organizes music into the semblance of organic movement. However, when Langer speaks of rhythm, she does not mean simply the periodicity or regular recurrence of sounds or events. Rather, she explains, rhythm results when the human mind organizes the recurrent sounds or events into a temporal form.[57]

The concept of rhythm is more a relation between tensions than a matter of equal divisions of time, as in musical meter. It is a recurring pattern of setting up new tensions by resolving former ones. Therefore, such musical tensions as harmonic progressions and the resolution of dissonances serve as rhythmic agents. This pattern occurs, not only in music, but also in ritual activity, and in such physiological processes as breathing and the heartbeat, and simpler metabolisms.[58] As a rhythmic agent, ritual music provides a link between our physical existence and our ritualizing by expressing the rhythmic continuity that is the basis of organic unity and change.[59]

The final consideration regarding the positional dimension of the chants is the location of their performance. The singing of the chants occurs in the great Church of Reconciliation which is positioned both physically and existentially at the center of the pilgrimage experience. The brothers, in turn, are positioned in the center of the church. The music-making, like the icons and candles placed within the church, contributes to an experience of the building as a sacred space. That is, singing the Taizé chants pervades the ritual prayer to such an extent that it can be said to create a sonic environment in which the doing of the ritual takes place. Walter Ong describes this phenomenon as "acoustic space," explaining that besides visual tactile space there is also acoustic space apprehended in terms of sound and echoes.[60] Therefore, just as the presence of an assembly of worshipers can define a space as sacred, and just as the placement of sacred objects can contribute to defining a

---

[57] Susanne K. LANGER, *Feeling and Form: A Theory of Art* (New York: Charles Scribner's Sons, 1953), 126. Langer's comment is another instance of the interpretive approach also used by Chauvet and Lawler which focuses on the importance of the subject in the creation of a symbol's meaning.

[58] LANGER, *Feeling and Form*, 127-129.

[59] LANGER, *Feeling and Form*, 127.

[60] ONG, *The Presence of the Word*, 163.

space as sacred,[61] so too, the singing of the Taizé chants can create a sonic environment which contributes to apprehending the Taizé church building as sacred space.

Furthermore, by providing this sonic environment of sacred space, ritual music-making, that is, active involvement in singing, playing, dancing, listening, or moving with the rhythms of music – creates a space of ideal time which allows for an experience of the already/not yet of ritual. That is, the music allows the worshiper to step outside of *chronos* into a space "between and betwixt,"[62] for the duration of the music-making. In this space, the music provides an experience of transcending barriers, not only between pilgrims, but also between the human and the divine. In this sense, Taizé liturgy provides worshipers with sacred symbols and cultural structures, e.g. the Berthier chants, which can facilitate communion with the God of Jesus Christ.

Thus the activity of singing provides both aspects of anti-structure and generativity which, although enacted within the liturgical setting, lends motion to the overall pilgrimage process. By situating pilgrims in an activity where everyone can join in singing despite differences defined by social structures, the music-making – in the act of singing – contributes to the elimination of those structures as boundaries.

In addition, by engaging the participation of the pilgrims, the music-making provides the generative dimension which enables the pilgrims to negotiate connections and become integrated into the group in which they have begun taking an active part. In this way, the activity of music-making becomes the location for the negotiation of reconciliation and the building of "communitas."

Kelleher points out that questions which inquire about the exegetical, operational, and positional dimensions of symbols "disclose a position which believes that verbal or textual language, although a very significant mediator of meaning, is only one part of a complex system of meaning when it is employed in ritual."[63] Such an observation reflects Turner's view that "texts not only animate and are animated by contexts but are processually inseverable from them."[64]

---

[61] See *Environment and Art in Catholic Worship,* 2, 28, and 63.

[62] The phrase is used by Arnold van Gennep to describe the experience of liminality.

[63] KELLEHER, "Liturgical Theology," 14.

[64] TURNER, "Process, System, and Symbol," 151. These conclusions regarding the interplay of text, as ritual symbol, with other ritual symbols corresponds with the conclusions of semioticians such as Willem Speelman and Armen Marsoobian who interpret the texts as part of a larger network of meaning. See chapter three.

Employing Turner's three dimensions of significance to interpret Taizé liturgy as a symbolic process and Berthier's chants as ritual symbol makes it possible to study some of the aspects involved when Taizé music is sung within a ritual context. However, it is not possible to exhaust all the potential meanings which might be generated within the ritual context. There are two reasons for this. The first is because music-making is symbolizing activity of subjects operating from within particular experience-domains. The second is that it is symbolizing activity to which an infinite complex of interpretants is linked.[65]

The pilgrimage setting at Taizé provides structures which tap the potential of ritual to create, during the pilgrimage process, an experience of provisional reconciliation and "communitas." However, the ultimate purpose of Taizé rituals reaches far beyond that. For as liminality is "the creative fond not only for ritual but for culture in general,"[66] so the symbolic "rehearsal" of behavior where distinctions of wealth, status, and denomination are reversed, reinterpreted, or replaced – mediated through the singing of the chants – provides the possibility of imagining a church and a culture where this unity can one day be realized. In this way singing Berthier's chants can be understood as symbolic activity mediating meaning on four levels: liturgy, pilgrimage, church, and culture.

Conclusions

This chapter has examined singing the Berthier chants as symbolic activity within the context of Taizé liturgy and the Taizé pilgrimage process. Several conclusions can be drawn from this analysis. The first is that Taizé prayer is part of a larger set of rituals which we have called the Taizé pilgrimage process. This process involves the interaction of a community of brothers and international pilgrims. Secondly, Taizé liturgy is a symbolic process which involves the interaction of a complexus of symbols that mediate the Christian identity of those who participate in the liturgies at the great Church of Reconciliation. Thirdly, the Taizé pilgrimage process enables pilgrims to enter into a liminal state that situates them outside the ordinariness of their everyday lives. This liminality provides for "anti-structural moments of reversal" which suspend

---

[65] See NATTIEZ, *Music and Discourse,* 8-10.
[66] GRIMES, *Beginnings in Ritual Studies,* 149.

social barriers and promote an experience of "communitas" and reconciliation which is at the source of unity and universality.

In addition, several aspects of Turner's ritual theory enable us to interpret the role of Berthier's chants in the Taizé liturgies. Turner's three
dimensions of significance provide a method for interpreting how
Berthier's music interacts with other ritual symbols in the generation of
meaning. In addition, they make it possible to interpret music-making's
ability to structure the worshiping assembly, negotiate relationships, and
mediate Christian identity in the Taizé liturgies.

Victor Turner's method of processual symbolic analysis focuses on ritual as meaningful performance. In keeping with that approach, this
study has thus far concerned itself with an analysis of Taizé music as
symbolic action. The following chapter will pursue this investigation a
step further by using J.L. Austin's performative language theory to investigate the role of music-making as ritual speech acts.

CHAPTER FIVE

INTERPRETING TAIZÉ PRAYER IN LIGHT OF J.L. AUSTIN'S PERFORMATIVE LANGUAGE THEORY

Introduction

Examining several theories and theologies of symbol in chapter three and Turner's ritual theory in chapter four has surfaced questions regarding the role of language in ritual, and the possibility of treating music as a type of language. Chapter three considered the argument that, since ritual is more closely akin to the arts than to propositional discourse, the language of ritual can be described as exhibitive rather than as assertive. Chapter four considered Turner's method of processual symbolic analysis as a way to approach ritual music-making as symbolic activity."[1]

Since ritual is a combination of both "articulate speech and purposeful action,"[2] an approach which views ritual language as action can provide a framework for interpreting music-making as an example of ritual speech acts. J.L. Austin's performative language theory provides an important perspective on ritual language because it is built on the premise that, in certain instances, language as action takes precedence over language as assertion. This insight is important for investigating ritual music's power to generate meaning because it provides the possibility of locating meaning in articulations other than assertions or truth claims. For if, as Kramer asserts, "meaning begins with (forms around, clings to) a truth claim (implicit or explicit, real or fictive), then music has no meaning in the ordinary sense."[3] If, however, meaning can be found, not only in a grid of assertions, but embedded in "a field of humanly significant actions,"[4] then there is the possibility of using performative language theory to locate meaning in ritual music-making.

In order to use performative language theory to interpret music, it is necessary to justify approaching music as a type of language. Jean-Jacques

---

[1] TURNER, "Process, System, and Symbol," 151.
[2] WHEELOCK, "The Problem of Ritual Language," 50.
[3] KRAMER, *Music as Cultural Practice*, 5.
[4] KRAMER, *Music as Cultural Practice*, 6.

Nattiez has observed that "since music is not, after all, language in the lit-eral sense, the use of linguistic theory in musicology is always metaphori-cal, so that its value is heuristic … "[5]

Justin London has used speech act analysis to interpret musical struc-tures as compositional utterances made by composers. He argues that, "as a result of our enculturated belief that music is a kind of language, we can and often do treat music as a linguistic phenomenon. That is, we acquire our mechanisms for dealing with intentional communicative behavior through our acquisition of a linguistic framework."[6] In other words, London believes that it is possible to use speech act analysis to interpret music because language is the prototypical framework we have adopted in order to deal with other kinds of meaningful communicative behavior.[7]

London explains that it is possible to describe musical structures in terms of language and linguistic behavior because a MUSIC IS LAN-GUAGE metaphor[8] structures the actions a listener performs in appre-hending music. As long as this metaphor is operative, it is possible to treat a composer and his or her works in the same way in which we would treat a speaker and his or her utterances.[9] This metaphor, Lon-don explains, is acquired in musical childhood and becomes so estab-lished in the way a person learns to listen to music that it becomes wholly transparent. As a result, a person takes his or her knowledge structure of language and maps it onto a musical target. However, the listener is unaware of the fact that the MUSIC IS LANGUAGE METAPHOR functions as a basic conceptual metaphor since this type

---

[5] Jean-Jacques NATTIEZ, *Fondements d'une sémiologie de la musique* (Paris: Union Générale d'Editions, 1975), 400. Cited in Francis SPARSHOTT, "Aesthetics of Music," in *What Is Music? An Introduction to the Philosophy of Music,* ed. Philip ALPERSON (Univer-sity Park, Pennsylvania: The Pennsylvania State University Press, 1987), 79.

[6] Justin LONDON, "Musical and Linguistic Speech Acts," *The Journal of Aesthetics and Art Criticism* 54 (Winter 1996): 49.

[7] LONDON, "Musical and Linguistic Speech Acts," 49.

[8] LONDON, "Musical and Linguistic Speech Acts," 50. Throughout his essay, Lon-don types all phrases referring to metaphors in capitals according to the notation used by George LAKOFF and Mark JOHNSON in such works as *Metaphors We Live By* (Chicago: University of Chicago Press, 1980; and *More Than Cool Reason: A Field Guide to Poetic Metaphor* (Chicago: University of Chicago Press, 1989). When speaking of metaphor, London does not mean the figure of speech which can be described as an abbreviated simile. Rather, he views ordinary thinking and acting as fundamentally metaphorical.

[9] LONDON, "Musical and Linguistic Speech Acts," 49-50.

of metaphor is shared by members of a culture and usually used unconsciously and automatically.[10]

One of the advantages of the MUSIC IS LANGUAGE metaphor is that is allows us to evaluate musical gestures as we would linguistic gestures. In his own work, London uses the MUSIC IS LANGUAGE metaphor in order to be able to interpret musical structures as compositional utterances made by a composer/speaker. His purpose is to recover the composer's intent in choosing a particular musical gesture in a particular musical context. In this chapter, we are adopting London's notion of the MUSIC IS LANGUAGE metaphor in order to be able to interpret music-making in the liturgy as speech acts in light of the performative language theory of J.L. Austin.

J.L. AUSTIN'S PERFORMATIVE LANGUAGE THEORY

Introduction

In his book, *How to Do Things with Words,* the British philosopher, J. L. Austin, offers a key insight when he points out that the uttering of a sentence can be the doing of an action.[11] Initially, Austin made distinctions between statements that represented a situation and those which effected a situation. According to his theory, every speech act consists of a "locutionary act," an "illocutionary act," and a "perlocutionary act." The first is the simple production of an utterance; the second is the effect the speaker intends the utterance to produce in the hearer, and the third is the actual effect the sentence has on the hearer.[12] Later in his career, Austin came to see that all utterances have a performative aspect. In other words, the speaking of a sentence is the doing of an action.[13]

While subsequent philosophers have further nuanced Austin's categories and distinctions, they are in general agreement that there is a category of utterances which not only says something but actually does

---

[10] LONDON, "Musical and Linguistic Speech Acts," 51. Examples London offers to support his thesis include such common statements as "The principal theme is *stated* in the violins" and "The flute *answers* the *guestioning* oboe."

[11] John Langshaw AUSTIN, *How to Do Things with Words* (Cambridge, Massachusetts: Harvard University Press, 1962), 5.

[12] WHEELOCK, "The Problem of Ritual Language," 52.

[13] WHEELOCK, "the Problem of Ritual Language," 52-53.

something in the saying. Such a conclusion has significant ramifications for ritual studies. In the first place, it acknowledges the fact that the purpose of language goes beyond the simple utterance of propositions which can be proven true or false. Secondly, it provides a framework for looking at the function of liturgical language in a new way.

In his own research and analysis, G.J. Warnock nuanced Austin's performative language theory by saying that "*sometimes* saying is doing."[14] Distinguishing those cases which count as doing from those which don't depends on conventions in virtue of which saying counts as doing. These conventions are extra-linguistic.[15]

John Searle continued to develop the work begun by J.L. Austin by focusing on the absolute centrality of the concept of the speech act in the analysis of language. For Searle, the unit of linguistic communication is not the symbol or word or sentence, but "the production or issuance of the symbol or word or sentence in the performance of the speech act."[16] Furthermore, Searle reaffirms Austin's point that it is the illocutionary force of an utterance – language's power to produce the intended effect in the act of speaking – that is the most important concept for analyzing speech acts.

In analyzing the illocutionary force in speech acts, John Searle makes some important distinctions. He explains that each sentence has a propositional indicator and an illocutionary force indicator. It is the illocutionary force indicator with which he is concerned in looking at statements as speech acts. He explains that the illocutionary force indicator shows what illocutionary act the speaker is performing in uttering the sentence. He lists as devices which serve as these illocutionary force indicators the following: word order, stress, intonation contour, punctuation, the mood of the verb, and the so-called performative verbs. He adds that often the context of the actual speech situations makes the illocutionary force clear without invoking it explicitly. For example, a speaker's tone of voice may give his statement the force of a warning, without his having to begin by saying, "I warn you ..."[17]

---

[14] Geoffrey James WARNOCK, "Some Types of Performative Utterance," in *Essays on J.L. Austin,* ed. Isaiah BERLIN, et al. (London: Oxford University Press, 1973), 69.

[15] WARNOCK, "Some Types of Performative Utterance," 73.

[16] John R. SEARLE, *Speech Acts: An Essay in the Philosophy of Language* (Cambridge: Cambridge University Press, 1969), 16.

[17] SEARLE, *Speech Acts: An Essay in the Philosophy of Language*, 30.

Elsewhere Searle reiterates this point in another way when he says:

> The principle that the meaning of a sentence is entirely determined by the meanings of its meaningful parts I take as obviously true; what is not so obviously true, however, is that these include more than words (or morphemes) and surface word-order. The meaningful components of a sentence include also its *deep syntactic structure* and the *stress* and *intonation contour* of its utterance. Words and word-order are not the only elements which determine meaning (emphasis added).[18]

To summarize John Searle's point, performative language theory acknowledges that in certain instances utterances possess what has been termed "illocutionary force," the power to effect what is being stated. This force is produced not simply by the words or the word order, but also by deep syntactic structure, stress, and intonation-contour. Lastly, Jacques Derrida's critique of Austin's speech act theory provides a decisive corrective when he points out that all acts of communication presuppose the possibility of being repeated in new contexts. In other words, in order to function at all, a speech act must be *iterable*. This means that the speech act is capable of functioning in situations other than the occasion of its production, among persons other than those involved in its original production.[19]

This focus on the iterability or repeatability of all acts of communication is pertinent to an analysis of ritual performance since, by its very nature ritual is behavior which displays observable repetition in its structural and chronological framework.[20] In addition, by its nature ritual involves communicating some message by means of a dynamic interaction of several symbol systems. Within this context, ritual communication, whether it be in the form of speaking, singing, or gesturing is intimately and essentially connected with the action context of the ritual. As a result, ritual activity becomes not just an instrument for conveying ideas, but a means to accomplish the ends of the ritual. That is, ritual performance is an instance when saying something counts as

---

[18] John R. SEARLE, "Austin on Locutionary and Illocutionary Acts," in *Essays on J.L. Austin*, ed. Isaiah BERLIN, et al. (London: Oxford University Press, 1973), 151.

[19] KRAMER, *Music as Cultural Practice*, 8. See also Jacques DERRIDA, *Margins of Philosophy*, trans. Alan BASS (Chicago: The Chicago University Press, 1982), 307-330. Stanley FISH also discusses this at length in his essay "With the Compliments of the Author: Reflections on Austin and Derrida," in *Critical Inquiry* 8 (1982): 693-722.

[20] George S. WORGUL, Jr., "Ritual," in *The New Dictionary of Sacramental Worship*, ed. Peter E. FINK, (Collegeville: The Liturgical Press, 1990), 1101.

doing because by its nature ritual includes those extra-linguistic conventions which enable saying to count as doing.[21]

Implications for Liturgical Language

Before using performative language theory as a tool for interpreting liturgical music, it will be helpful to examine efforts which have already been made to interpret liturgical language using J.L. Austin's theory. This section will consider efforts by Wade T. Wheelock, Jean Ladrière, and Joseph Schaller to use performative language theory as an interpretive tool.

Wade T. Wheelock has taken Austin's theory and John Searle's development of it and applied his conclusions to the study of ritual language. As a result of his synthesis, Wheelock defines ritual language as "that set of utterances which is intimately and essentially connected with the action context of a ritual. Ritual language is not just an instrument for conveying ideas, but is directly used in accomplishing the ends of the ritual operation."[22]

Wheelock's definition identifies the key distinction between propositional discourse and ritual language: the first is a locutionary act while the second is an illocutionary act. According to Wheelock, the most essential difference between ritual utterances and ordinary language is the purpose of the two. On the one hand, the purpose of making a propositional statement is to communicate information that the hearer doesn't already know. Ritual utterances, on the other hand, are speech acts that convey little or no information. Rather, they are meant to create and allow participation in a known and repeatable situation. Instead of information, repetition is the norm and metaphors and ambiguity abound.[23]

Wheelock reasons that if the conditions governing the performance of a ritual speech act are different from ordinary speech, then the purpose or illocutionary force of the two must be different. In effect, Wheelock concludes, the language of any ritual must be primarily understood and described as *situating* rather than *informing speech.*[24]

What does Wheelock mean when he says that ritual language is situating speech? He means that the speaking of the text presents the situation, expresses and actually helps to create the situation, and/or facilitates

---

[21] WARNOCK, "Some Types of Performative Utterance," 73.
[22] WHEELOCK, "The Problem of Ritual Language," 50.
[23] WHEELOCK, "The Problem of Ritual Language," 56-59.
[24] WHEELOCK, "The Problem of Ritual Language," 59.

the recognition of the situation. Furthermore, situating speech has the capacity to constantly repeat the transformations it brings about. Situations represent "being" or "action" rather than simply knowing. They must and can be concretely realized at every repetition, since they are the chief means by which the physical and cultural entities unite in the production of a situation.[25]

In his efforts to discover how liturgical language works, Jean Ladrière has also applied the findings of J.L. Austin and John Searle to his own linguistic analysis. Ladrière's concern is to discover ways in which linguistic analysis can be used to understand the expression of Christian faith in liturgy.[26] In order to do so, he identifies a threefold performativity of liturgical language: that of an "existential induction," that of an "institution," and that of a "presentification."[27]

By existential induction, Ladrière means an operation by means of which "an expressive form awakens in the person using it a certain affective disposition which opens up existence to a specific field of reality."[28] An effect is produced. The question is what kind of language function enables it to produce an effect. Ladrière's explanation is that the function of language is not to indicate the existence of the attitude nor to describe it, but to *speak the attitude* [emphasis added]. This is done through the use of personal pronouns and such characteristic performative verbs as "pray" and "give thanks." In other words, the language makes the attitude exist by virtue of the illocutionary act underlying its enunciation.[29]

Ladrière refers to the second aspect of performativity as an institution. By institution, Ladrière means the effect whereby liturgical language not only disposes individuals to welcome that which it suggests, but, by the same means, institutes a community. In other words, language is the location in which and the instrument by means of which the community is constituted.[30]

Ladrière considers the third aspect, presentification, to be the most fundamental aspect of the performativity of liturgical language. He

---

[25] WHEELOCK, "The Problem of Ritual Language," 59-63.

[26] Jean LADRIÈRE, "The Performativity of Liturgical Language," in *Liturgical Experience of Faith*, ed. H. SCHMIDT and David N. POWER, Concilium series, no. 82 (New York: Herder and Herder, 1973), 50.

[27] LADRIÈRE, "The Performativity of Liturgical Language," 55.

[28] LADRIÈRE, "The Performativity of Liturgical Language," 56.

[29] LADRIÈRE, "The Performativity of Liturgical Language," 56-57.

[30] LADRIÈRE, "The Performativity of Liturgical Language," 58-59.

explains it this way: "By all those acts which it effects, this language makes present for the participants, not as a spectacle, but as a reality whose efficacy they take into their very own life, that about which it speaks and which it effects in diverse ways ... "[31]

According to Ladrière, Christian liturgy, as ritual activity engaging language, produces this effect by means of repetition, proclamation, and sacramentality.[32] By repetition, Ladrière means that the liturgy repeats texts which announce events yet to occur or which have already occurred in Jesus Christ. This repetition is not a mere quotation of the past, but the resumption into speech acts of today of words written or spoken in the past. In this way, by re-forming the words which announce the mystery of salvation, the community actively enters into that mystery.[33]

For Ladrière, the confession of faith is the culmination of this process of repetition. That is, it is an act of proclamation whose illocutionary power is that of an attestation, ratification and commitment. In declaring the mystery of salvation, it becomes active and present.[34]

Ladrière admits that linguistic analysis cannot suffice to explain sacramental performativity. However, he points out that language is a kind of structuring field which enables faith to express itself in accordance with the exigencies of the reality to which it corresponds.[35]

As a result of this three-fold performativity, therefore, liturgical language expresses faith and awakens its full flowering in the community constituted by its very expression and also in the individual. Thus it acts as a kind of structuring field which gives voice to faith, echoes the Word made flesh, and becomes the location of his presence.[36]

Building on the work of Wheelock and Ladrière, Joseph Schaller points out that performative language theory is a helpful tool in liturgical studies because it provides a method which "focuses the question of the relationship of *meaning* and *text* in the context of ritual,[37] an approach often more productive in the study of liturgy than textual

---

[31] LADRIÈRE, "The Performativity of Liturgical Language," 59-60.

[32] LADRIÈRE, "The Performativity of Liturgical Language," 60-61.

[33] LADRIÈRE, "The Performativity of Liturgical Language," 60.

[34] LADRIÈRE, "The Performativity of Liturgical Language," 60.

[35] LADRIÈRE, "The Performativity of Liturgical Language," 62.

[36] LADRIÈRE, "The Performativity of Liturgical Language," 62.

[37] In this study, the term "liturgy" is being used as the more specific example of the more general category of "ritual." See the Introduction of this study for more specific qualifications of the terms ritual, worship, and liturgy.

criticism which attends exclusively to the discursive contents of texts."[38] In addition, the theory is pertinent to the study of liturgy because it views language more as "doing" than simply communicating *about* a state of affairs. Rather, a state of affairs is *established* in communicating.[39] By interpreting liturgical language as speech acts, Schaller concludes that the act of pronouncing liturgical texts has the potential to effectively change the existential situation of the participating members of a community.[40]

Because performative language theory focuses primarily on performative rather than propositional discourse, it can be successfully employed to interpret liturgical language as speech acts. By using the MUSIC IS LANGUAGE metaphor outlined by Justin London, it is possible to approach liturgical music-making as a type of liturgical language. Thus, by using linguistic theory metaphorically, it is possible to interpret liturgical music-making as a performative speech act. This possibility will be the subject of the next section of this chapter.

IMPLICATIONS FOR LITURGICAL MUSIC

If, as is evident in the work of Wheelock, Ladrière, and Schaller, several principles of performative language theory can serve as useful tools in investigating the nature of ritual language and its function in the liturgy, these same principles should be able to be applied to an investigation of the nature of ritual music in general and Taizé music in particular. Those principles can be summarized as follows: (1) that speaking an utterance can be the doing of something, since, by virtue of its illocutionary force, language has the power to produce an intended effect, (2) that, because of its illocutionary force, ritual language is situating rather than informing speech; and (3) that the meaningful components of a sentence include deep syntactic structure and the stress and intonation contour of its utterance.

Our intention is to employ these principles in an analysis of Taizé music. Reformulating them to apply to the Taizé chants, they read as follows: (1) that singing the Taizé chants can be the doing of something,

[38] Joseph J. SCHALLER, "Performative Language Theory: An Exercise in the Analysis of Ritual," *Worship* 62 (September 1988), 415.

[39] SCHALLER, "Performative Language Theory," 416.

[40] SCHALLER, "Performative Language Theory," 416.

since by virtue of its illocutionary force, ritual song has the power to produce an intended effect, (2) that, because of its illocutionary force, ritual music is situating rather than informing discourse; and (3) that the meaningful components of a song include deep syntactic structure and the stress and intonation contour of its utterance.

Certain parameters need to be identified before pursuing this analysis. In the first place, although the proclamation of Scripture and the praying of various prayers are an important part of Taizé prayer, the greatest percentage of each liturgy is by design comprised of the singing of the chants. Since the object of this study is the nature of liturgical music, any reference to texts will be to those which serve as the lyrics to the Taizé chants.

Furthermore, the focus of performative language theory is not on language as an object, but language as an activity. Both J.L. Austin and John Searle develop this notion in their writings. Austin's initial insight that the uttering of a sentence can be the doing of something and Searle's point that it is not the symbol or word, but the *production* of the symbol or word that is the unit of linguistic communication indicate that it is the activity of speaking itself that is their central concern. Therefore, just as performative language theory does not focus on language as an object, but as an activity of speaking, so, too, is our focus on the act of music-making rather than on music as an object that can be captured in a written score or in a recording.

In his effort to develop a musical hermeneutics, Lawrence Kramer provides a rationale for applying performative language theory to musical processes when he says:

> Any act of expression or representation can exert illocutionary force provided, first, that the act is iterable and, second, that in being produced the act seeks to affect a flow of events, a developing situation. In their illocutionary dimension, therefore, speech acts exemplify a larger category of expressive acts through which illocutionary forces pass into general circulation. Musical processes clearly count as expressive acts according to the terms just given. If we can learn to recognize them as such, to concretize the illocutionary forces of music as we concretize its harmonic, rhythmic, linear, and formal strategies, we can then go on to interpret musical meaning.[41]

---

[41] KRAMER, *Music as Cultural Practice*, 9.

Based on the criteria Kramer gives for an act of expression to exert illo-cutionary force, liturgical music-making possesses illocutionary force because it is an example of an iterable act which has the potential to affect the flow of the liturgical event. Music-making affects the flow of ritual particularly by means of illocutionary force indicators identified by John Searle, that is, stress and intonation contours. In terms of per-formative language theory, these illocutionary forces are the key to inter-preting musical meaning.

Earlier in this chapter, we argued that performative language theory can be used successfully to interpret ritual music-making because cul-turally music is approached from within linguistic frameworks. At this point, it is helpful to look at additional aspects of J.L. Austin's theory to discover more specifically how music-making can be interpreted as a speech act.

J.L. Austin distinguishes five general categories of speech acts: com-missives, expositives, verdictives, exercitives, and behabitives.[42] The first two, commissives and expositives, are dependent on language because they require the use of tenses or propositional components. For this rea-son, Justin London points out, they cannot be mapped onto music since music cannot fulfill the requirements of tense and/or predication.[43] Commissives are typified by promising. They *commit* a person to doing something. They also include declarations of intention. Expositives, on the other hand, indicate how our utterances fit into a conversation. They are expository and can include such expressions as "I reply," and "I concede."[44]

Verdictives, exercitives, and especially behabitives are less dependent on language and so offer the possibility of being expressed as musical speech acts.[45] Verdictives are typified by giving a verdict, usually by someone in an official capacity such as an umpire, jury, or priest. Similarly, exercitives are the giving of a decision either in favor of or against a course of action.[46] Thus, both verdictives and exercitives require that these speech acts be uttered by someone speaking in a specifically-defined institutional

---

[42] AUSTIN, *How to Do Things with Words*, 150. I have rearranged the order in which Austin discusses these five categories in order to discuss them in terms of their depen-dence on language.

[43] LONDON, "Musical and Linguistic Speech Acts," 56-57.

[44] AUSTIN, "How to Do things with Words," 150-151.

[45] LONDON, "Musical and Linguistic Speech Acts," 56.

[46] AUSTIN, "How to Do things with Words," 152-154.

role, as, for example, speaker-as-umpire or speaker-as-priest.[47] In Justin London's judgment, musical gestures cannot be described in these terms because composers do not fulfill these institutional roles.[48] However, in the liturgy, worshipers and other ministers can take on specifically-defined institutional roles in the singing of certain ritual elements. Therefore, in the case of ritual music, musical speech acts have the potential to operate as verdictives and exercitives.

However, the fifth category, behabitives appear to offer the greatest potential for being mapped onto music. Austin describes behabitives as a very miscellaneous group that have to do with attitudes and *social behavior.* Examples include apologizing, commending, thanking, and blessing.[49]

There are two reasons why behabitives offer the best possibility for treating music gestures as speech acts. The first is that behabitives often involve little or no propositional content, and as the coins of social exchange are usually produced in the present tense, or in a tenseless fashion. The second is the fact that behabitives are strongly marked by intonation and other paralinguistic features. In other words, behabitives involve those musical qualities of pitch, tone of voice, loudness, rhythm, and articulation which specify the illocutionary act.[50] These are the very features which John Searle pointed out are among the illocutionary indicators in speech acts.[51]

The use of stress and variation of voice pitch has always assisted in the communication of meaning, even in spoken utterance. Once again, Joseph Gelineau's comment on the role of musical elements in ritual speech in pre-Christian and early Christian usage provides an important insight:

> As soon as speech turned to poetry, or when public and ceremonial speaking was involved, rhythmic and melodic features were incorporated which today would be classified as musical or at least pre-musical. Music and singing could be present even though none of the vocabulary associated with musical performance might be met with.[52]

---

[47] LONDON, "Musical and Linguistic Speech Acts," 57.
[48] LONDON, "Musical and Linguistic Speech Acts," 57.
[49] AUSTIN, *How to Do things with Words,* 151, 159.
[50] LONDON, "Musical and Linguistic Speech Acts," 57.
[51] See John SEARLE, 17, n. 18 above.
[52] GELINEAU, "Music and Singing," 444.

In other words, the incorporation of rhythmic and melodic features is more likely to occur in situations which can be described as ritual activity. The result is the enhancement of the speech act by what performative language theory calls the illocutionary force indicators of stress and intonation. Because music possesses these components, it is an important partner with language in the communication of meaning.

Returning, then, to the three principles of performative language theory which can elucidate the role of music in ritual, we will begin by investigating how singing the Taizé chants can be said to be the doing of something in the particular ritual called Christian liturgy.[53]

First Principle: Liturgical Singing as Doing

The "Constitution on the Liturgy" states that the purpose of Christian liturgy is twofold: the "glory of God and the sanctification of the faithful."[54] The issue is whether the singing of the Taizé chants within the Taizé liturgies can be described as "doing something" that in some way accomplishes one or both of the purposes of the liturgy.

Like the category of speech acts which J.L. Austin calls behabitives, singing the Taizé chants is the speaking of attitudes. In other words, singing the chants draws the worshipers into the action of praying and becomes the vehicle for speaking attitudes of prayer. As a result, the action of singing is fundamentally confessional because, in the context of the liturgy, it speaks or expresses faith in God and in the possibility of a relationship with him. The repetition and accessibility of the chants facilitates the confession of faith and structures its expression.

According to Ladrière's notion of existential induction, it is possible to say that such singing of attitudes of praise, thanksgiving, contrition, and petition awaken in the person singing "a certain affective disposition which opens up existence to a specific field of reality."[55] The effect which is produced, through the repetition of singing the attitude, is a gradual transformation whereby the singer becomes a person who, for example, is thankful or contrite. When Don Saliers asserts that liturgical song has the power of transformation by forming over time, the

---

[53] See chapter four for a more detailed discussion of the two types of Taizé liturgies.
[54] *Sacrosanctum Concilium,* 10, 112.
[55] LADRIÈRE, "The Performativity of Liturgical Language," 56.

imagination and affectivity of the Christian assembly, he is referring to the illocutionary dimension of singing without using the term.[56]

In light of performative language theory, then, we can say that singing such Christian attitudes of prayer is an act of prayer which gives glory to God. In addition, by enabling participation in a known and repeatable act, singing the chants can bring about transformation, that is, the sanctification of the worshipers, by forming them, over time, in those Christian dispositions which are expressed in the act of singing.

Attitudes of praise, thanksgiving, contrition, and petition may be expressed through the singing of the chants by individual worshipers, even in cases where the language is unfamiliar to the singers. This is possible because, in the case of ritual speech acts, the language – e.g. Latin – is not the unique and often not even the primary means of conveying the ritual's message.[57] Rather, ritual activity is set in motion by the interaction of a complexus of symbols such as Scripture, icons, the music, the community of brothers, and postures of reverence or meditation which together mediate meaning.

It is possible to say that in the case of the Taizé chants, understanding the language is not always critical because the most distinguishing feature of ritual utterances as speech acts is that they convey little or no information. In the case of liturgy, the ritual includes memorized sets of utterances or traditionally prescribed patterns that are known or accessible to the worshipers before they engage in the prayer. The actual singing of the Taizé chants, for example, does not convey information that the participants do not already know. This is because the purpose in singing them is different from the purpose of ordinary language utterances.[58]

Second Principle: Liturgical Singing as Situating Speech

Wheelock's thesis that the language of ritual must be primarily understood as *situating* rather than *informing* speech is especially pertinent to liturgical song. In performing the Taizé chants, members of the assembly create an acoustic space in which they become *situated*. The music

---

[56] See SALIERS, "The Integrity of Sung Prayer," 293. Salier's argument is presented in greater detail in chapter three.

[57] WHEELOCK, "The Problem of Ritual Language," 57.

[58] WHEELOCK, "The Problem of Ritual Language," 58-59.

which they make fills the space and surrounds those who are present within it.

Because of their structure and mode of performance, the Taizé chants as music can be said to situate the assembly in very specific ways. In the first place, the chants provide a sonic environment in which the assembly engages in prayer. Walter Ong, whose idea of "acoustic space"[59] was noted in chapter four in discussing the positional dimension of symbols, describes the dynamic this way:

> Habits of auditory synthesis give rise to a special sense of space itself. For besides visual-tactile space there is also acoustic space (which, through voice and hearing, has its own associations with the kinesthetic and tactual not quite the same as the kinesthetic and tactual associations of sight). We can apprehend space in terms of sound and echoes ... Space thus apprehended has qualities of its own. It is not spread out in front of us as a field of vision but diffused around us. Sound ... can be apprehended from any direction, so that the hearer is *situated* [emphasis added] in a center of an acoustic field, not in front of it (so that it is indeed hardly a field).[60]

This ability of music to *situate* worshipers in a sonic environment provides an experience, not only of the worship space, but also of the activity of music-making and of the worshiping assembly engaged in that activity. It is in this way that singing as situating speech creates and allows participation in the liturgy.

But more can be said than simply saying that the making of the music situates the assembly in a sonic environment. The characteristics of that sonic environment can be further delineated as to content and form. An examination of a specific Taizé chant will facilitate the demonstration of this point.

Wait for the Lord, whose day is near.

---

[59] See chapter four for additional discussion of Ong's notion.
[60] ONG, *The Presence of the Word*, 163.

Musique: Jacques Berthier – © Ateliers et Presses de Taizé, 71250 Taizé-Communauté, France

Fig. 1. "Wait for the Lord"[61]

The ostinato "Wait for the Lord" situates the assembly in an attitude of patient expectancy by various musical and textual means. The eight measure response is sung at a slow tempo, designated *lento* in the score. This tempo creates an unhurried atmosphere which is reinforced by the repetition of the phrase, "Wait for the Lord," sung twice in the eight measures. Furthermore, the choice of note values – two dotted half notes, eight half notes, two quarter notes, and two eighth notes indicates a preference for more sustained, that is, longer, note values.

In both instances, the attitudes of waiting, hoping, and expectation are clearly articulated by a great economy of text. Key words such as "wait" and "Lord" are on the longest notes; the insignificant article, "the," is sung to the shortest note value, the eighth note. Thus the attitude of patient waiting is not disturbed by a "busyness" of text or musical construction.

"Wait for the Lord" is an example of one of the variations in the ostinato genre which includes the possibility of employing verses. However, in this case, the piece is so designed that the verses are not sung simultaneously with the refrain as is the case with such pieces as "Laudate Dominum" and "Bonum est confidere."[62] Instead, the assembly waits while the cantor sings a verse before repeating the ostinato response. In this way, the musical form expresses the text and the spiritual attitude thus articulated.

The instrumental accompaniment, as well as the choral humming which accompanies the cantor's verses are characterized by such sustained

---

[61] *Chants de Taizé,* no. 2. See Berthier, vol. 2, vocal, 78, for the original text of this piece. In the version printed here in Fig. 1, the last phrase is "keep watch, take heart," instead of the original which was "be strong, take heart!" This is further evidence of the practice of constantly revising the chants even after many years of singing.

[62] BERTHIER, *Music from Taizé,* vol. 1, vocal, 10-11; BERTHIER, *Music from Taizé,* vol. 2, vocal, 12-13. See chapter two for discussion of the two methods for singing ostinati with verses.

notes as whole notes, dotted half notes and half notes. This type of accompaniment further reinforces the slowness of the tempo and embodies a kind of patient waiting.

The greatest amount of movement in the piece is found in the solo parts, both the cantor's verses and the instrumental solos. The cantor's verses include scripture texts which serve as gentle encouragement. There are more quarter notes and eighth notes both in the cantor's verses and in the instrumental solos than either in the assembly's response or in the keyboard accompaniment. This serves to alleviate the slow pace of the song and provides a sense of forward movement to the piece. The possibility of an indeterminate amount of repetition of the ostinato further situates the assembly in an attitude of hopeful waiting and mutual encouragement.

The second flute solo (see Fig. 2) provided for "Wait for the Lord," is a good example of the preponderance of shorter note values in the solo parts.

Musique: Jacques Berthier – © Ateliers et Presses de Taizé, 71250 Taizé-Communauté, France

Fig. 2. Flute solo for "Wait for the Lord"[63]

Whereas the refrain sung by the assembly (see Fig. 1) includes only two eighth notes in the melodic line, the flute solo (see Fig. 2) includes twenty-seven eighth notes in the same eight measure segment.

In general, the strong rhythmic movement and repetition of the chants have the ability to draw individual members into its movement, thereby enabling them to become a part of the whole. In this way, the singing of the chants situates the singers in a community thus bonded by the act of singing. This phenomenon corresponds to Ladrière's description of *institution,* his term for the second aspect of performativity of liturgical language. Ladrière explains:

> Language is not the expression of a community constituted before it and apart from it and is not the description of what such a community would

---

[63] BERTHIER, *Music from Taizé,* vol. 2, instrumental, 108.

be, but the *location* [emphasis added] in which and the instrument by means of which the community is constituted. In so far as it gives to all participants – as co-locutors – the chance to take on the same acts, it establishes between them that operative reciprocity which constitutes the reality of a community.[64]

This community aspect is an essential element both in an understanding of language as a speech act and of an understanding of ritual music. Just as language becomes the location and instrument of community, so too, the making of the music is the means by which the community is constituted.

Music-making embodies the experience of community by providing the assembly with a physical and psychological experience of unity and harmony. Not only the sense of hearing and seeing, but the intellect, emotions and the entire body are taken up into the rhythms, melody, and harmony of the music. The music thus mediates an embodied experience of that community or "People of God." In no other experience of liturgical art can each individual member of the assembly be so drawn into an awareness of and a participation in the larger group.

This experience of community in many ways corresponds to Turner's notion of *communitas* discussed in chapter four. Through participation in the singing, the worshipers experience a oneness whereby distinctions of wealth, class, gender, race, and denomination are suspended in favor of unity and harmony.[65] In this way, the singing of the Taizé chants does more than communicate *about* a given state of affairs. Rather, as Schaller has pointed out, a state of affairs is established *in* communicating.[66] Furthermore, it is this establishment of a "state of affairs" which creates and allows participation in a known and repeatable situation.[67]

Lastly, liturgical music-making – that is active involvement in singing, playing, dancing, listening, or moving with the rhythms of liturgical song – situates worshipers in the experience of the already/not yet of ritual. This is possible because the situation thus enacted in liturgy is idealized.[68] In the case of Taizé, for example, the situation of unity, although experienced in the liturgy, is not yet fully achieved.

---

[64] LADRIÈRE, "The Performativity of Liturgical Language," 59.
[65] See TURNER, *The Ritual Process,* 83, 114.
[66] See SCHALLER, "Performative Language Theory," 416.
[67] SCHALLER, "Performative Language Theory," 416.
[68] WHEELOCK, "The Problem of Ritual Language," 105.

Third Principle: The Illocutionary Force Indicators

Thus far we have examined how singing the Taizé chants as liturgical songs can be said to speak attitudes of prayer and situate the worshiping assembly so that they can participate both individually and corporately in the liturgical action. In the particular case of the Taizé chants, this is possible, even when the text of the chants is in an unfamiliar language, because the purpose of the singing is not to convey information. Rather, the purpose is to invite and enable participation in a known and repeatable situation.

Furthermore, J.L. Austin's five categories of speech acts provides for the possibility of mapping certain speech acts onto music, particularly music which has the ability to express or "speak" attitudes and involve such social behavior as apologizing, commending, thanking, and blessing. These behabitives serve as "coins of social exchange" and are strongly marked by such musical qualities as stress and intonation. Many of the Taizé chants in unfamiliar languages qualify as behabitives because they speak such attitudes of prayer as praising, thanksgiving, contrition, petition, and confession which, exchanged among the worshipers, produce the intended effect of praising, etc.

However, when the language codes of the Taizé chants are available to the worshipers, those chants will serve even more powerfully to focus the illocutionary force of the singing. In these cases, the music provides the illocutionary force indicators, that is, the heightened stress and intonation contours which, interacting with the text produce the illocutionary effect.

The previous analysis of "Wait for the Lord" was carried out for the purpose of demonstrating how singing the Taizé chants can be situating speech. In the process, the analysis involved attending to the illocutionary force indicators of that ostinato response.

To highlight music's role as an illocutionary force indicator in the wedding of text and music in song, an additional analysis is provided below.

A - do - ra - mus te Chri - ste be - ne - di - ci - mus ti - bi,

qui - a   per   cru - cem   tu - am   re - de - mi - sti   mun - dum,

qui - a   per   cru - cem   tu - am   re - de - mi - sti   mun - dum.

Musique: Jacques Berthier – © Ateliers et Presses de Taizé, 71250 Taizé-Communauté, France

Fig. 3. "Adoramus Te Christe"[69]

The English translation of the Latin text reads as follows: "We adore you, O Christ, and we bless you, because by your cross you have redeemed the world."[70] An analysis of the text reveals that it contains those elements described by J.L. Austin as characteristic of behabitives. For as J.L. Austin explains, behabitives include the notion of reaction to other people's behavior and expressions of attitudes to someone else's past conduct or imminent conduct.[71] The text of the chant is expressing the attitudes of adoration and blessing in response to Christ's having redeemed the world. While the words "we thank" are not explicitly stated, the attitude of gratitude underlies those of adoration and blessing.

The speaking of the text constitutes a speech act since it accomplishes the speaking of the attitudes of adoration, blessing and thanksgiving. However, enhanced by the stress and intonation contour of the music, the syncretic discourse possesses greater illocutionary effect. An analysis

---

[69] BERTHIER, *Music from Taizé*, vol. 2, vocal, 2.

[70] This chant is set only to a Latin text. However, in the 1995 edition of the songbook used at Taizé, a translation of the text is provided in seven languages. This is an example of a Taizé chant whose meaning is interpreted, not only by the Latin text, but through such piecemeal or exegetic interpretations which are provided to assist understanding. See TURNER, "Symbols and Social Experience," 11; COLLINS, "Ritual Symbols," 343.

[71] AUSTIN, *How to Do Things with Words*, 159.

of how the musical elements of stress and intonation contour enhance the meaning of the text will demonstrate how Berthier's music together with the text produce the illocutionary effects of the chant.

In "Adoramus te Christe," the parallelism and brevity of the first two phrases provides a strong focus on the word "Christus" (Christ), which is the object of both verbs, "adoramus" (adore) and "benedicimus" (bless). The repetition of the same pitch and the lowness of the pitch in each voice, provide a weightiness to both phrases. The words, "adoramus te" (we adore you), are sung on the lowest pitch of the song in each voice, a melodic device that parallels such gestures as kneeling or bowing. By contrast, the highest pitches of the first two phrases are for singing the words "Christus" (Christ) and "tibi" (you) in reference to Christ, again a possible melodic device for expressing Christ's exalted position as Son of God.

The syncopated rhythm of the third phrase relieves the heaviness of the first two phrases. The text, "quia per crucem tuam" (because by your cross), is set to a lilting phrase expressing an attitude of joy and wonder without actually using those words.

The fourth phrase, "redemisti mundum" (you have redeemed the world), begins on the lowest pitch of the melody line, the dominant note, and ends on the tonic. Underlying the melodic movement, there is a parallel harmonic movement from dominant to tonic that creates a sense of rest or resolution. The third and fourth phrases are repeated with each single performance of the complete ostinato. Thus, each time the assembly expresses adoration and blessing, they repeat the reason twice.

The linguistic and musical elements work together to express the attitudes of adoration, blessing, faith, and gratitude. Furthermore, several means are employed to reinforce the illocutionary force of the ostinato. For example, in each case, the verbs are placed on the downbeat at the beginning of each new phrase.[72] In addition, the contour of the melody highlights the sense of the text and the underlying attitude. Lastly, the choice of the minor key of f-sharp minor, the use of repeated notes, and

---

[72] This feature of this chant is an example of why Berthier felt that translating the texts of his chants into other languages was not a desirable option. In the case of "Adoramus te Christe," the Latin verb comes first and is sung on the strong beat, that is the downbeat. In English, the pronoun would come first, thereby moving the verb to a weak beat.

the low tessitura[73] provide a somberness which is balanced by the syncopated rhythm and the ascent of the melodic line in three of the four phrases.

As in the case of the first two principles of performative language theory, the third principle regarding the illocutionary force of stress and intonation contour is also influenced by context. The singing of the chant "Adoramus te Christe" interacts with other ritual symbols in the creation of meaning. This includes the fact that the chants are sung by a group of believers who generally can be expected to come from various Christian denominations. Furthermore, as outlined in chapter four, the chant is sung in the context of ritual prayer which includes other chants, prayers, Scripture readings, and the visibility of sacred icons, particularly the Taizé crucifix. As these elements change or are rearranged, the illocutionary power of the singing can also change.

This chapter has examined the performative language theory of J.L. Austin and its possibilities for interpreting liturgical singing at Taizé as a speech act. Because the liturgical prayer at Taizé is ritual activity, the role of language as performative and situating activity has enabled us to interpret the singing of Berthier's chants as an instance when singing is the doing of something. What is accomplished is the speaking of attitudes which, because of their illocutionary power can, over time, bring about the transformation of those who participate in the liturgy. Furthermore, singing the chants situates the worshipers in a sonic environment which draws individual participants into its movement and situates them in a community. Lastly, the musical elements of the chants serve as illocutionary force indicators which give the singing of the chants the power to effect what is being sung.

This chapter has emphasized the fact that the purpose of the liturgy is not to provide information or make assertions, but to allow participation in a known and repeatable situation. The next and final chapter will explore the potential meanings mediated through this participatory activity.

---

[73] Tessitura is a musical term used to describe the range of a vocal compass in which most of a piece is located. It does not include the total range of the piece. So, for example, one may say the tessitura of the soprano was either low or high, depending on where in the range the voice most consistently sang.

CHAPTER SIX

TAIZÉ MUSIC AS A MEDIATION OF ECCLESIAL MEANING

RECAPITULATION

The present study of Taizé music was initiated in order to address two questions: 1) how the act of music-making is intended to work as ritual symbol through its interplay with text and assembly in the production of the ritual event; and 2) what ecclesial meanings might be mediated in the intended ritual process. Chapter one began to address the first question by examining official statements on music's relation to the liturgy as it has been articulated in official church documents and in the corporate responses of professional groups of musicians and liturgists. Chapter two examined Berthier's Taizé chants as a particular case of music interacting with text and assembly in the production of the ritual event. Chapter three examined various theories and theologies of symbol in order to discover in what way the Taizé chants might be operating as ritual symbol. Chapter four drew upon Victor Turner's ritual theory in order to interpret the Taizé pilgrimage experience and the symbolic function of music-making within Taizé liturgies. Chapter five examined aspects of J.L. Austin's performative language theory in order to determine how Taizé music-making might be an example of ritual speech acts.

Thus far I have determined that Berthier's music for Taizé is an example of how music operates as ritual symbol in the liturgy. This chapter will explore potential ecclesial meanings which may be mediated in the celebration of Taizé prayer. This task begins with the premise that there is an integral relationship between the celebration of the liturgy and the generation of theological meaning. This assertion lays the foundation for the subsequent claim that liturgical music-making can be integral to the process of expressing and shaping ecclesial meaning.

The notion that there is a relationship between the church's prayer and the church's theology is certainly not a new idea. What this study intends to argue, however, is that as ritual symbol, liturgical music-making is an integral agent in mediating the church's self-expression and ongoing transformation.

LITURGY AS *THEOLOGIA PRIMA*

The fifth century writer, Prosper of Aquitaine, is generally credited with coining the phrase *legem credendi lex statuat supplicandi,* that is, the law of faith is the law of prayer. Sometimes the phrase has been shortened simply to *lex orandi, lex credendi.* The pre-baptismal catecheses and the post-baptismal mystagogic catecheses of Cyril of Jerusalem, John Chrysostom, and Theodore of Mopsuestia are good examples of how the church's "law of prayer" influenced patristic explanations of the church's "law of belief."[1] The writings of these Fathers indicate that it was not simply in the liturgical texts, but in the ritual whole that the disclosure of theological and spiritual meaning was believed to unfold.[2]

In the early Church, especially in the East, the liturgy was referred to as *theologia prima* while dogmatic speculation was referred to as *theologia secunda.* Furthermore, the first meaning of "orthodoxy" was right praise (*ortho-doxia*) in the liturgy. It is only in the secondary, derived sense that "orthodoxy" came to be understood as right teaching.[3]

Don Saliers explains liturgy as orthodoxy in this way:

> *Ortho-doxa* means right praise to God. *Doxa,* of course, has the wonderful ambiguity of referring both to human belief and to something intrinsic to God: doxa as the divine glory. *Ortho-doxa* is the practice of right ascription of honor and praise and glory to the One to whom all such ascription is due.[4]

The term *orthodoxy,* then, points to one of the two purposes of the liturgy identified in article 10 of *Sacrosanctum Concilium,* to praise and glorify God in the midst of his Church.

---

[1]   See CYRIL of JERUSALEM, "Catechetical Lectures," in *The Faith of the Early Fathers,* vol. 1, trans. W.A. JURGENS, 347-371 (Collegeville: The Liturgical Press, 1970); John CHRYSOSTOM, "Baptismal Catechesis," 99-101 and THEODORE of MOPSUESTIA, "Catechetical Homilies," 81-84, both in *The Faith of the Early Fathers,* vol. 2, trans. W.A. JURGENS (Collegeville: The Liturgical Press, 1979).

[2]   Kevin W. IRWIN, "Liturgical Theology," in *The New Dictionary of Sacramental Theology,* ed. Peter E. FINK, 721-733 (Collegeville: The Liturgical Press, 1990), 722.

[3]   Gerard LUKKEN, "The Unique Expression of Faith in the Liturgy," trans. David SMITH, in *The Liturgical Experience of Faith,* ed. Herman SCHMIDT and David POWER, Concilium: Religion in the Seventies Series, no. 82 (New York: Herder and Herder, 1973), 19.

[4]   Don E. SALIERS, *Worship as Theology: Foretaste of Glory Divine* (Nashville: Abingdon Press, 1994), 40.

By engaging in *ortho-doxy,* or right praise, an assembly is drawn into the ethos of the liturgy and through it comes to know God's glory. This glory is the shared life of glory in God, that is, the divine *perichoresis.*[5] When an assembly of believers participates in the liturgy, then, two dynamics are operative. On one hand, engaging in the liturgy is learning to give to God the glory, or *doxa,* due God's name. On the other hand, giving God the glory by participating in the liturgy as *ortho-doxy* draws the assembly into a participation in the life of this God of glory.[6]

The liturgy, therefore, can be understood as an action which expresses both faith and praise. However, while praise is undoubtedly the climax of the liturgical expression of faith, the ability to fully express this element requires a humanity capable of experiencing reality by engaging the whole person. Scholars such as Han Fortmann have identified humanity's increasing "disincarnation" as a crucial problem of Western civilization. By "disincarnation," Fortmann means our inability to experience reality freely because our bodies and senses play an increasingly minor role in our understanding of reality. To achieve its end of giving glory to God, then, the liturgy must engage the whole person – intellect, emotions, body, and senses.[7]

Furthermore, liturgical confession of faith originated in the early Church as a hymn or doxology, that is, as a praise (*logos*) of God's glory (*doxa*). In fact, the tradition of expressing confessions of faith in the hymn form can be traced as far back as such New Testament examples as Eph. 1.3-14, Phil. 2.6-11 and Col. 1.15-20. Originally the emphasis was not on the doctrinal content but on the expression of praise. After the Council of Chalcedon (451 A.D.), however, the emphasis changed until the confession of faith became less a liturgical doxology and more a formulation of doctrine, a development which reached its peak with the Tridentine confession of faith in the sixteenth century.[8]

---

[5] The Greek term *perichoresis* refers to the mutual interdependence of the three persons of the Blessed Trinity.

[6] SALIERS, *Worship as Theology,* 40-41.

[7] Han (Henricus) FORTMANN, *Wat is er met de mens gebeurd?* (Bilthoven: Uitgeverij Ambo, 1971): 9-18; idem, *Discovery of the East: Reflections on a New Culture,* trans. Patrick GAFFNEY (Notre Dame, Indiana: Fides Publishers, Inc., 1971): 13-14. Originally published in Dutch as *Oosterse Renaissance* (Bilthoven: Uitgeverij Ambo, 1970), 13-14. Both writings are cited in LUKKEN, "The Unique Expression," 11.

[8] LUKKEN, " The Unique Expression," 16-17.

If then the purpose of the liturgy is to give glory to God, and if the law of prayer is the law of belief, then the celebrating of liturgy is indeed *orthodoxia prima,* that is, a theological event. The terms *theologia* and *orthodoxia prima* describe the liturgy as an activity in which faith is expressed and from which teaching is derived as from the first source and norm. In this way, the nature of liturgy as right praise requires not the formulation of doctrine, but the engagement of whole human persons in an activity which is more akin to the artistic or the poetic than to the noetic.[9] Thus it is that through the mediation of a variety of symbols in dynamic interaction, God gives himself completely to humanity and humanity abandons itself to God in Jesus and through the Holy Spirit.[10]

LITURGY AS *THEOLOGIA ECCLESIA*

If doing liturgy can be described as an action which generates theological meaning, and if the subject of that liturgical action is the Christian community as church, then, as Yves Congar points out, questions regarding the nature of the liturgy are fundamentally ecclesiological questions.[11] Liturgy's role in manifesting the true nature of the church is aptly expressed in article two of *Sacrosanctum Concilium* which states that "it is through the liturgy, especially, that the faithful are enabled to express in their lives and manifest to others … the real nature of the true Church." Liturgical symbols mediate this expression and manifestation.

Liturgy: An Act of Ecclesial Performative Meaning

In her work in liturgical theology, Margaret Mary Kelleher has developed the thesis that the liturgy expresses ecclesial meaning. Accordingly,

---

[9] Even when we are contrasting text and music in the liturgy, it is important to remember, as John BLACKING points out in "The Structure of Musical Discourse: The Problem of the Song Text," 18, that poetry is by its nature closely aligned with music. The language of ritual is not, after all, propositional, but more often like music redundant, illocutionary and performative.

[10] LUKKEN, "The Unique Expression," 16, 20.

[11] Yves M.J. CONGAR, "L'Ecclesia ou communauté chrétienne, sujet intégral de l'action liturgique," in *La Liturgie après Vatican II: Bilans, Études, Prospective,* ed. Jean-Pierre JOSSUA and Yves M.J. CONGAR (Paris: Les Éditions du Cerf 1967): 241, 268.

she defines liturgy as "an act of ecclesial performative meaning in which the church symbolically mediates itself."[12] Basing her definition on Lonergan's understanding of human subjectivity, Kelleher applies the term "collective subject" to the church. Just as images and symbols play an important role in the operations of the human subject, so, too, do they play the same important role in the operations of the collective subject.[13] Thus we can "think of the church as a community whose knowledge is mediated by symbols, whose actions are informed by symbols, and whose commitments are specified by symbols."[14] It is liturgical performance which provides the opportunity for a community to symbolically mediate their understanding of their participation in the mystery of being church and of the rule and reign of the Kingdom of God already come and not yet come to fullness.[15]

Liturgy as Ritual Action

Chapter four of this study drew upon the ritual theory of Victor Turner in order to interpret the Taizé pilgrimage experience as social drama. The rituals of Taizé, including the daily liturgies, are aspects of that social drama which give expression to the different needs and goals of the pilgrimage experience. In the light of Turner's ritual theory, Kelleher offers another definition of liturgy as "a social, symbolic process which has the ability to communicate and create meaning."[16] This definition identifies important key elements for analyzing liturgical activity.

Defining liturgy as a *social* process highlights the fact that it is an activity of a social entity called *church*. This social entity is itself *in process* as it communicates and creates meaning regarding its own identity.[17]

Defining liturgy as a *symbolic* process highlights the fact that its basic units are ritual symbols. Interacting within the ritual process, these symbols become the agents which express the church's self-understanding. In other words, as ritual activity, the liturgy communicates and creates

[12] Margaret Mary KELLEHER, "Liturgy: An Ecclesial Act of Meaning," *Worship* 59 (November 1985): 482.
[13] KELLEHER, "Liturgy: An Ecclesial Act of Meaning," 483-485.
[14] KELLEHER, "Liturgy: An Ecclesial Act of Meaning," 487.
[15] SALIERS, *Worship as Theology*, 145-146.
[16] KELLEHER, "Liturgy: An Ecclesial Act of Meaning," 488.
[17] KELLEHER, "Liturgy: An Ecclesial Act of Meaning," 488.

meaning by means of a dynamic system of symbols which serve to disclose the "beliefs, values, commitments, relationships, memories and
hopes which are constitutive of the church as a community."[18]

In performing the liturgy, therefore, the church is performing itself.
In other words, Kelleher concludes that it is possible to say that the
church itself is the reality which is being mediated in liturgical celebrations. The notion that the liturgy as symbolic process mediates recognition within a community or social world is consistent with both
Polanyi's and Chauvet's understanding of symbol.[19]

Asserting that the church is the reality mediated by the liturgy is
not a denial of the fact that one of the primary roles of the liturgy is
to communicate the Christian message. However, since the Christian
message plays a constitutive role in the ongoing realization of the
Christian community, the community mediates the message as it
transforms itself in an ongoing process of self-realization. As Kelleher
explains, "The Christian message is the word of a community, a word
which provides a world of meaning set out in symbol, language, art,
lives, story, Scripture, rituals, and creeds. It is within this world of
meaning that persons gradually become Christians and achieve collective subjectivity."[20] Furthermore, local communities are particular
realizations of the church. Therefore, it is the church itself which is
mediated in the liturgical celebrations of each liturgical assembly.[21]
Doing the liturgy, therefore, enables the church to both express its
identity as the Body of Christ and form itself ever more in conformity
to Christ.

Another way Kelleher frames her understanding of the liturgy as an
act of ecclesial meaning is by using Lonergan's notion of horizon[22] to
interpret the church as a collective subject. According to Lonergan,
everyone has a horizon or boundary of meaning within which he or she
lives. The horizon of the church, then, would be a corporate horizon
consisting of a web of shared meaning. It is this corporate horizon

---

[18] KELLEHER, "Liturgy: An Ecclesial Act of Meaning," 491.

[19] CHAUVET, *Symbol and Sacrament*, 112; POLANYI, *Meaning*, 71-73.

[20] KELLEHER, "Liturgy: An Ecclesial Act of Meaning," 487.

[21] KELLEHER, "Liturgy: An Ecclesial Act of Meaning," 493.

[22] Chapter three of this study discusses Nattiez's definition of meaning as that which
exists "when an object is situated in relation to a horizon." Cf. above. Nattiez equates
this horizon with what he calls an individual's lived experience. This is analogous to
Lonergan's use of the term.

which is mediated by symbols in liturgical praxis and plays a role in mediating the church. The nature of those symbols and the manner in which they appear in the liturgical action are influential in shaping the corporate horizon and determining its role in the ongoing creation and transformation of the church. This corporate horizon, in turn, determines the living tradition which plays a formative role in the lives of individual members and communities.[23]

Focusing on the reality of the church's corporate horizon does not ignore the fact that within that horizon there exists a diversity of personal horizons. Furthermore, the mediation of the church's horizon is influenced, not only by each individual's personal appropriation of the meanings carried in the corporate horizon, but also by the culture and history of the particular local community celebrating the liturgy. It is because of the multivocality of the symbols that the liturgy is able to mediate meaning among diverse collective subjects. However, because each local assembly is also part of a larger reality – the wider horizon of a "world church"[24] – local assemblies are challenged to be faithful to both of these dimensions of the ecclesial horizon.[25]

The Role of Liturgical Music-Making in Mediating Ecclesial Meaning

Thus far this chapter has shown that there is an important connection between the doing of liturgy and the generating of theological meaning. It has further shown that because liturgy is the action whereby the collective subject, or church, mediates itself in mediating the Christian message, the meaning generated is to a great extent ecclesial meaning. Since liturgy is ritual activity, ecclesial meaning is mediated through the dynamic interplay of a complexus of symbols whose message engages the whole person – body, senses, intellect, and emotions – in an activity described as *ortho-doxia* or right praise to God.

---

[23] KELLEHER, "Liturgy: An Ecclesial Act of Meaning," 494-495.

[24] Karl RAHNER first used the term "world church" in "Towards a Fundamental Interpretation of Vatican II," *Theological Studies* 40 (1979): 716-727. Rahner's thesis in this essay is that Vatican II is the first major official event in which the church actualized itself as a *world church*. By this he meant that Vatican II marked a transition in the history of the church from operating as a Christianity of Europe with its American annexes to beginning to see itself as a truly global religion.

[25] KELLEHER, "Liturgy: An Ecclesial Act of Meaning," 496.

The symbols of the liturgy include the texts, music, gestures, sacred objects, and environment. All of them support and illuminate each other in order to mediate the sacred mysteries.[26] In interpreting the theological meaning of the liturgy in the past, there has sometimes been an exclusive concentration on texts. Today, however, most scholars would support Don Saliers observation that it is necessary to go beyond the text and investigate the symbols in liturgy and liturgy as symbol.[27] He explains:

> To focus solely on the verbal or surface language of liturgical prayer is to neglect the very way that the language gains meaning and depth. Liturgical language is radically dependent upon what is not verbal for meaning and significance.[28]

Salier's comment highlights the complex interrelationship that exists between liturgical language and the various other liturgical symbols. It is the interplay of both verbal and non-verbal symbols that mediates meaning in ritual activity.

Saliers's point corroborates our use of performative language theory to interpret the liturgy. For in ritual speech acts, their code and medium of contact – for example, the use of the Greek or Latin language and the medium of sound – are often not the primary means of conveying ritual meaning. Rather, there may be a set of a particular tradition's key symbols, including the visual, the aural, the kinesthetic, and the olfactory, which interplay with language to communicate meaning.[29] This interplay is mutual rather than hierarchic. For as Wheelock points out, "it is not a simple case of language's being augmented by accompanying gestures or facial expressions which serve to convey some message of mood or emphasis that explicates the verbal message. The situation is often just the reverse, with the verbal message being used to clarify and augment the independent symbolic expressions in the other media."[30]

---

[26] These "sacred mysteries" include the mystery of the church, the mystery of Christ, and ultimately the Paschal Mystery which designates the essential aspects of Christian redemption. However, as liturgical performance is an instance of primary theology, not secondary theology, articulations of these mysteries are symbolic and revelatory, not propositional.

[27] SALIERS, *Worship as Theology,* 140.

[28] SALIERS, *Worship as Theology*, 140.

[29] WHEELOCK, "The Problem of Ritual Language,"57.

[30] WHEELOCK, "The Problem of Ritual Language," 57.

If this is the case, then we are justified in concluding that, as ritual symbol, liturgical music-making – specifically the singing of the Taizé chants – contributes to the mediation of ecclesial meaning. This ecclesial meaning includes the many facets of the church's life and of its members' memories and experiences of it. In addition to the general focus on ecclesial meaning, however, two more specific questions can be asked: 1) Is there a particular ecclesiology that is being disclosed in the liturgical celebrations of Taizé? and 2) How do the Taizé chants assist in disclosing that particular ecclesiology? In order to begin to address these questions, the next two sections of this chapter will explore how Taizé music as ritual symbol mediates ecclesial meaning and how contemporary ecclesiologies have influenced the creation and use of Taizé music.

TAIZÉ MUSIC: RITUAL SYMBOL MEDIATING ECCLESIAL MEANING

Singing as a Mediation of Identity

Chapter three explored Louis-Marie Chauvet's understanding of the role of symbol in mediating identity and recognition. By negotiating connections and mediating relationships, symbols permit individuals or the group as a whole to recognize one another and thereby discover their identity and their place within the group.[31]

Singing the Taizé chants at the liturgies in the great Church of Reconciliation enables members of the assembly to negotiate several connections and discover old and new relationships. These connections can occur on both the physical and spiritual level. One of the primary connections is the fact that singing the chants puts individuals in touch with their own bodies and emotions. This is significant, since, as Chauvet points out, the body is the primordial and arch-symbolic form of mediation and the basis for all subjective identification.[32] Since the body is the entry place where the entire symbolic order takes root in us as human beings,[33] the activity of music-making facilitates our ability to enter into the meanings mediated by symbols. In addition, as Foley points out, singing mediates a participatory knowledge that allows our

---

[31] CHAUVET, *Symbol and Sacrament*, 84-85.
[32] CHAUVET, *Symbol and Sacrament*, 147.
[33] CHAUVET, *Symbol and Sacrament*, 147.

bodies and our spirits to breath and move with its rhythms in such a way that there is a physical, palpable connection with all those who are present and singing with us.[34]

On the spiritual level, singing the chants connects all the pilgrims who are expressing the same faith through their engagement in the same activity of prayer. In another way, singing the chants connects them with the God whom they are addressing in sentiments which may include, among others, praise, petition, thanksgiving, or repentance. This expression of the Christian faith through song enables them as individuals to experience themselves as persons who confess the Christian faith and are in communion with others who confess the same faith.

At the same time that this dynamic is occurring on the individual level, the music-making as symbol is likewise mediating the identity of the entire group or assembly. A group identity emerges of persons who are in relationship with each other through a common Christian faith. Instead of viewing the other participants as members of different Christian denominations or different countries or races, the pilgrims are enabled to view themselves as part of a social entity defined by the common activity of singing prayer to a God in whom they share a common belief.

In this setting the participants can experience a church in which dogmatic differences are set aside and common elements of the Christian faith are highlighted. Focus is on the Christ praised and petitioned in song, portrayed in the icons and proclaimed in the Scriptures, rather than the Christ defined by the dogmas of a particular denomination. These emphases make it possible for an individual to find his or her place in the group and recognize the group as a social entity to which he or she belongs.

The accessibility of the Taizé chants is one of the primary characteristics which enables participants to negotiate connections and thereby mediate identity and recognition. The simplicity and repetition of the musical format has the potential to draw in even the most hesitant of singers. The music is arranged in several voices with optional vocal and instrumental parts. This multiplicity of melodic and harmonic elements, as well as the variety of languages employed, communicates the idea that diversity is not only tolerated but welcomed. All voice parts have a role in creating the total sound, a sound which by design accommodates a great deal of

---

[34] FOLEY, "Sound Theology," 126.

variation. Furthermore, opportunities are provided for numerous native tongues to find expression in the chants. That spirit of hospitality and openness which is incorporated into the songs serves to bridge national differences, not by eliminating them, but by celebrating them. Such a dissolution of boundaries promotes the message that the church, as it is experienced at Taizé, is a world church in the sense spoken of by Rahner.[35] It is a church which seeks to find its voice in the diversity and multiplicity of its local expression as a way of realizing its true catholicity or universality.

The aleatory nature of the chants, which includes the possibility of undetermined repetition and numerous combinations of vocal and instrumental arrangements, provides an aspect of provisionality and openendedness to the musical compositions. Such provisionality, in turn, provides an experience of church which is dynamic or in process. It is a pilgrim church, journeying toward the realization of the Kingdom, present, but not yet fully realized. The Taizé chants are songs for the journey, songs of a pilgrim people, moving toward the goal of perfect harmony or union with God and with each other.

Singing the chants of Berthier, then, can be understood as participating in a symbolizing activity which has the potential to mediate ecclesial identity. This potential can be more fully realized when the singing is performed within a liturgical context.

Singing as the Performance of Ritual Speech Acts

Chapter five explored the performative language theory of J.L. Austin which argued that the uttering of a sentence can be the doing of an action. Using Austin's theory in order to speak of music-making as the doing or accomplishing of something, we concluded that singing the Taizé chants can be the doing or accomplishing of a ritual action.

In his interpretation of J.L. Austin's performative language theory, John Searle identifies that aspect of an utterance which possesses the power to effect what is being stated the "illocutionary force." This force is produced not simply by words or word order, but also by deep syntactic structure, stress, and intonation contour. The thesis of this study is that music, as a symbol interacting with text in song, assists especially in providing those elements of stress and intonation contour which empower the singers to *do something* in the act of singing.

---

[35] RAHNER, "Towards a Fundamental Interpretation," 724-727.

Furthermore, we considered how the act of singing a Taizé chant might be said actually to accomplish something in the singing by looking at singing as the speaking of an attitude. Our conclusion was that the singing of a chant, as part of the process of performing the ritual and interacting with other symbols, produces an effect.

The conclusions of that analysis can be applied to the singing of the Taizé chants in general. That is, the act of singing the chants is the doing of the ritual. The ritual includes such actions as praising, thanking, and petitioning God and responding to the Scriptures. The chants, as a combination of music and text, possess an illocutionary power to accomplish these actions in the very act of singing.

Furthermore, it is the assembly, as church, which is performing these actions in the singing of the chants. Therefore, we can say that singing the chants in the context of the liturgy mediates a Church which praises, thanks, and petitions God and responds to the Scriptures. The chants provide a vehicle which enables these actions to be repeated by engaging body, mind, and emotions.

In addition to viewing the singing of the Taizé chants as the *doing or accomplishing of an action,* the singing of Taizé chants, interpreted through the lens of performative language theory, can be said also to assist in the *creation of the situation* in which the praying assembly finds itself. In other words, *a state of affairs is established* in the singing. It is a state of affairs where, while the music-making is occurring, the assembly as a local representation of the church, *prays as one church.* Unity is accomplished – for the duration of the music – where separated Christians are united in heart, mind, body, and emotions in worshiping God. For the duration of the singing, the unity which is so elusive to the table of ecumenical dialogue is achieved and celebrated around the table of the word.

In this way, singing the Taizé chants serves to create a particular environment which situates individuals and groups in relationship to each other. The state of affairs which results may be described as one which places the pilgrims of Taizé in a situation of mutual respect and hospitality where a common Christian faith is celebrated within the context of cultural differences. By situating the members of the assembly in this dynamic interplay of commonality and diversity, the Taizé chants enable the assembly to embody a concrete expression of the "communitas" spoken of by Victor Turner.[36]

---

[36] See TURNER, *The Ritual Process,* 83.

Furthermore, the genres of the Taizé chants serve as "structuring structures"[37] situating members of the assembly in specific relationships to each other within the performance of the music. That is, the chants situate the assembly as the primary minister of the prayer. The performance of this ministry is characterized by a mutuality of service rather than a hierarchy of office.

At the same time that singing the Taizé chants serves to structure the community and establish a state of affairs, it is also true that symbols are not only *agents,* but also *products* of their culture. In other words, while the singing of the Taizé chants mediates an ecclesial identity and forms a community in "deep dispositions over time"[38] it is also true that symbols, as cultural products express or reflect the reality of those who use them. If that is the case, and if the liturgies of Taizé can be said to be authentic, then it should be possible to draw some correlation between the ecclesiology mediated in ritual performance and the ecclesiology articulated in the lives and writings of those who celebrate those rituals.

CONTEMPORARY THEOLOGIES OF CHURCH

The Ecclesiology of Vatican II

No event in the twentieth century has so influenced contemporary ecclesiology, both within the Roman Catholic church and within other Christian denominations as the Second Vatican Council. Of the sixteen documents promulgated by the council, two are specifically pertinent to the concerns of this chapter. The key document, *Lumen Gentium*[39] opens with a chapter devoted to articulating a theology of the mystery of the church. According to *LG,* the church is "a sign and instrument ... of communion with God and of unity among all men [and women]."[40]

---

[37] See KRAMER, *Music as Cultural Practice*, 10. Chapter two of this study provides a more detailed discussion of Kramer's notion of structural tropes.

[38] SALIERS, *Worship as Theology,* 147.

[39] *Lumen Gentium* is the Latin title of the Vatican II document whose English title is *Dogmatic Constitution on the Church.* Hereafter *LG.*

[40] Sacrosanctum Oecumenicum Concilium Vaticanum, "Constitutio Dogmatica de Ecclesia," in *Constitutiones, Decreta, Declarationes,* 93-219 (typis Polyglottis Vaticanis, 1966), 1. In this study the English translation is quoted from Austin FLANNERY, gen. ed., "Dogmatic Constitution on the Church," in *Vatican Council II: The Conciliar and*

The source of the universal Church's unity is derived from "the unity of the Father, the Son and the Holy Spirit" (*LG* 4). The mission of the church is one of "proclaiming and establishing among all peoples the kingdom of Christ and of God ... [even as] she is, on earth, the seed and the beginning of that kingdom" (*LG* 5). Finally, if the Church is to be faithful to the Lord Jesus, "the author of salvation and the principle of unity and peace," it must become for every person "the visible sacrament of this saving unity" (*LG* 9).

Clearly, the theme of communion is central to the Council's understanding of the mystery of the Church. This communion, furthermore, has as its source the communion of the Trinity, revealed to us through the Lord Jesus, who calls every person to be a visible witness of that unity.

On the same day that the Council promulgated the "Dogmatic Constitution on the Church," it also promulgated the "Decree on Ecumenism." This decree, entitled *Unitatis Redintegratio,*[41] reiterates the Council's focus on Christian unity when it asserts that "[T]he restoration of unity among all Christians is one of the principal concerns of the Second Vatican Council."[42] This concern, the council fathers point out, is shared by large numbers everywhere who "have felt the impulse of this grace and among our separated brethren also there increases from day to day a movement, fostered by the grace of the Holy Spirit, for the restoration of unity among all Christians. Taking part in this movement, which is called ecumenical, are those who invoke the Triune God and confess Jesus as Lord and Saviour" (*UR* 1).

This decree signals both an awareness of a growing ecumenical spirit and a willingness on the part of the Church to participate wholeheartedly in ecumenism in obedience to the promptings of the Holy Spirit. Not coincidentally, at the time of the promulgation of this decree in November 1964, the small community of brothers in the Burgundian

---

Post Conciliar Documents, 350-423, revised edition (Grands Rapids, Michigan: William B. Eerdmans Publishing Company, 1984), 1.

[41] Hereafter, *UR.*

[42] Sacrosanctum Oecumenicum Concilium Vaticanum, "Decretum de Oecumenismo," in *Constitutiones, Decreta, Declarationes,* 243-274 (typis Polyglottis Vaticanis, 1966), 1. In this study the English translation is quoted from Austin FLANNERY, gen. ed., "Decree on Ecumenism," in *Vatican Council II: The Conciliar and Post Conciliar Documents,* 452-532, revised edition (Grands Rapids, Michigan: William B. Eerdmans Publishing Company, 1984), 1.

hills of Taizé, France was already living their response to the promptings of the same Spirit.

The Ecclesiology of Taizé

Christian unity and the reconciliation of all humankind are two aspects of the same passion which has inspired Brother Roger Schutz's entire life at Taizé. It is the central theme of all of his writings and the font from which and toward which all his energy and thinking is directed.[43]

In the spiritual directives which follow the Rule of Taizé, Schutz describes the brothers of Taizé as men living an "ecumenical vocation" whereby they are called to "seek unity in all things" and "show forth fellowship in their daily life."[44] Schutz is quick to point out that the unity about which he is speaking is not just a spiritual unity.[45] What is necessary and vital to the church is the *visible* unity of all Christians.[46]

Schutz's quest for unity, however, is not blind to the existence of pluralism. Instead of denying pluralism or attempting to eliminate it, he advocates a unanimity which embraces diversity. Brother Roger explains:

> To live unanimity, planted in the heart of pluralism, is to bind oneself to that which continues to be primary for every community and for the community of communities, namely the Church. To live unanimity in pluralism is to seek the pivot that is common to all, the pivot around which diversity is built up in a plurality of expressions, in a freedom of existence which is all the greater as the unanimity is more certain.[47]

Schutz makes an important distinction here between unanimity and uniformity. He points out that uniformity only creates the appearance of unity. Unanimity, on the other hand, presupposes pluralism.[48]

---

[43] DAVIS, "The Ecumenical Ecclesiology of Max Thurian," 38.

[44] Roger SCHUTZ, *The Rule of Taizé: in French and in English* (Taizé: Les Presses de Taizé, 1965), 101.

[45] Roger SCHUTZ, *Unity: Man's Tomorrow* (New York: Herder and Herder, 1963), 74. Published originally in French as *L'Unité, Esperance de Vie* (Taizé: Les Presses de Taizé, 1962).

[46] SCHUTZ, *The Rule of Taizé*, 101; SCHUTZ, *Unity*, 74.

[47] Roger SCHUTZ, *Unanimity in Pluralism*, trans. David FLOOD, Brother PASCHAL, and Brother THOMAS (Chicago: Franciscan Herald Press, 1967), ix-x. Published in French as *Unanimite dans le Pluralisme* (Taizé: Les Presses de Taizé, 1966).

[48] SCHUTZ, *Unanimity in Pluralism*, 14.

The brothers of Taizé seek to achieve this visible unity of which Brother Roger so frequently speaks by working toward unanimity both in community life and community prayer. Brother Roger's singleness of purpose is revealed when he explains: "What do we want to be other than men living the common life? We have come together in a life committed to follow in the footsteps of Christ, in order to be an existential sign of the Church's unity."[49]

As in their community life, so, too, is unity central to the prayer life of the brothers. The introductory section of the first Taizé Office available in English explains how this focus is rooted in the tradition of the Church even as it looks forward to the realization of a future unity:

> The Taizé Office is the fruit of an experience of community prayer, rooted in the ecumenical tradition of the Church. It belongs to the group of liturgies dating back to the early times of the Church. Its sources are manifold, but the different streams become a unity in the living experience of a community. ... This Office does not claim to be an official liturgy. It represents a stage in the liturgical research of the Church and the expectation of visible unity for all Christians. It is intended to serve this research and this unity, while already being the Office of a community.[50]

The original Taizé Office was, by design, rooted in the diversity of the church even as it sought to be an agent of unity. A later edition, published in French under the title "La Louange des Jours," reiterates the community's original intention to integrate its search for unity into its life of prayer. The brothers of Taizé approach their present form of common prayer as one which is still evolving and provisional.[51]

This characterization of their common prayer as *provisional* introduces yet another important aspect of Taizé's efforts to promote visible Christian unity. Schutz sees the dynamic of provisionality operative within his own community and also within the Church. It is part of his theology of hope, a way of living in expectation of a unity yet to be achieved.

The life of the Taizé community is provisional in that it is continually developing and evolving. Its goal is not to achieve some final point of

---

[49] SCHUTZ, *Unanimity in Pluralism*, 9. See chapter four for a discussion of the way in which the brothers are a visible witness to unity even in the manner in which they come together for daily prayer in the great Church of Reconciliation.

[50] *The Taizé Office*, 9.

[51] *Praise God*, 7.

stability or establishment. Rather, the brothers of Taizé hope that their efforts to achieve unity in the Church will eventually make the very existence of Taizé obsolete. In fact, the community looks with joyful hope to its own disappearance.[52] Schutz reflects on this possibility of the community's disappearance when he says:

> Our liturgy leads us to a unanimity in faith and supports a strong hope. It makes us live, as on the evening of Emmaus, in the presence of the Risen One whom our eyes are kept from seeing. And yet, is not this a provisional state, which is destined to disappear on the day of visible unity?[53]

Those living in expectation of Christian unity, Schutz explains, must be willing to pay the price of that unity. For him that means the willingness to go beyond present positions towards the fullest realization of ecumenism.[54] This requires, not a movement "going back" or "returning" to the past, but rather, a movement forward to the future, a unity to be fully realized only in the final unity of the Kingdom of God.[55]

One of the original brothers of Taizé, Max Thurian (1921-1996),[56] developed an understanding of this movement toward unity as a "going beyond" in his theology of dépassement. In Thurian's judgment, this was also the approach taken by the Second Vatican Council. He explains:

> Our modern ecumenism must be a mutual, spiritual and theological help to evangelize the modern world that God loves. This is perhaps the way in which we will progress into the last stage of visible unity for Christians, no longer looking at each other with love or suspicion, but looking together at the world for which Christ died and for which we, together, are called to sacrifice our ecclesial and confessional comfort, united so that the world may believe.[57]

---

[52] DAVIS, "The Ecumenical Ecclesiology of Max Thurian," 45.

[53] Robert SCHUTZ, *The Power of the Provisional*, trans. Philip PARSONS and Timothy WILSON (London: Hodder and Stoughton, 1969), 67.

[54] SCHUTZ, *The Power of the Provisional*, 59.

[55] DAVIS, "The Ecumenical Ecclesiology of Max Thurian," 248.

[56] DAVIS, "The Ecumenical Ecclesiology of Max Thurian," 1. Max Thurian joined Roger Schutz and a third brother in 1944. He was one of the original seven who pronounced lifetime vows on Easter Sunday, April 17, 1949. He served as sub-prior of the Taizé community and was engaged in theological and liturgical research and writing. He has published several books and articles on a variety of theological themes.

[57] Max THURIAN, *The One Bread*, trans. Theodore DUBOIS (New York: Sheed and Ward, 1969), 110.

Once again, this excerpt highlights the several themes of Taizé's ecumenical mission: promoting a unity which is visible, which is forward looking, and which is essential to any effort to evangelize the world.

Like Schutz, Thurian cautions that unity does not imply uniformity. Rather, he envisions a living variety, an organic bond among all the regional churches in their valid diversity to be a sign of the Holy Spirit quickening and enriching the Church in unity.[58]

The writings of both Roger Schultz and Max Thurian capture the theology and spirituality which enlivens the life and ministry of the brothers of Taizé. Their ministry, however, is not directed solely toward the reunification of ecclesial institutions. Rather, it is also directed toward the reconciliation of all who find themselves separated or alienated from their fellow human beings.[59] By channeling their efforts to being present to the world as a "living 'parable' of unity," the brothers of Taizé seek to fully embrace what they understand to be the vocation of all Christians: the call to be witnesses, in a torn and individualistic world, to a mutual unity that overcomes all barriers.[60]

TAIZÉ'S RITUALIZATION OF ITS ECCLESIOLOGY

The ecclesiologies articulated by the Second Vatican Council and the community of Taizé both focus on the importance of working toward achieving Christian unity. Since Vatican II, several initiatives have been undertaken by the churches to work actively toward that goal. The Taizé community, true to its own emphasis on the importance of achieving a *visible Christian unity,* has been conspicuous in this effort.

Taizé has evolved within a Christian milieu that is rife with divisions, but one that has renewed hope that those divisions may be overcome. The ecclesiology which it espouses shapes its community life and its prayer life. In this respect we can say that the Taizé liturgy is an expression of its ecclesiology. From the earliest days of its ministry to pilgrims, Taizé has searched for a form of prayer which might gather together

---

[58] Max THURIAN, "L'unité visible," *Verbum Caro* XVI (1962): 153; Max THURIAN, *Love and Truth Meet,* trans. C. Edward HOPKINS (Philadelphia: Pilgrim Press, 1968), 65.

[59] DAVIS, "The Ecumenical Ecclesiology of Max Thurian," 247.

[60] John HEIJKE, *An Ecumenical Light on the Renewal of Religious Community Life: Taizé,* Duquesne Studies: Theological Series no. 7 (Pittsburgh: Duquesne University Press, 1967), 99.

people from different races, countries, and denominations. The team effort of Brother Robert Giscard and Jacques Berthier to create a form of liturgical song which might enable all to participate was inspired by this same commitment to inclusivity and hospitality as prerequisites for unity. The result of their effort is a corpus of music which mediates a tangible experience of unity in the activity of singing the chants.

On the other hand, not only has Taizé's ritual prayer and ritual song evolved through the living out of its ecclesiology, but it is also possible to say that Taizé ritual prayer has been an agent promoting and shaping its ecclesiology. In other words, the fact that thousands of pilgrims make their way to Taizé each year to *pray* as *one* Church is an important step toward realizing that hoped for unity.

Gerard Lukken's insight regarding the primacy of *theologia* and *orthodoxia prima* can well be applied to Taizé:

> A conversion to authentic liturgical practice might, after all, be the right way of bringing and keeping Christians together in *one* Church. The *communio* of all believers with the one Lord and with each other is experienced and expressed in a unique way in the liturgy and we should not underestimate the ecumenical significance of this.[61]

This *communio* about which Lukken speaks is ritualized at Taizé three times a day, every day, by large numbers of pilgrims.

This ongoing, regular ritual performance of acts expressive of unity is not inconsequential. On the contrary, as Susanne Langer points out, such a "constant reiteration of sentiments toward first and last things … is not a free expression of emotions, but a disciplined rehearsal of 'right attitudes.'"[62] Applying Langer's remark to Christian liturgy, we can conclude, like Don Saliers, that it is *over a period of time* that liturgy shapes and expresses a community so that its capacity to make connections is deepened and it is formed in the deep dispositions of the Christian life.[63] *Over time* the singing of the Berthier chants can exert a powerful influence in expressing and shaping that unity toward which the church strains by forming those who sing the chants in that disposition of *communio* which is the ultimate goal of Christ's church.

---

[61] LUKKEN, "The Unique Expression," 21.
[62] LANGER, *Philosophy in a New Key*, 153.
[63] SALIERS, "Sung Prayer," 293; SALIERS, *Worship as Theology*, 143-147.

SINGING THE TAIZÉ CHANTS IN OTHER LOCAL COMMUNITIES

The focus of this study has been on the intended performance of the Taizé chants at the site of the great Church of Reconciliation in Taizé, France. Since the early days of collaboration between Brother Robert Giscard and Jacques Berthier, however, the music has spread to local worshiping communities throughout the world and is currently being sung in approximately twenty languages. The fact that these chants have been adopted with such enthusiasm by such great numbers suggests that these songs have the power to embody meaning in settings other than the Taizé community. How does such a possibility impact on the thesis of this study? Can meaning be transferred from one context to another?

In asserting that the Taizé chants operate as ritual symbol in the liturgies at Taizé, we are asserting that music performed within the context of ritual performance interacts with other symbols to generate theological meaning. Because the subjects engaged in the liturgy are engaged as collective subjects, we are further asserting that when the ritual performance is Christian liturgy, the theological meaning is fundamentally ecclesial.

This study has presented theorists who have demonstrated that symbolic discourse, and specifically musical discourse, is not simply an objective or neutral reality. In Nattiez's schema, the neutral or immanent dimension interacts with the poietic and esthesic dimension.[64] The poietic is determined by the creator of the music. This may be the composer, but in the case of Taizé, it can also be the performers of the music because of its aleatory nature. At the same time, the esthesic dimension is determined by the listeners who, in the case of worshiper-participants, can also be the performers of the music.

In other words, interpreting music as ritual symbol is a process of discovering how human subjects create meaning through interaction with a piece of music in a ritual setting. That interaction involves subsidiary clues – to use the language of Polanyi – which gather together diffuse memories of human subjects in such a way that they are carried away by their meaning.[65] Or, to use the language of Peirce, we can say that the

---

[64] NATTIEZ, *Music and Discourse*, 16-18, 28-32. The three dimensions are defined and discussed in greater detail in chapter three.

[65] POLANYI, *Meaning*, 71-73.

interaction is determined by an infinite number of interpretants which are drawn from the lived experience of the symbol's users.[66]

Because symbols are multivalent, they have the power to mediate many layers of meaning. This is what enables music, as well as other symbols, to communicate across cultural boundaries. It is also what enables music to embody new meanings in repeated instances of music-making or in new contexts. Identical meanings will not be communicated in each instance of performance. Rather, meaning is dependent on the ritual context and the horizons of the human subjects using the symbols. Since both the ritual contexts and the horizons of the human subjects are dynamic rather than static, the meaning mediated is in constant flux.

In each new performance of the Taizé chants, in each new local community, there is the potential for music to mediate new meaning as human subjects surrender their whole existence, lived as members of the church, into the music they are making. It is the diffuse and boundless memories of the church's existence and of their life in it that give the music meaning by becoming embodied and fused in it.

What enables music to transcend cultural boundaries is not some innate power of music to operate as a "universal language." Rather, it is because human subjects "are able to make sense of a piece of music on their own terms"[67] that music can mean many things to many people. The symbolic nature of music enables that to happen by mediating the identity of the subjects and allowing them to make sense of their world by finding their place in it.[68] In the specific case of ritual music, it is the ritual setting and the interplay of other ritual symbols that provides the specific context for mediating ecclesial meaning.

Yet, this mediation of meaning is not a purely subjective activity. Included in the process are the creative impulses of the composer/performers as well as the musical composition itself. In addition, a certain level of competence in negotiating the cultural codes is required of the worshipers. The "symbolon" must be recognized as a part of the whole. In this case, the whole is the social/cultural reality we call "church."

The widespread adoption of the chants of Taizé for ritual prayer attests to the ability of liturgical song to mediate ecclesial recognition,

---

[66] NATTIEZ, *Music and Discourse,* 10.
[67] BLACKING, "Structure of Musical Discourse," 21.
[68] CHAUVET, *Symbol and Sacrament,* 84-85.

identification, and transformation when Christians engage in ritual prayer. In the end, God is glorified in the lives of those who surrender to the power of symbols to "carry them away" or "draw them out of their private agendas," not only into the larger act of Christ in the community, but also into the divine *perichoresis*. In that way, participation in ritual performance draws human subjects into the font of God's glory where lives are transformed in the "marvelous exchange" (*admirabile commercium*) between God and humankind which we call grace.[69]

CONCLUSION:
TOWARD A CRITICAL THEORY OF MUSIC AS RITUAL SYMBOL

The purpose of this study has been to investigate the thesis that it is because music operates as ritual symbol that it is both ministerial and integral to the liturgy. By examining various theories and theologies of symbol and using them to interpret Taizé music, we have determined that ritual music-making is symbolic activity. Our final task is to explain how music's symbolic property enables it to be both ministerial and integral to the liturgy.

Official church documents since *Sacrosanctum Concilium* have used the term "ministerial" either explicitly or implicitly to describe music's various roles within the liturgy. Since contemporary Roman Catholic usage understands ministry as *diakonia* or mutual service, the purpose of these various services can be viewed as working toward the building up of the community of believers for the sake of the Kingdom.

Music as symbolic activity serves the community by evoking participation, not only in the ritual action, but also, on a deeper level, by evoking participation in the common work of becoming and being transformed into a community of faith. By negotiating relationships among the community and between the community and the God whom they worship, music-making allows individuals and the assembly as a social group to orient themselves, that is, to discover their identity and their place within their world.[70]

---

[69] CHAUVET, *Symbol and Sacrament*, 99-100.
[70] CHAUVET, *Symbol and Sacrament*, 110-111.

Music as symbolic performance likewise serves the community when it provides a vehicle for the "rehearsal" of right attitudes whereby transformation or sanctification becomes possible.[71] As speech acts that are strongly characterized by intonation, pitch, rhythm, and articulation, the singing of acclamations and other responses possess the illocutionary force to "do something" in the act of singing. This repeated performance of expressions of praise, thanksgiving, repentance, or other sentiments appropriate to living the Christian vocation can serve, over time, to transform those who perform these musical speech acts.

In addition to building up the community of believers, church documents have described music as ministerial when it serves the texts of the liturgy and the ritual itself. However, like music, texts and the various elements of the liturgy, including ritual gestures, sacred objects, vestments, and architecture are also ritual symbols. Therefore, they, too, have a ministerial function. The stone of the altar, the wood of the cross, the words that proclaim the good news – all these symbols interact in order to mediate the liturgy's meaning. They are not ends in themselves. Their service is mutual and grounded in the community for the sake of building the Kingdom. The ultimate purpose of all these ritual symbols is mediating the revelation of the God of Jesus Christ and the community's response to that revelation.

But if there is a mutuality of service, and if a complexus of ritual symbols interact in the production of the liturgical event, in what way can music's symbolic service be described as integral? That is, if something is "integral" when it participates in making a whole by being a part of it, what unique contribution does music, as ritual symbol, provide in the liturgy?

Since the liturgy is by its very nature symbolic process and since the process of symbolizing is eminently "sensory and bodily," the human body is the entry place where the entire symbolic order takes root in us as human beings.[72] Music-making, whether it be singing, dancing or moving with the rhythms of a song, playing musical instruments, or ululating enables worshipers to ritualize their very bodiliness and to involve their whole persons in the act of worship.

---

[71] See LANGER, *Philosophy in a New Key*, 153; SALIERS, "The Integrity of Sung Prayer," 293; SALIERS, *Worship as Theology*, 143-147.
[72] CHAUVET, *Symbol and Sacrament*, 140, 147.

Furthermore, since ritual speech is exhibitive rather than assertive and more closely aligned with music and poetry than propositional discourse, expressing gestures and speech musically is inherent to the liturgical process. Music provides elements of stress and intonation contour which constitute the illocutionary force required to *accomplish* an action in the *saying* of something. It is music which provides the illocutionary force that situates the assembly in a sonic environment which draws worshipers into its movement, enabling participation in a known and repeatable action within an "acoustic space."[73]

All of these characteristics of music-making as symbolic process contribute to the overall integrity of the liturgical process. By mutual interaction, ritual symbols enhance the power of all symbols to mediate meaning. Music's characteristics of stress and rhythm, intonation contour and pitch provide a unique means for involving the body, emotions, and memory of those who worship and enhancing the symbolizing activity of other liturgical elements.

Lastly, the meaning mediated by music can be discovered when, like all symbols, it is interpreted in relationship with the whole of which it is a part. Hence the importance of accounting for context, cultural codes and the experience-domain of the community, as individuals, and as a social group.

Once the power of music to operate symbolically is understood, other questions regarding its use in the liturgy can be addressed. These pertain to criteria for determining music's appropriateness and excellence and the way in which these affect *how* and *what* music symbolizes. Such questions, while not the topic of this study, are currently being debated in several forums.

Music-making has the potential to integrate Christian identity and Christian transformation as it mediates the revelation of God's self-communication to humankind and humankind's response to that self-communication. The challenge is to promote music-making that has the power to bear the weight of the mystery it is called upon to mediate and the power to communicate it within a given cultural and social context. Ritual music-making may provide a "nobler aspect" to the rites or "a more graceful expression to prayer,"[74] but a more complex dynamic is being described when music is said to be ministerial and integral to the

---

[73] ONG, *The Presence of the Word*, 163.
[74] *Musicam Sacram*, 5.

liturgy. Understanding music's role as ritual symbol can provide the foundation for an approach to the ministry of music which enables liturgical music-making to be truly integral and ministerial. Such an approach will ensure that the ministry of music promotes the purpose of liturgical prayer: the glory of God and the sanctification of humankind.[75] Otherwise, the music of the liturgy can be reduced to an object manipulated without vision or understanding.

---

[75] *Sacrosanctum Concilium,* 112.

BIBLIOGRAPHY

A. PRIMARY SOURCES

1. Books

Communauté de Taizé. *Praise God: Common Prayer at Taizé.* Translated by Emily CHISHOLM. New York: Oxford University Press, 1977. Originally published as *La Louange de Taizé.* Taizé: Les Presses de Taizé, 1971.

Communauté de Taizé. *The Rule of Taizé: in French and in English.* Taizé: Les Presses de Taizé, 1965.

Communauté de Taizé. *The Taizé Office.* London: The Faith Press, 1966. Originally published as *Office de Taizé.* Taizé: Les Presses de Taizé, 1963.

SCHUTZ, Roger. *Living Today for God.* Translated by Stephen MCNIERNEY and Louis EVRARD. Baltimore: Helicon Press, 1962. Originally published as *Vivre l'Aujourd'hui de Dieu.* Taizé: Les Presses de Taizé, 1961.

SCHUTZ, Roger. *The Power of the Provisional.* Translated by Philip PARSONS and Timothy WILSON. London: Hodder and Stoughton, 1969. Originally published as *Dynamique du Provisoire.* Taizé: Les Presses de Taizé, 1965.

SCHUTZ, Roger. *Unanimity in Pluralism.* Translated by David FLOOD, Brother PASCHAL, and Brother THOMAS. Chicago: Franciscan Herald Press, 1967. Originally published as *Unanimité dans le Pluralisme.* Taizé: Les Presses de Taizé, 1966.

SCHUTZ, Roger. *Unity: Man's Tomorrow.* New York: Herder and Herder, 1963. Originally published as *L'Unité, Espérance de Vie.* Taizé: Les Presses de Taizé, 1962.

THURIAN, Max. *The Eucharistic Liturgy of Taizé.* Translated by John ARNOLD. London: The Faith Press, 1962.

THURIAN, Max. *Love and Truth Meet.* Translated by C. Edward HOPKIN. Philadelphia: Pilgrim Press, 1968. Originally published as *Amour et Vérité se rencontrent.* Taizé: Les Presses de Taizé.

THURIAN, Max. "L'unité visible." *Verbum Caro* XVI (1962): 150-160.

THURIAN, Max. *The One Bread.* Translated by Theodore DUBOIS. New York: Sheed and Ward, 1969. Part I originally published as *Le pain unique,* 1967 and part II as *La foi en crise,* 1968. Taizé: Les Presses de Taizé.

2. Documents

Bishops' Committee on the Liturgy. *Environment and Art in Catholic Worship.* Washington, D.C.: USCC Publications Office, 1978.

Bishops' Committee on the Liturgy. *Liturgical Music Today*. Washington, D.C.: USCC Publications Office, 1982.

Bishops' Committee on the Liturgy. *Music in Catholic Worship*. Washington, D.C.: USCC Publications Office, 1972.

Documents on the Liturgy 1963-1979: Conciliar, Papal, and Curial Texts. Collegeville: The Liturgical Press, 1982.

The Milwaukee Symposia for Church Composers: A Ten-Year Report. Washington, D.C.: The Pastoral Press and Chicago: Liturgy Training Publications, 1992.

PIUS X. "Tra le sollecitudini." In *Acta Sanctae Sedis* 36 (1904): 329-339. Translation in *The New Liturgy: A Documentation, 1903-1965*, ed. R. Kevin SEASOLTZ, 3-10. New York: Herder and Herder, 1966.

Sacred Congregation of Rites. "Musicam Sacram." In *Acta Apostolicae Sedis* 60 (1967): 300-320. Translation in *Documents on the Liturgy 1963-1979: Conciliar, Papal, and Curial Texts,* no. 1293-1306. Collegeville: The Liturgical Press, 1982.

Sacrosanctum Oecumenicum Concilium Vaticanum. "Constitutio Dogmatica de Ecclesia." In *Constitutiones, Decreta, Declarationes,* 93-219. Typis Polyglottis Vaticanis, 1966. Translation in Austin FLANNERY, gen. ed. "Dogmatic Constitution on the Church." In *Vatican Council II: The Conciliar and Post Conciliar Documents,* 350-423. Revised edition. Grand Rapids, Michigan: William B. Eerdmans Publishing Company, 1984.

Sacrosanctum Oecumenicum Concilium Vaticanum. "Constitutione de sacra liturgia." In *Constitutiones, Decreta, Declarationes,* 3-70. Typis Polyglottis Vaticanis, 1966. Translation in Austin FLANNERY, gen. ed. "The Constitution on the Sacred Liturgy." In *Vatican Council II: The Conciliar and Post Conciliar Documents,* 1-37. Revised edition. Grands Rapids, Michigan: William B. Eerdmans Publishing Company, 1984.

Sacrosanctum Oecumenicum Concilium Vaticanum. "Decretum de Oecumenismo." In *Constitutiones, Decreta, Declarationes,* 243-274. Typis Polyglottis Vaticanis, 1966. Translation in Austin FLANNERY, gen. ed. "Decree on Ecumenism." In *Vatican Council II: The Conciliar and Post Conciliar Documents,* 451-532. Revised edition. Grands Rapids, Michigan: William B. Eerdmans Publishing Company, 1984.

"The Snowbird Statement on Catholic Liturgical Music." In *Pastoral Music* 20 (February-March 1966): 13-19.

Universa Laus. *Musiques et liturgie*. Paris: Les Editions du Cerf, 1988. Translation in Claude DUCHESNEAU and Michel VEUTHEY, eds. *Music and Liturgy: the Universa Laus Document and Commentary*. Translated by Paul INWOOD. Washington, D.C.: The Pastoral Press, 1992.

3. Interviews

BERTHIER, Germaine. Interview by author, 29 May 1996, Paris, France.

BERTHIER, Jacques. "Jacques Berthier: Un serviteur de la musique liturgique." Interview by Pierre FAURE and Didier RIMAUD. *Célébrer* no. 236 (Janvier 1994): 3-16.

CASTALDI, Brother JOHN. Interview by author, 23 May 1996, Taizé, France.

DIRK, Brother. Interview by author, 22 May 1996, Taizé, France.

GELINEAU, Joseph. Interview by author, 28 May 1996, Ecuelles, France.

SABÉ GRIFUL, Nuria. Interview by author, 24 May 1996, Taizé, France.

4. Music

BERTHIER, Jacques. *Bénissez le Seigneur: 27 Chants de Taizé avec versets de solistes et accompagnements*, ed. Frère ROBERT. Taizé: Les Presses de Taizé, 1990.

BERTHIER, Jacques. *Cantos de Taizé*. Volume 1. Edición Vocal, ed. Hermano ROBERTO. Chicago: G.I.A. Publications, Inc., 1986.

BERTHIER, Jacques. *Music from Taizé*. Volume 1. Vocal edition and instrumental edition, ed. Brother ROBERT. Chicago: G.I.A. Publications, Inc., 1981.

BERTHIER, Jacques. *Music from Taizé*. Volume 2. Vocal edition and instrumental edition, ed. Brother ROBERT. Chicago: G.I.A. Publications, Inc., 1984.

BERTHIER, Jacques, et al. *Songs and Prayers from Taizé*, ed. Brother ROBERT. Basic edition and accompaniment edition for cantor and instruments. Chicago: G.I.A. Publications, Inc., 1991.

BERTHIER, Jacques. Unpublished Music. The Community of Taizé: Taizé, France.

BERTHIER, Jacques, et al. *Chantez le Seigneur: 33 Chants de Taizé avec versets de solistes et accompagnements*, ed. by Communauté de Taizé. Taizé: Les Presses de Taizé, 1994.

Chants de Taizé. Taizé: Ateliers et Presses de Taizé, 1995.

Radość Serca: Śpiewy z Taizé. Śpiewnik. Katowice: Wydawnictwo Columb Sp zo. o, 1992.

ROBERT, Brother, ed. *Songs and Prayers from Taizé*. Basic edition and accompaniment edition for cantor and instruments. Chicago: G.I.A. Publications, Inc., 1991.

Śpiewy z Taizé. Głosy solowe. Taizé: Les Presses de Taizé, 1993.

B. SECONDARY SOURCES

ALBERIGO, Giuseppe. "The Christian Situation after Vatican II." In *The Reception of Vatican II*, ed. Giuseppe ALBERIGO, Jean-Pierre JOSSUA, and Joseph A. KOMONCHAK, 1-24. Translated by Matthew J. O'CONNELL. Washington, D.C.: The Catholic University of America Press, 1987.

ALPERSON, Philip. "Introduction: New Directions in the Philosophy of Music." *The Journal of Aesthetics and Art Criticism* 52 (Winter 1994)· 1-11

ALPERSON, Philip, ed. *What Is Music? An Introduction to the Philosophy of Music.* University Park, Pennsylvania: The Pennsylvania State University Press, 1987.

ARISTOTLE. *The Politics.* Edited by Stephen EVERSON. Cambridge: The University of Cambridge Press, 1988.

Aristotle's Poetics. Translated by S.H. BUTCHER. Introduction by Francis FERGUSON. New York: Farrar, Straus and Giroux, 1961.

AUSTIN, John Langshaw. *How to Do Things with Words.* Cambridge, Massachusetts: Harvard University Press, 1962.

BALADO, J.L. Gonzalez. *The Story of Taizé.* Third revised edition. Collegeville, Minnesota: The Liturgical Press, 1988.

BEARDSLEY, Monroe C. "Understanding Music." In *On Criticizing Music: Five Philosophical Perspectives,* ed. Kingsley PRICE, 55-73. Baltimore: The John Hopkins University Press, 1981.

BELLAH, Robert N. *Beyond Belief: Essays on Religion in a Post Traditional World.* New York: Harper and Row, 1970.

BLACK, George. "Church Musician in France: Taizé." *Music: The AGO-RCCO Magazine* 10 (April 1976): 44-46.

BLACK, George. "Church Musician in France: Part II, Canons at Taizé." *The American Organist* 14 (July 1980): 36-37.

BLACKING, John. *How Musical Is Man?* The John Danz Lectures. Seattle: University of Washington Press, 1973.

BLACKING, John. "The Structure of Musical Discourse: The Problem of the Song Text." *Yearbook for Traditional Music* 14 (1982): 15-23.

BLOCH, Ernst. *Essays on the Philosophy of Music.* Translated by Peter PALMER. Cambridge: Cambridge University Press, 1974, 1985.

BOADT, Lawrence. "Problems in the Translation of Scripture as Illustrated in ICEL's Project on the Liturgical Psalter." In *Shaping English Liturgy: Studies in Honor of Archbishop Denis Hurley,* ed. Peter C. FINN and James M. SCHELLMAN, 405-429. Washington, D.C.: The Pastoral Press, 1990.

BOILÉS, Charles. "Processes of Musical Semiosis." *Yearbook for Traditional Music* 14 (1982): 24-44.

BOURDIEU, Pierre. *Outline of a Theory of Practice.* Translated by Richard NICE. Cambridge: Cambridge University Press, 1977.

BRINKLEY, Timothy. "Langer's Logical and Ontological Modes." *Journal of Aesthetics and Art Criticism* 28 (Summer 1970): 455-464.

BROOKS, Robert R. "Music and Worship of the Taizé Community." Masters thesis, Southwestern Baptist Theological Seminary, Fort Worth, Texas, 1984.

BROWN, Frank Burch. *Religious Aesthetics: A Theological Study of Making and Meaning.* Macmillan Studies in Literature and Religion series, gen. ed. David JASPER. London: The Macmillan Press Limited, 1990.

BROWN, Raphael. "Taizé Community." In *The New Catholic Encyclopedia,* vol. 13, 917-918. Washington, D.C.: The Catholic University of America Press, 1967.

BYNUM, Caroline Walker. "Women's Stories, Women's Symbols: A Critique of Victor Turner's Theory of Liminality." In *Anthropology and the Study of Religion,* ed. Robert L. MOORE and Frank E. REYNOLDS, 105-125. Chicago: Center for the Scientific Study of Religion, 1984.

CAGLIO, Ernest Moneta. "Chapter VI: Sacred Music." *The Commentary on the Constitution and on the Instruction on the Sacred Liturgy,* ed. Annibale BUGNINI and Charles BRAGA, 244-267. Translated by Vincent P. MALLON. New York: Benzinger Brothers, 1965.

CASSIRER, Ernst. *An Essay on Man: An Introduction to a Philosophy of Human Culture.* New Haven: Yale University Press, 1944.

CHAUVET, Louis-Marie. *Symbol and Sacrament: A Sacramental Reinterpretation of Christian Existence.* Translated by Patrick MADIGAN and Madeleine E. BEAUMONT. Collegeville: The Liturgical Press, 1995.

CHEW, Geoffrey. "Acclamation." In *The New Grove Dictionary of Music and Musicians,* ed. Stanley SADIE, vol. 1, 35-36. London: Macmillan Publishers Limited, 1980.

COKER, Wilson. *Music and Meaning: A Theoretical Introduction to Musical Aesthetics.* New York: The Free Press, 1972.

COLLINS, Mary. "Glorious Praise: The ICEL Liturgical Psalter." *Worship* 66 (July 1992): 290-310.

COLLINS, Mary. "Ritual Symbols and the Ritual Process: The Work of Victor W. Turner." *Worship* 50 (July 1976): 336-346.

CONGAR, Yves. "L'Ecclesia ou communauté chrétienne, sujet intégral de l'action liturgique." In *La Liturgie après Vatican II: Bilans, Études, Prospective,* ed. Jean-Pierre JOSSUA and Yves M.J. CONGAR, 241-282. Paris: Les Éditions du Cerf, 1967.

CONGAR, Yves. "Reception as an Ecclesiological Reality." Translated by John GRIFFITHS. In *Election and Consensus in the Church,* ed. Giuseppe ALBERIGO and Anton WEILER, 43-68. Concilium: Religion in the Seventies Series, no. 77. New York: Herder and Herder, 1972.

DAVIES, Horton. "Worship at Taizé: A Protestant Monastic Servant Community." *Worship* 49 (January 1975): 23-34.

DAVIS, Edward. "The Ecumenical Ecclesiology of Max Thurian, Brother of the Community of Taizé: A Catholic Appraisal." Ph.D. diss., The Catholic University of America, 1970.

DEISS, Lucien. *Spirit and Song of the New Liturgy.* Revised edition. Cincinnati: World Library Publications, Inc., 1976.

DEISS, Lucien. *Visions of Liturgy and Music for a New Century.* Translated by Jane M.- A. BURTON. Collegeville: The Liturgical Press, 1996.

DERRIDA, Jacques. *Margins of Philosophy.* Translated by Alan BASS. Chicago: The University of Chicago Press, 1982.

DETELS, Claire. "Autonomist/Formalist Aesthetics, Music Theory, and the Feminist Paradigm of Soft Boundaries." *The Journal of Aesthetics and Art Criticism* 52 (Winter 1994): 113-126.

DOLGIN, Janet L., David S. KEMNITZER, and David M. SCHNEIDER, eds. "Introduction: 'As People Express Their Lives, So They Are ...'" In *Symbolic Anthropology: A Reader in the Study of Symbols and Meanings.* New York: Columbia University Press, 1977.

DRIVER, Tom F. *The Magic of Ritual: Our Need for Liberating Rites that Transform Our Lives and Our Communities.* San Francisco: HarperCollins Publishers, 1991.

DULLES, Avery, *The Craft of Theology: From Symbol to System.* New York: The Crossroad Publishing Company, 1992.

DULLES, Avery. *Models of Revelation.* Garden City, New York: Doubleday and Company, Inc., 1983.

DULLES, Avery. "The Symbolic Structure of Revelation." *Theological Studies* 41 (1980): 51-73.

ECO, Umberto. *A Theory of Semiotics.* Advances in Semiotics series, gen. ed. Thomas A. SEBEOK. Bloomington: Indiana University Press, 1976.

ÉMILE, Brother. "Taizé Community." In *Dictionary of the Ecumenical Movement,* ed. Nicholas LOSSKY et al. Grand Rapids, Michigan: William B. Eerdmans Publishing Company, 1991.

EPPERSON, Gordon. *The Musical Symbol: A Study of the Philosophic Theory of Music.* Ames, Iowa: Iowa State University Press, 1967.

FAURE, Marie-Pierre. "Jacques Berthier, a Friend of God." *Liturgy: Cistercians of the Strict Observance* 29 (1995): 83-86.

FELLERER, Gustav. *The History of Catholic Church Music.* Translated by Francis A. BRUNNER. Baltimore: Helicon Press, 1961.

FISH, Stanley. "With the Compliments of the Author: Reflections on Austin and Derrida." *Critical Inquiry* 8 (1982): 693-721.

FOLEY, Edward. *Music in Ritual: A Pre-Theological Investigation.* American Essays in Liturgy series, no. 1. Washington, D.C.: The Pastoral Press, 1984.

FOLEY, Edward. "Musical Forms, Referential Meaning and Belief." *Worship* 69 (July 1995): 314-333.

FOLEY, Edward. "Toward a Sound Theology." *Studia Liturgica* 23 (1993): 121-139.

FORTMANN, Han (Henricus). *Discovery of the East: Reflections on a New Culture.* Translated by Patrick GAFFNEY. Notre Dame, Indiana: Fides Publishers, Inc., 1971. Originally published in Dutch as *Oosterse Renaissance.* Bilthoven: Uitgeverij Ambo, 1970.

FORTMANN, Han. *Wat is er met de mens gebeurd?* Bilthoven: Uitgeverij Ambo, 1971.

GAJARD, Dom Joseph. *The Solesmes Method: Its Fundamental Principles and Practical Rules of Interpretation.* Translated by R. Cecile GABAIN. Collegeville: The Liturgical Press, 1960.

GELINEAU, Joseph. "Music and Singing in the Liturgy." In *The Study of the Liturgy,* ed. Cheslyn JONES, Geoffrey WAINWRIGHT and Edward YARNOLD, 440-454. New York: Oxford University Press, 1978.

GELINEAU, Joseph. *Voices and Instruments in Christian Worship.* Translated by Clifford HOWELL. Collegeville: The Liturgical Press, 1964.

GOEHR, Lydia. *The Imaginary Museum of Musical Works: An Essay in the Philosophy of Music.* New York: Oxford University Press, 1992.

GOEHR, Lydia. "Political Music and the Politics of Music." *The Journal of Aesthetics and Art Criticism* 52 (Winter 1994): 99-112.

GRIFFITHS, Paul. "Aleatory." In *The New Grove Dictionary of Music and Musicians,* ed. Stanley SADIE, vol. 1, 237-242. London: Macmillan Publishers Limited, 1980.

GRIMES, Ronald L. *Beginnings in Ritual Studies.* Revised edition. Studies in Comparative Religion, gen. ed., Frederick M. DENNY. Columbia: University of South Carolina Press, 1995.

GRIMES, Ronald. "Liturgical Supinity, Liturgical Erectitude: On the Embodiment of Ritual Authority," *Studia Liturgica* 23 (1993): 51-69.

GRIMES, Ronald. "Reinventing Ritual." *Soundings* 75 (Spring 1992): 21-41.

GROUT, Donald Jay. *A History of Western Music,* 3d ed. New York: W.W. Norton and Company, 1980.

HAGBERG, Gary. *Art as Language: Wittgenstein, Meaning, and Aesthetic Theory.* Ithaca: Cornell University Press, 1995.

HANSLICK, Eduard. *On the Musically Beautiful: A Contribution Towards the Revision of the Aesthetics of Music.* Translated and edited by Geoffrey PAYZANT from the eighth edition (1891) of *Vom Musikalisch-Schönen: ein Beitrag zur Revision der Ästhetik der Tonkunst.* Indianapolis: Hacket Publishing Company, 1986.

HARVEY, Mark Sumner. "Rhythm, Ritual, and Religion: Postmodern (Musical) Agonistes." *Black Sacred Music: A Journal of Theomusicology* 8 (Spring 1994): 178-201.

HAYBURN, Robert F. *Papal Legislation on Sacred Music: 95 A.D. to 1977 A.D.* Collegeville: The Liturgical Press, 1979.

HEFNER, Philip. "Editorial." *Zygon* 21 (March 1986): 5.

HEIJKE, John. *An Ecumenical Light on the Renewal of Religious Community Life: Taizé.* Duquesne Studies, ed. Henry J. KOREN, Theological Series no. 7. Pittsburgh: Duquesne University Press, 1967.

HICKS, Douglas A. "The Taizé Community: Fifty Years of Prayer and Action." *Journal of Ecumenical Studies* 29 (Spring 1992): 202-214.

HIGGINS, Kathleen Marie. *The Music of Our Lives*. Philadelphia: Temple University Press, 1991.

HUCKE, Helmut. "The Concept of Church Music in History." Translated by Gordon E. TRUITT. In *Aide-Mémoire UL: Excerpts from the UL Bulletin 1979-1983*. Washington, D.C.: Universa Laus and the National Association of Pastoral Musicians, 1996.

HUDSON, Richard. "Ostinato." In *The New Grove Dictionary of Music and Musicians*, ed. Stanley SADIE, vol. 14, 11-12. London: Macmillan Publishers Limited, 1980.

HUGLO, Michel, Peter le HURAY, and David NUTTER. "Litany." In *The New Grove Dictionary of Music and Musicians*, ed. Stanley SADIE, vol. 11, 75-78. London: Macmillan Publishers Limited, 1980.

INNIS, Robert E. "Art, Symbol, and Consciousness: A Polanyi Gloss on Susan Langer and Nelson Goodman." *International Philosophical Quarterly* 17 (December 1977): 455-476.

IRWIN, Kevin W. "Liturgical Theology." In *The New Dictionary of Sacramental Worship*, ed. Peter E. FINK, 721-733. Collegeville: The Liturgical Press, 1990.

"Jesus Prayer, The." In *The Oxford Dictionary of the Christian Church*, 2d ed. F.L. CROSS and E.A. LIVINSTONE, 738. Oxford: Oxford University Press, 1974.

JONCAS, J. Michael. "Rereading *Musicam Sacram*: Twenty-five Years of Development in Roman Rite Liturgical Music. *Worship* 66 (May 1992): 212-231.

JONCAS, J. Michael. "Musical Semiotics and Liturgical Musicology: Theoretical Foundations and Analytic Techniques." *Ecclesia Orans* 8 (1991): 181-206.

JUNGMANN, Josef Andreas. "Constitution on the Sacred Liturgy." Translated by Lalit ADOLPHUS. Chap. in *Commentary on the Documents of Vatican II*, ed. Herbert VORGRIMLER, 1-30. New York: Herder and Herder, 1967.

JURGENS, W.A., ed. and trans. *The Faith of the Early Fathers*. Vol. 1. Collegeville: The Liturgical Press, 1970.

JURGENS, W.A., ed. and trans. *The Faith of the Early Fathers*. Vol. 2. Collegeville: The Liturgical Press, 1979.

KELLEHER, Margaret Mary. "Liturgical Theology: A Task and a Method." *Worship* 62 (January 1988): 2-25.

KELLEHER, Margaret Mary. "Liturgy: An Ecclesial Act of Meaning." *Worship* 59 (November 1985): 482-497.

KELLEHER, Margaret Mary. "Ritual." In *The New Dictionary of Theology*, ed. Joseph A. KOMONCHAK, Mary COLLINS, and Dermot A. LANE, 906-907. Collegeville: The Liturgical Press, 1991.

KELLEHER, Margaret Mary. "Worship." In *The New Dictionary of Theology*, ed. Joseph A. KOMONCHAK, Mary COLLINS, and Dermot A. LANE, 1105-1106. Collegeville: The Liturgical Press, 1991.

KRAMER, Lawrence. *Music as Cultural Practice, 1800-1900*. Berkeley: University of California Press, 1990.

KRAUSZ, Michael, ed. *The Interpretation of Music: Philosophical Essays*. New York: Oxford University Press, 1993.

LADRIÈRE, Jean. "The Performativity of Liturgical Language." In *Liturgical Experience of Faith*, ed. H. SCHMIDT and David N. POWER, 50-62. Concilium series, no. 82. New York: Herder and Herder, 1973.

LANGER, Susanne K. *Feeling and Form: A Theory of Art Developed from Philosophy in a New Key*. New York: Charles Scribner's Sons, 1953.

LANGER, Susanne K. *Problems of Art: Ten Philosophical Lectures*. New York: Charles Scribner's Sons, 1957.

LANGER, Susanne K. *Philosophy in a New Key: A Study in the Symbolism of Reason, Rite and Art*, 3d edition. Cambridge, Massachusetts: Harvard University Press, 1967.

LAWLER, Michael. *Symbol and Sacrament: A Contemporary Sacramental Theology*. New York: Paulist Press, 1987.

LOMAX, Alan. "Song Structure and Social Structure." *Readings in Ethnomusicology*, ed. David P. McALLESTER, 227-252. New York: Johnson Reprints, 1971.

LONDON, Justin. "Musical and Linguistic Speech Acts." *The Journal of Aesthetics and Art Criticism* 54 (Winter 1996): 49-64.

LUKKEN, Gerard M. "Liturgy and Language: An Approach from Semiotics." *Questions Liturgique* 73 (1992): 36-52.

LUKKEN, Gerard M. "Semiotics and the Study of Liturgy." *Studia Liturgica* 17 (1987): 108-117.

LUKKEN, Gerard M. "The Unique Expression of Faith in the Liturgy." Translated by David SMITH. In *The Liturgical Experience of Faith*, ed. Herman SCHMIDT and David POWER, 11-21. Concilium: Religion in the Seventies Series, no. 82. New York: Herder and Herder, 1973.

LUKKEN, Gerard and Mark SEARLE. *Semiotics and Church Architecture: Applying the Semiotics of A.J. Greimas and the Paris School to the Analysis of Church Buildings*. Liturgia condenda, vol. 1. Kampen, The Netherlands: Kok Pharos Publishing House, 1993.

MANN, Alfred and J. Kenneth WILSON. "Canon." In *The New Grove Dictionary of Music and Musicians*, ed. Stanley SADIE, vol. 3, 689-693. London: Macmillan Publishers Limited, 1980.

MARGOLIS, Joseph. "On the Semiotics of Music." In *What Is Music?: An Introduction to the Philosophy of Music*, ed. Philip ALPERSON, 211-236. University Park, Pennsylvania: The Pennsylvania State University Press, 1987.

MARSHALL, Robert L. "Chorale." In *The New Grove Dictionary of Music and Musicians*, ed. Stanley SADIE, vol. 4, 312-321. London: Macmillan Publishers Limited, 1980.

MARSOOBIAN, Armen T "Saying, Singing, or Semiotics: '*Prima la Musica e poi le Parole*' Revisited." *Journal of Aesthetics and Art Criticism* 54 (Summer 1996): 269-277.

MEYER, Leonard B. *Music, the Arts, and Ideas: Patterns and Predictions in Twentieth Century Culture.* Chicago: The University of Chicago Press, 1967.

MITCHELL, Nathan. "Symbols Are Actions, Not Objects." *Living Worship* 13 (February 1977): 1-4.

MOLINO, Jean. "Fait musical et sémiologie de la musique." *Musique en jeu* 17(1975): 37-62.

MORRIS, Charles. "Foundations of the Theory of Signs." In *Foundations of the Unity of Science: Toward an International Encyclopedia of Unified Science,* vol. 1, nos. 1- 10, ed. Otto NEURATH, Rudolf CARNAP, and Charles MORRIS, 77-137. Chicago: The University of Chicago Press, 1969.

MORRIS, Charles. *Signification and Significance: A Study of the Relations of Signs and Values.* Cambridge, Massachusetts: The M.I.T. Press, 1964.

MURRAY, David W. "Ritual Communication: Some Considerations Regarding Meaning in Navajo Ceremonials." In *Symbolic Anthropology: A Reader in the Study of Symbols and Meanings,* ed. Janet L. DOLGIN, David S. KEMNITZER, and David M. SCHNEIDER, 195-220. New York: Columbia University Press, 1977.

NATTIEZ, Jean-Jacques. "The Contribution of Musical Semiotics to the Semiotic Discussion in General." In *A Perfusion of Signs,* ed. Thomas A. SEBEOK, 121- 142. Bloomington: Indiana University Press, 1977.

NATTIEZ, Jean-Jacques. *Fondements d'une sémiologie de la musique.* Série "Esthétique" ed. Mikel DUFRENNE. Paris: Union Générale d'Editions, 1975.

NATTIEZ, Jean-Jacques. *Music and Discourse: Toward a Semiology of Music.* Translated by Carolyn ABBATE. Princeton, New Jersey: Princeton University Press, 1990.

NATTIEZ, Jean-Jacques. "Reflections on the Development of Semiology in Music." Translated by Katharine ELLIS. *Music Analysis* 8 (1989): 21-75.

NELSON, Angela M.S. "Text, Texture, and Context in Theological Perspective." *Black Sacred Music: Journal of Theomusicology* 8 (Spring 1994): 64-77.

NEWCOMB, Anthony. "Sound and Feeling." *Critical Inquiry* 10 (1984): 614-643.

NIETZSCHE, Friedrich. *The Birth of Tragedy.* In *Basic Writings of Nietzsche.* Translated and edited by Walter KAUFMANN. New York: The Modern Library, 1968.

"Nunc Dimittis: Brother Robert of Taizé." *GIA Quarterly* 4 (Summer 1993): 9.

O'MEARA, Thomas F. "Ministry." In *The New Dictionary of Theology,* ed. Joseph A. KOMONCHAK, Mary COLLINS, and Dermot A. LANE, 657-661. Collegeville: The Liturgical Press, 1991.

ONG, Walter. *The Presence of the Word: Some Prolegomena for Cultural and Religious History.* New York: Simon and Schuster, 1970.

ORTIGUES, Eugene. *Le discours et le symbole.* Paris: Aubier-Montaigne, 1962.

POLANYI, Michael and Harry PROSCH. *Meaning.* Chicago: The University of Chicago Press, 1975.

POTTMEYER, Hermann J. "A New Phase in the Reception of Vatican II: Twenty Years of Interpretation of the Council." In *The Reception of Vatican II*, ed. Giuseppe ALBERIGO, Jean-Pierre JOSSUA, and Joseph A. KOMONCHAK, 27-43. Translated by Matthew J. O'CONNELLL. Washington, D.C.: The Catholic University of America Press, 1987.

QUASTEN, Johannes. *Music and Worship in Pagan and Christian Antiquity.* NPM Studies in Church Music and Liturgy. Translated by Boniface RAMSEY. Washington, D.C.: The Pastoral Press, 1983.

RAHNER, Karl. *The Church and the Sacraments.* Translated by W.J. O'HARA. Herder and Herder, 1963.

RAHNER, Karl. "The Theology of Symbol." In *Theological Investigations,* vol. 4, *More Recent Writings,* trans. Kevin SMYTH. Baltimore: Helicon Press, 1966.

RAHNER, Karl. "Towards a Fundamental Interpretation of Vatican II." *Theological Studies* 40 (1979): 716-727.

ROBERT, Brother. "Taizé Music … A History." *Pastoral Music* 11 (February-March 1987): 19-22.

ROBERTS, Louis. *The Achievement of Karl Rahner.* New York: Herder and Herder, Inc., 1967.

SALIERS, Don E. "The Integrity of Sung Prayer." *Worship* 55 (July 1981): 290-303.

SALIERS, Don E. *Worship as Theology: Foretaste of Glory Divine.* Nashville: Abingdon Press, 1994.

SCHALLER, Joseph J. "Performative Language Theory: An Exercise in the Analysis of Ritual." *Worship* 62 (September 1988): 415-432.

SCHECHNER, Richard. "Victor Turner's Last Adventure." Preface in *The Anthropology of Performance,* 7-20. New York: Performing Arts Journal, Inc., 1986.

SCHUTZ, Alfred. "Making Music Together: A Study in Social Relationship." In *Symbolic Anthropology: A Reader in the Study of Symbols and Meanings*, ed. Janet L. DOLGIN, David S. KEMNITZER, and David M. SCHNEIDER, 106-119. New York: Columbia University Press, 1977.

SCHUTZ, Brother Roger. "An Interview with Brother Roger of Taizé. Interview by Patrick SAMWAY. *America* 148 (January 22, 1983): 46-50.

SEARLE, John R. "Austin on Locutionary and Illocutionary Acts." In *Essays on J.L. Austin,* ed. Isaiah BERLIN, et al. London: Oxford University Press, 1973.

SEARLE, John R. *Speech Acts: An Essay in the Philosophy of Language.* Cambridge: Cambridge University Press, 1969.

SEARLE, Mark. "Ritual and Music." *Pastoral Music* 11 (February-March 1987): 13-18.

SEASOLTZ, R. Kevin. *The New Liturgy: A Documentation, 1903-1965.* New York: Herder and Herder, 1966.

SEASOLTZ, R. Kevin. *New Liturgy, New Laws.* Collegeville: The Liturgical Press, 1980.

SECKEL, Clyde. "How Can Music Have Theological Significance?" *Black Sacred Music: A Journal of Theomusicology* 8 (Spring 1994): 13-35.

SKELLEY, Michael. *The Liturgy of the World: Karl Rahner's Theology of Worship,* foreword by Rembert G. WEAKLAND. Collegeville: The Liturgical Press, 1991.

SÖHNGEN, Oskar. "Music and Theology: A Systematic Approach." In *Sacred Sound: Music in Religious Thought and Practice,* ed. and trans. Joyce IRWIN. Journal of the American Academy of Religious Thematic Studies, 50 (1983): 1-19.

SÖRBOM, Göran. "Aristotle on Music as Representation." *The Journal of Aesthetics and Art Criticism* 52 (Winter 1994): 37-46.

SPARSHOTT, Francis. "Aesthetics of Music: Limits and Grounds." In *What Is Music?: An Introduction to the Philosophy of Music,* ed. Philip ALPERSON, 33-98. University Park, Pennsylvania: The Pennsylvania State University Press, 1987.

SPEELMAN, Willem Marie. *The Generation of Meaning in Liturgical Songs: A Semiotic Analysis of Five Liturgical Songs as Syncretic Discourse.* Liturgia condenda 4. Kampen: Kok Pharos Publishing House, 1995.

SPINK, Kathryn. *A Universal Heart: The Life and Vision of Brother Roger of Taizé.* San Francisco: Harper and Row Publishers, 1986.

STEFANI, Gino. "Essai sur les communications sonores dans la liturgie." *Paroisse et liturgie* 52 (1970): 99-106, 232-242, 319-336.

"Taizé Community." In *The New Catholic Encyclopedia Supplement 1978-1988.* Vol. 18, 503. Washington, D.C.: The Catholic University of America Press, 1989.

TILLICH, Paul. "Art and Ultimate Reality." In *Art, Creativity and the Sacred,* ed. Diane APOSTOLOS-CAPPADONA, 219-235. New York: The Crossroad Publishing Company, 1984.

TILLICH, Paul. *Dynamics of Faith.* New York: Harper and Row, Publishers, 1957.

TURNER, Victor W. *The Anthropology of Performance.* New York: Performing Arts Journal, Inc., 1986.

TURNER, Victor W. *Dramas, Fields, and Metaphors: Symbolic Action in Human Society.* Symbol, Myth, and Ritual Series, gen. ed., Victor TURNER. Ithaca: Cornell University Press, 1974.

TURNER, Victor W. *The Forest of Symbols: Aspects of Ndembu Ritual.* Ithaca: Cornell University Press, 1967.

TURNER, Victor W. "Passages, Margins, and Poverty: Religious Symbols of Communitas." *Worship* 46 (August-September 1972): 390-412 and (October- November 1972): 482-494.

TURNER, Victor W. "Process, System, and Symbol: A New Anthropological Synthesis." In *On the Edge of the Bush: Anthropology as Experience,* ed. Edith L.B. TURNER, 151-173. Tucson: The University of Arizona Press, 1985.

TURNER, Victor W. *The Ritual Process: Structure and Anti-Structure.* Chicago: Aldine Publishing Company, 1969.

TURNER, Victor W. "Symbols and Social Experience in Religious Ritual." In *Worship and Ritual: In Christianity and Other Religions,* Studia Missionalia, 1-21. Rome: Gregorian University Press, 1974.

TURNER, Victor W. "Symbols in African Ritual." In *Symbolic Anthropology: A Reader in the Study of Symbols and Meanings,* ed. Janet L. DOLGIN, David S. KEMNITZER, and David M. SCHNEIDER, 183-194. New York: Columbia University Press, 1977.

TURNER, Victor and Edith L.B. TURNER. "Pilgrimage as a Liminoid Phenomenon." In *Image and Pilgrimage in Christian Culture: Anthropological Perspectives,* 1- 39. New York: Columbia University Press, 1978.

VAN GENNEP, Arnold. *The Rites of Passage.* Translated by Monika B. VIZEDOM and Gabrielle L. CAFFEE. Chicago: The University of Chicago Press, 1960.

WACHSMANN, Klaus P. "Folk Music." In *The New Grove Dictionary of Music and Musicians,* ed. Stanley SADIE, vol. 6, 693. London: Macmillan Publishers Limited, 1980.

WARNOCK, Geoffrey James. "Some Types of Performative Utterance." In *Essays on J.L. Austin,* ed. Isaiah BERLIN, et al., 69-89. London: Oxford University Press, 1973.

WEAKLAND, Rembert. *Themes of Renewal.* Laurel, Maryland: The Pastoral Press, 1995.

WHEELOCK, Wade T. "The Problem of Ritual Language: From Information to Situation." *The Journal of the American Academy of Religion* 50 (1982): 49-71.

WORGUL, George S., Jr. "Ritual." In *The New Dictionary of Sacramental Worship,* ed. Peter E. FINK, 1101-1106. Collegeville: The Liturgical Press, 1990.

ZUCKERKANDL, Victor. *Sound and Symbol,* vol. 2. Translated by Willard R. TRASK. Princeton, New Jersey: Princeton University Press, 1969.